International Practitioner's Deskbook Series

International Labor and Employment Law

A Practical Guide

Editors
Philip M. Berkowitz
Thomas Müller-Bonanni

ABA — Defending Liberty Pursuing Justice

ABA Section of International Law
Your Gateway to International Practice

Section of International Law
American Bar Association

Cover design by ABA Publishing.

Printed in the United States of America

10 09 08 07 06 5 4 3 2 1

Library of Congress Cataloging-in-Publication Data

International labor and employment law / [edited] by Philip M. Berkowitz, Thomas Müller-Bonanni.
p. cm.—(International practitioner's deskbook series)
Includes bibliographical references and index.
ISBN 1-59031-640-1 (alk. paper)
1. Labor laws and legislation. 2. Labor laws and legislation, International.
I. Berkowitz, Philip M. II. Müller-Bonanni, Thomas. III. American Bar Association.
Section of International Law. IV. Series.

K1705.I53 2006
344.01—dc22

2006010304

CONTENTS

About the Editors

Philip M. Berkowitz is a partner with Nixon Peabody LLP in New York City, where he chairs the firm's international labor and employment team. He received his B.A. from the State University of New York at New Paltz and his J.D. from Northwestern School of Law. Mr. Berkowitz's extensive labor and employment experience includes discrimination and harassment, whistleblowing, wrongful dismissal, ERISA violations, executive compensation, and breach of contract and restrictive covenants. He has defended litigations in federal and state courts and administrative agencies across the United States, as well as arbitrations before the National Association of Securities Dealers, the American Arbitration Association, and the International Chamber of Commerce. Mr. Berkowitz is the senior advisor to the International Employment Law Committee of the ABA Section of International Law and is the management co-chair of the New York State Bar Association's International Labor and Employment Law Committee.

Dr. Thomas Müller-Bonanni, LL.M., is a partner with Freshfields Bruckhaus Deringer based in Germany. He specializes in labor and employment law with a special focus on mass lay-offs, restructurings, outsourcings, mergers and acquisitions, and privatizations. Dr. Müller-Bonanni also has broad experience in advising on pension schemes and remuneration systems, including stock options. He was born in 1968 and received his legal education at the universities of Cologne, Germany, Geneva, and Lausanne, Switzerland. Dr. Müller-Bonanni holds an LL.M. degree from New York University and was a scholar of the German Academic Exchange service. He is a regular lecturer at HR specialist seminars, both at the national and international levels, and is the author of numerous legal publications.

About the Contributors

BELGIUM

Carl Bevernage is a partner of the employment law, compensation and benefits, and pensions practice group of Loyens. He is involved in industrial relations law, individual employment law, and national insurance and pension schemes under Belgian and European law. His specializations also include civil and criminal proceedings and arbitrations, pharmaceuticals and medical products law, and WTO issues. In addition to his professional activities, Mr. Bevernage is head of the Belgian Delegation with the Council of European Bars (CCBE), a member of the Belgian High Council of Justice, and a member of the American Bar Association's Section of International Law and the Section of Labor and Employment Law. He is also the senior editor of and a contributor to *International Labor and Employment Laws* (BNA 2003) and president of the Belgian-Dutch Association. Mr. Bevernage was president of the Brussels Bar in 1990–1992. He holds a law degree (Katholieke Universiteit Leuven, 1967), and LL.M. (Tulane University, USA, 1968). He is a member of the Brussels Bar and speaks Dutch, French, English, and German.

Henry-David Hachez is a Belgian attorney at the law firm of Loyens and has extensive experience in Belgian employment, labor, and immigration law. He has advised foreign and Belgian companies on general employment and labor law matters, transfers of undertakings, collective dismissals, reorganizations, Social Security matters, individual dismissals, self-employment matters, labor and employment disputes, and immigration matters. Mr. Hachez is a regular speaker on selected topics of Belgian employment, labor, and immigration law at both client and other seminars. He is a member of the Brussels Bar and holds the following degrees: Lic. Jur. (University of Leuven, 1996), Degree in Economic and Employment Law (University of Ghent, 1997), and LL.M. (Georgetown University Law Center, 2001). Mr. Hachez is fluent in French, Dutch, and English.

BRAZIL

Isabel C. Franco is a senior partner of the Brazilian law firm Demarest e Almeida. Her practice is concentrated predominately on matters of business law. She provides general assistance to multinational clients in their investments in her native Brazil, advising on matters relating to Brazilian laws, especially with regard to corporate mergers and acquisitions, contracts, employment, and telecommunications. In 1990, Ms. Franco launched Demarest e Almeida's New York office. Ms. Franco graduated from Universidade de São Paulo – School of Law in 1978 with an LL.B., and in 1996 received an LL.M. from Fordham Law School. She is admitted to the Brazilian Bar and is licensed under New York law as a foreign legal consultant and completed the Program of Instruction of Lawyers at Harvard University in 1992. Ms. Franco was the chair of the New York State Bar Association (Section of International Law and Practice) in 2001. She was a director of the Brazilian-American Chamber of Commerce in New York. In Brazil, Ms. Franco serves on the Committee of International Relations of the Brazilian Bar Association on both the state and federal levels. She is on the board of directors of the American Chamber of Commerce for 2003–2006, on the Executive Committee, and also in the position of legal counsel since 2003.

CANADA

Stuart S. Aronovitch joined the Canadian law firm Heenan Blaikie LLP in 2001 as a member of its Labor and Employment Law Group. His practice involves most areas of labor and employment law, with particular emphasis on employment contracts, restrictive covenants, confidentiality agreements, and dismissals. He represents a broad range of clients before civil courts and administrative tribunals, and has developed a particular expertise in wrongful dismissal suits and injunction proceedings. Mr. Aronovitch received his B.C.L./LL.B. from McGill University in 1993 and his B.A. from McGill University in 1989. He is a director of the Lord Reading Law Society, and is affiliated with the Canadian Bar Association and Barreau du Québec.

Jonathan L. Dye, B.A. (Hons.), LL.B., M.B.A, LL.M., works in Heenan Blaikie LLP's Toronto office. His litigation practice involves a range of issues such as wrongful dismissal, workplace discrimination, statutory employment standards, and enforcement of employment contracts. He also advises employers on these issues and regularly works with the firm's corporate attorneys to deal with employee issues in corporate transactions. Mr. Dye is a prolific writer and speaker, and currently serves on both the Labour Relations Section of the Ontario Bar Association and the Leadership of the Employment Law Committee of the Defense Research Institute (DRI).

CHINA

Qi (Adam) Li is a partner of Jun He Law Offices, focusing on international mergers and acquisitions in China, international financial transactions, and capital markets. Mr. Li has practiced law for fifteen years and is admitted in both China and New York. He is a graduate of Columbia Law School in New York and Fudan University in China. Mr. Li has been named one of the ten best lawyers in China by the Ministry of Justice, a Leading Lawyer by *Asian Law & Practice,* and one of the 30 Hottest Lawyers in China by *Asia Legal Business.*

Hong Zhang is an associate of Jun He Law Offices. She graduated from East China University of Politics and Law. She is a member of the Association of the Bar of All-China Lawyers Association and the Shanghai Bar Association. Since joining Jun He Law Offices, Ms. Zhang has worked on providing views and advice on general corporate matters, mergers and acquisitions, and labor and employment in China for local and international clients.

FRANCE

Salli A. Swartz has practiced international business law in Paris since 1979. Ms. Swartz specializes in international arbitrations and mediations. She also regularly advises French and other European subsidiaries of major American multinational companies in connection with their business activities in Europe and the Middle East, the Foreign Corrupt Practice Act, anti-boycott laws, and the OECD Convention on Combating Bribery of Foreign Public Officials. Ms. Swartz has lectured extensively on international business law issues and teaches intellectual property at the Ecole National Superieur des Arts & Metiers in Paris and international arbitration and mediation at the French business school Hautees Etudes Commercials. She is the author of numerous articles and publications, and is co-editor and author of a chapter in *Careers in International Law* published by the ABA in 2002. She is also the author of the chapter "Selling Products in Foreign Countries—International Sales" in *Negotiating and Structuring International Commercial Transactions* published by the ABA in 2003. Ms. Swartz is a member of the Pennsylvania and Paris Bars, with specializations in the law of international relations and commercial law, is admitted to practice before the French Courts, the U.S. Court of Appeals for the Federal Circuit, the U.S. Court of International Trade, and the U.S. Supreme Court. She is also the ABA liaison to the Union Internationale des Avocats.

GERMANY

Dr. Thomas Müller-Bonanni, LL.M., is a partner with Freshfields Brickhaus Deringer based in Germany. He specializes in labor and employment law with a special focus on mass lay-offs, restructurings, outsourcings, mergers and acquisitions, and privatizations. Dr. Müller-Bonanni also has broad experience in advising on pension schemes and remuneration systems, including stock options. He was born in 1968 and received his legal education at the universities of Cologne, Germany, Geneva, and Lausanne, Switzerland. Dr. Müller-Bonanni holds an LL.M. degree from New York University and was a scholar of the German Academic Exchange service. He is a regular lecturer at HR specialist seminars, both at the national and international levels, and is the author of numerous legal publications.

ITALY

Alberto Maggi is a partner in the Milan office of the international law firm Gianni, Origoni, Grippo & Partners, where he heads the Labor Law Department. Mr. Maggi graduated in 1985 with a law degree from the University of Pavia. He specializes in employment law and industrial relations, with a focus on transfer of undertakings, layoffs, and general labor-related issues connected with reorganizations and restructuring processes with companies. Mr. Maggi provides advice on a regular basis to many Italian and foreign multinational groups.

Silvia Tozzoli is an associate in the Labor Law Department of Gianni, Origoni, Grippo & Partners in the Milan office. Ms. Tozzoli earned a degree in law and a PhD in labor law and industrial relations from the University of Pavia, and an

LL.M. in labor law from the London School of Economics and Political Science. She is currently an honorary research and teaching fellow at the University of Pavia. Ms. Tozzoli's main areas of activity are employment and trade union law, dealing with both contentious and non-contentious work. She has also gained experience in private and public pension matters. Ms. Tozzoli recently has advised on labor law aspects related to insolvency procedures.

JAPAN

Hideki Thurgood Kano is a Japanese lawyer and partner of Anderson Mori & Tomotsune. He has been practicing in the area of labor and employment since 1995 and devotes his practice extensively to this area. Mr. Kano acts of behalf of both Japanese and non-Japanese multinational companies on all aspects of labor and employment, including ways to avert formal labor and employment disputes, and litigation. He has written and lectured extensively on labor and employment matters in addition to matters in other areas of law. He is a graduate of Tokyo University and received an LL.M. from Cornell University.

James M. Minamoto is an American lawyer and the Senior Foreign Counsel of Anderson Mori & Tomotsune. Mr. Minamoto's practice includes cross-border corporate transactions and litigation, and he primarily assists non-Japanese, overseas companies by coordinating their business activities in Japan, including establishing a business presence, supply and distribution, labor and employment, antimonopoly and competition regulation, joint ventures, mergers and acquisitions, and strategic alliances. Mr. Minamoto is a graduate of Cornell University and received his J.D. from the University of Pennsylvania Law School.

MEXICO

Jorge G. De Presno, partner in the Mexico City office of Thacher Proffitt & Wood, is head of the labor and employment law practice. He is a litigator and counsel in individual and collective matters. Mr. De Presno is a professor of labor law at the Universidad Iberoamericana in Mexico City and a member of the board of the Mexican Bar Association and the Interamerican Bar Association. He is a speaker in several forums in Mexico and abroad in matters related to labor and employment law, litigation, and constitutional issues.

THE NETHERLANDS

Maartje M. Govaert, born in 1972, is a Dutch *advocaat,* admitted to the Rotterdam Bar in 1999 and an associate at De Brauw Blackstone Westbroek as of that year. She is presently active within the Amsterdam employment and employee benefits department and hence now admitted to the Amsterdam Bar. In the past she has worked in the mergers and acquisitions department in the Rotterdam and Amsterdam offices of De Brauw. Ms. Govaert's current practice consists of both litigation and rendering advice on employment matters in general and employment-related issues in merger and acquisitions deals.

Liesbeth (E). Th.M. Sneek, born in 1959, is a Dutch *advocaat,* admitted to the Amsterdam Bar in 1984 and a partner at De Brauw Blackstone Westbroek since

1992. She is presently the coordinating partner of De Brauw's employment and employee benefits department in Amsterdam. Her practice consists of both litigation and rendering advice on employment (and pension) matters in general and employee consultation issues (works councils) in particular, whereby her previous experience in transnational merger and acquisitions work proves to be useful. Ms. Sneek is counsel to many of the prominent clients of De Brauw Blackstone Westbroek in various industry sectors.

SPAIN

Vicente Calle is a partner with the Spanish law firm Garringues. He received his law degree from Complutense University in 1989. Mr. Calle's practice comprises primarily of labor law, and he is a specialist in major restructuring operations. He belongs to the Madrid Bar Association and is fluent in Spanish and English.

Alfredo Aspra Rodríguez has been with the firm Garringues since 2001 and has over five years of professional experience. He specializes in the labor area. Mr. Rodríguez gained a Masters degree in labor law from the Centro Europeo de Estudios Empresariales Garrigues in 2000–2001. He has been an active participant in collective bargaining and restructuring processes at large companies, an area in which he has specialized in recent years and in which he has extensive experience. He also specializes in providing advice in labor and Social Security matters to Spanish and international companies, particularly with regard to labor audits for all types of transactions, in the areas of Social Security, immigration, nationality, hiring, and collective bargaining.

UNITED KINGDOM

Nicholas Dent is a senior associate at Barlow Lyde & Gilbert, one of London's premier litigation firms with its core client base drawn from the professional services and insurance sectors. Mr. Dent's practice at BLG and at the two other leading city employment practices where he has worked has always been focused on the financial and professional services sector, advising major institutions on complex discrimination and other Employment Tribunal cases and the full range of advisory, contentious, and transactional issues. He has a particular specialty in advising on collective redundancies, as well as outsourcing and insolvency-related issues.

UNITED STATES

Philip M. Berkowitz is a partner with Nixon Peabody LLP in New York City, where he chairs the firm's international labor and employment team. He received his B.A. from the State University of New York at New Paltz and his J.D. from Northwestern School of Law. Mr. Berkowitz's extensive labor and employment experience includes discrimination and harassment, whistleblowing, wrongful dismissal, ERISA violations, executive compensation, and breach of contract and restrictive covenants. He has defended litigations in federal and state courts and administrative agencies across the United States, as well as arbitrations before the National Association of Securities Dealers, the American Arbitration Association, and the International Chamber of Commerce. Mr. Berkowitz is the senior advisor to the International Employment Law Committee of the ABA Section of

International Law and is the management co-chair of the New York State Bar Association's International Labor and Employment Law Committee.

Anders Etgen Reitz is an associate with the firm Bech-Bruun in Copenhagen. He received his Master of Laws in 2000 and his LL.M. in 2005 and was admitted to practice in September 2003. Mr. Reitz practices in employment and labor law, litigation, and corporate law, and is a specialist in litigation, legal proceedings and arbitration, employees' legal position in business transfers, share options and share schemes, and salaried employee law.

INTRODUCTION

The field of international labor and employment law is developing rapidly and changing to fit the needs of increasingly global businesses. Human resources play an increasingly important role in international business transactions. Counsel for multinational companies increasingly recognize the importance of having a global perspective in labor and employment law. They are searching for sources of practical assistance.

This book is meant to help fill that role. Part of the ABA's *International Practitioner's Deskbook Series,* it is presented in the friendly, usable format of a single-volume handbook.

Our aim has been to provide helpful, practical guidance to international corporate lawyers who confront labor and employment problems in structuring corporate transactions. Thus, we focus on practical issues: establishing a facility; hiring a workforce; drafting employment contracts; terminating or replacing employees; providing wages and benefits; dealing with unions; carrying out workforce reductions; selling the business; and paying severance. We also treat issues regarding discrimination and harassment, wrongful dismissal, and key labor issues on the horizon. It is our hope and expectation that we will revise this book periodically.

Our contributors are leading labor lawyers in numerous important jurisdictions.

We have sought to distinguish this book from others in the area of international labor and employment law that tend to be encyclopedic in scope and approach. We have focused not only on what the laws provide, but also on the perspective of on-the-ground counsel who have extensive day-to-day experience with these issues. We are aware that we have not treated every pertinent jurisdiction. We have focused, in this volume, on what we perceived to be the largest economies. We may have been somewhat arbitrary in making these determinations, and we hope to include other jurisdictions in a future volume.

We are very grateful for all of the contributors' hard work in finalizing this volume. We are particularly grateful for the assistance of Anders Etgen

Reitz of Bech-Bruun in Copenhagen in co-editing many of these chapters. Finally, we are grateful to the ABA for permitting us to contribute to its exciting *International Practitioner's Deskbook Series.*

Philip M. Berkowitz
Thomas Müller-Bonanni
January 2006

CHAPTER 1

Labor and Employment Law in Belgium

Carl Bevernage
Henry-David Hachez

SECTION I

My client wishes to establish a manufacturing facility in Belgium and will need to hire a workforce. What are the key legal issues involved?

Labor Legislation

Belgium is a federal constitutional monarchy. Labor and employment legislation is voted on and enacted at the federal level. The three regions, Flanders, Wallonia, and Brussels, have only limited powers in this field.

The two major trade unions (Christian-Democrat and Socialist) and the smaller Liberal union historically have enjoyed large membership. They are deemed by law to be "representative" and play a major role in shaping protective legislation. They also negotiate collective bargaining agreements with the national and sectoral employers' federations that define wages and working conditions at the federal level as well as in the various branches of trade and industry. Collective bargaining at the company level is rather unusual.

The broad issues of employment (maximum wage increases, flexible working time, early retirement, etc.) are determined every two years in negotiations between the unions and the national employers' federations. The result of their negotiations is implemented in collective bargaining agreements concluded at the sectoral level by joint bodies set up by law in all sectors of industry and trade, including the nonprofit sector.

The collective bargaining agreements are rendered generally binding by royal decree to all workers, regardless of whether they are unionized. An employer has practically no way of excluding union representation when such a demand is made.

Employees designated by the unions as members of the so-called Union Delegations (grievance committees) or elected to the Works Council (in companies employing at least 100 workers) or to the Committees for Prevention and Protection at Work (in companies employing at least 50 workers) enjoy considerable protection against layoff. This same protection extends to unsuccessful candidates at the elections.

Labor legislation is comprehensive in the areas set forth below and cannot, in most cases, be contracted away:

- Maximum working time;
- Public holidays and vacation (pay);
- Minimum wages;
- Automatic cost-of-living salary adjustments;
- Protection of salary;
- Work regulations;
- Dismissal rules;
- Early retirement schemes;
- Protection of maternity rights, parental leave, and time off for educational purposes, family care, etc.;
- Restrictions regarding noncompetition covenants;
- Nondiscrimination;
- Use of language (Dutch in Flanders, French in Wallonia, and a choice between the two in Brussels) in labor relations and mandatory documents; and
- Jurisdiction of the labor courts (arbitration in individual labor disputes is possible only with employees earning at least €52,836 per year (threshold 2004)).

Most legislation and collective bargaining agreements are enforced by penal law. However, in many instances, penal sanctions are replaced by civil penalties imposed by the Ministry of Labor.

A distinction is made between white-collar employees and blue-collar workers. The statutory rules that apply to each category of employees differ in many ways, the most important of which is that blue-collar workers can be dismissed with much shorter notice periods and can be subject to shorter trial periods as well.

Inbound cross-border assignments may be subject to foreign law; however, under the Rome Convention, which determines the law applicable to international employment contracts, the parties' choice of law must not deprive the employee of the protection granted by mandatory rules of law that would have applied if the parties had not agreed upon a choice of law. As a result, mandatory rules of Belgian labor law will apply to every labor relationship habitually carried out in Belgium, even if the parties chose another jurisdiction's law to govern their contract.

In addition, pursuant to the Posted Workers (EC) Directive (96/71/EC), most Belgian labor law provisions will apply as of the first day of any temporary reassignment to Belgium.

Social Security Contributions

Wages are subject to Social Security taxes. A white-collar employee's share is currently 13.07 percent, and the employer contributes about 34.70 percent of gross wages. The percentages for blue-collar workers differ because their extra vacation pay, called "double vacation pay," is financed through the Social Security system.

A limited reduction in Social Security charges is possible for certain categories of workers, such as long-term or elderly workers, or the first and second employee(s) recruited by small companies. Additional incentives may be available depending on the industry. Sector social funds may contribute financial support depending on the primary activity of the enterprise.

Social Security coverage includes unemployment benefits, medicare, sick pay, indemnities for occupational diseases, family allowances, and pensions.

Work Permits

Belgian employers are free to hire European Economic Area (EEA) nationals without a visa or work permit. Work permits from one of the regional Immigration Departments are required for other foreign workers. There are three categories of work permits:

- Permit A: Permits valid for all jobs and employers for an indefinite period;
- Permit B: Permits valid for a specific employer and for a fixed term (maximum 12 months but can be extended); and
- Permit C: Permits valid for all jobs and employers but for a fixed term (maximum 12 months but can be extended).

The requirements to obtain a work permit depend on the category of permit. A non-EEA national working in Belgium for the first time typically may apply for only Permit B. In practice it is not difficult to obtain a Permit B for highly qualified employees (generally determined by reference to their salary).

The entire application process takes about six to ten weeks. In all categories, the employer must have obtained the work permit before the worker comes to Belgium for the purpose of employment.

Employment Contracts

In principle, there is no requirement that an employment contract be in writing except for

- Contracts for a fixed term or for the completion of a specific task;
- Part-time contracts;
- Replacement contracts; and
- Contracts with a student or a home worker.

However, some clauses are valid only when agreed to in writing, such as a trial clause, a noncompetition clause, or a clause on the length of the notice period. Many employment terms and conditions need not be expressly agreed upon and result from statutory provisions, collective bargaining agreements, work regulations, and custom.

Working Hours

Weekly working hours may not exceed 38 hours, and daily working hours may not exceed eight hours, or 11 hours for shift work. Collective bargaining agreements concluded at the industry level and made compulsory by royal decree may reduce weekly working hours or allow for certain flexible-time arrangements. Night work and work on Sundays or on public holidays is prohibited, except in specific circumstances.

The statutory provisions regarding working hours do not apply to employees in a position of trust or management with the enterprise or to any person who has the authority to bind the enterprise vis-à-vis third parties.

Overtime is allowed but restricted by law; e.g., overtime pay and compensatory time off is required. The number of additional hours accumulated as overtime must not exceed 65 hours or 130 hours per year with union approval (in case, for example, of an exceptional workload).

Public Holidays and Vacation

Employees are entitled to ten paid public holidays per year and paid annual leave. The right to paid leave accrues on the basis of the days worked in the calendar year immediately preceding the calendar year in which an employee takes a holiday.

Employees who worked a full year are entitled to 20 days of holiday if they work a five-day week. This is the statutory minimum. Collective agreements in some industrial sectors expand this to paid leave.

Employees taking vacation days are entitled to their normal salary ("single vacation pay") plus 92 percent of their normal monthly salary ("double vacation pay").

Works Councils

A Works Council must be established in every enterprise defined as a "technical unit of operation" that employs on average at least 100 workers. Elections to Works Councils are organized every four years by the Ministry of Labor. Only recognized unions may present candidates.

An employer must consult with the Works Council or, in the absence thereof, with all its employees on various issues, including:

- Collective dismissals;
- Substantial changes in the structure of the enterprise; and
- Transfer of an enterprise.

Employers are not bound by the advice or suggestions of the employees' representatives on these matters but risk unrest among their workforce if consultation is not conducted in good faith and in a timely manner.

Committees for Prevention and Protection at Work

A Committee for Prevention and Protection at Work must be established in every enterprise defined as a "technical unit of operation" that employs on average at least 50 workers. Elections to the Committees are organized every four years by the Ministry of Labor at the same time as the elections to the Works Council. The next elections will be held in May 2008. Only recognized unions may present candidates.

The Committee for Prevention and Protection at Work has broad power to monitor employer compliance with a myriad of statutorily imposed health and safety rules and may make recommendations to improve the observance thereof.

Union Delegations

The Unions may designate among the personnel of companies employing on average at least 20 workers a Union delegation (grievance committee).

The following employees enjoy special protection against unfair dismissal:

- Members and candidates of the Works Council or the Committee for Prevention and Protection at Work;
- Members of the Union Delegation;
- Pregnant workers; and
- Employees who have lodged a gender discrimination complaint.

Maternity Rights

Pregnant employees are entitled to a maternity leave of 15 weeks. During this period, the employee receives a state maternity allowance. Maternity leave can be taken from the seventh week before the birth; at least one week must be taken before the expected date of birth. The remaining leave is taken after the date of birth.

Pregnant employees are protected against dismissal as of the date the employer is informed of the pregnancy until one month after the end of the maternity leave.

Paternity Rights

Employees are entitled to ten days paid paternity leave within 30 days of the birth.

Data Protection Rights

The Privacy Act of 1992 protects every person whose personal data is processed by a third party. Any person processing personal data must notify the Privacy Commission of the processing. Processing must be done in a fair way and, in principle, with the consent of the individual concerned. In addition, the information processed must be "adequate, relevant, and non-excessive." The Privacy Act allows an individual access to his or her processed data to check its accuracy and to request any correction.

These provisions apply to employers who process data about their employees. A notification to the Privacy Commission is not required in certain circumstances.

National Collective Bargaining Agreement No. 81 allows employers to control employee use of computers, including e-mail and the Internet, on the basis of three principles:

1. Fair objective;
2. Proportionality; and
3. Transparency.

The decision to control, the method of control, and the objective of control must be communicated to the employees through their representatives in the Works Council.

SECTION II

My client is acquiring an existing business in Belgium. How do I assess the existing workforce and consider changes?

Role of the Unions

At the enterprise level, negotiations and mandatory information or consultation are channeled through representative union-controlled bodies, such as Works Councils and Committees for Prevention and Protection at Work, for which nationwide social elections are organized every four years (the last elections were in May 2004) or through the Union Delegation.

The Joint Committees also play an important role in the event of a reorganization. They are set up at a sectoral level of industry, trade, service, and even the nonprofit sector (e.g., health care) and have jurisdiction over only salaried employees or blue-collar workers, or both, as the case may be. Many Joint Committees have established subcommittees in important industrial branches, such as the steel and food industries. Excluding the Joint Subcommittees, there are some 120 Joint Committees.

The Joint (Sub)Committees are composed of an equal number of union representatives and employer association representatives. The Chairman is an official of the Service of Collective Labor Relations organized within the Ministry of Labor.

Such committees primarily have a conciliatory role in order to prevent or settle disputes between employers and employees.

The importance of the representative unions is underscored by the fact that they are present in many public service companies, where they have received certain consultative and even administrative powers. Moreover, they act as intermediaries between the state and the people for the payment of various Social Security allowances (unemployment benefits, health care, family allowances, etc.), for which they receive fees from the government.

Unions are not incorporated. They are associations and are therefore not recognized by law. This means that they do not have any legal rights (except for those specifically provided for by law, as described hereinafter) and they are not an entity that can be sued in court. The legal basis for their existence is found in the principle of freedom of association as laid down in Article 20 of the Constitution.

Trade unions may initiate lawsuits against employers in well-defined fields of employment and labor but traditionally have not wished to involve the judiciary in disputes. Trade unions cannot be sued for damages by employers or third parties, for example, in cases of strike, third-party picketing, etc.

Special laws have been passed, however, to prevent exclusion of the unions from the legal field. Indeed, the representative unions:

- Have the right to conclude collective bargaining agreements;
- Are entitled to act in court on behalf of employees in employment litigation; and
- Can present candidates from the workforce of an enterprise at the "social elections."

Unions have the right to represent and defend employees in employment litigation before the labor courts.

At the company level, employees are represented in three different bodies, the members of which are either designated or elected. These bodies are the Union Delegation, the Works Council, and the Committee for Prevention and Protection at Work.

Union Delegation

The Union Delegation (Vakbondsafvaardiging—Délégation Syndicale) consists of employees designated or elected to represent the unionized employees vis-à-vis the employer. A collective bargaining agreement can extend this representation to nonaffiliated personnel.

The general status of the Union Delegation is regulated by the National Labor Council's Collective Bargaining Agreement No. 5 of May 24, 1971, as amended, concluded between the national confederation of employers and trade unions and implemented by sectoral collective bargaining agreements concluded by the various Joint Committees and Joint Subcommittees. As a result of such implementation, Union Delegations can be instituted in various sectors of industry and trade covered by such Committees, and they are mandatory intermediaries concerning the rights and grievances of their members within a given enterprise.

A Union Delegation should be formed as one or more "representative unions" require. A union may, however, present candidates for designation or election only if it can prove that it represents at least 10 percent of the enterprise's unionized personnel.

The Union Delegation is responsible for the following areas:

- Labor relations in general. This concerns the material aspects (salary, working hours, premiums, etc.) as well as the more immaterial aspects (employment conditions, human relations in the enterprise, etc.) of employment.
- Negotiating collective bargaining agreements and collective arrangements within the enterprise without prejudice to the collective bargaining agreements concluded at higher levels (i.e., by the Joint Committee or at the national level). It should be noted, however, that the Union Delegation is not competent to conclude collective bargaining agreements. This remains the prerogative of the representative unions.
- Application in the enterprise of labor and Social Security legislation, collective bargaining agreements, work regulations, and individual employment contracts.

Moreover, the Union Delegation represents the employees in individual and collective disputes with the employer. Finally, the Union Delegation has the right to provide employees any information pertaining to union activities.

When there is no Works Council in the enterprise, the Union Delegation takes over a number of the Works Council's powers. It is then entitled to receive information on the general prospects of the enterprise and intended major reorganizations and how these might impact employment.

Works Councils

Works Councils are regulated by the Laws of September 29, 1948, and August 4, 1996, and must be established by election if certain workforce size requirements, set forth by law and decree, are met.

A Works Council must be set up in each "enterprise" employing on average 100 or more employees. Enterprises in which a Works Council was or could have been in existence at the time of the last elections and that employ on an average basis between only 50 and 100 persons are also obliged to establish a Works Council. In such a case, however, there is no need to hold elections because the Committee for Prevention and Protection at Work will exercise its functions. In order to determine whether a Works Council and/or Committee for Prevention and Protection at Work must be established, the average workforce requirement is examined, taking into account the definition of "enterprise," which is "a technical operating unit."

A "technical operating unit" is characterized by social independence (i.e., the actual staffing or employment situation of a company, plant, division, or business unit) and economic independence (such as its relative autonomy or interdependence in economic, legal, or financial terms). The criteria for social independence, as interpreted by case law, takes precedence over the economic status of an enterprise.

The Works Council and the Committee for Prevention and Protection at Work are, in principle, composed of an equal number of employer and employee representatives. The employer representatives are designated by the employer and are chosen from management personnel. The employees' representatives are elected from candidates presented by the representative unions (plus the NCK-CNC, the National Union of Executives, for the election of the Works Council).

Reference must be made to EU Council Directive 5494/45/EEC of September 22, 1994, on the establishment of a European Works Council or a procedure in Community-scale undertakings and Community-scale groups of undertakings (hereinafter Community-scale groups) for the purposes of informing and consulting employees. The text of the Directive was introduced into Belgian law by means of Collective Bargaining Agreement No. 62 of February 6, 1996, which came into effect by the Royal Decree of March 22, 1996. In applying Article 13 of the Directive, Article 4 of Collective Bargaining Agreement No. 62 exempts from the obligations under the collective bargaining agreement Community-scale groups if an agreement on cross-border information and consultation of workers, concluded before September 23, 1996, exists within the Community-scale groups. Such agreement must be in writing and must cover the entire workforce of the Community-scale groups.

The Works Council may not interfere with the actual management of a business. It has an advisory role and is entitled to receive information on the business operations of the enterprise. The functions of the Works Council can be summarized as follows:

- Examine initiatives to increase cooperation between management and personnel and make recommendations on increasing productivity;
- Receive quarterly information relating to the productivity of the enterprise and annual information concerning the financial condition of the enterprise;
- Propose and amend work regulations;
- Advise on the standards for hiring and dismissing personnel;
- Ensure strict compliance with labor safety laws;
- Fix annual vacation periods with the consent of management; and
- Agree on the appointment of the statutory auditor.

Reorganization is itself a management decision and prerogative. However, the Works Council should receive information on situations that may affect employment conditions or involve collective transfers for economic or technical reasons. Such information should be provided before the decision is made by management. Indeed, a reorganization should not come as a surprise in companies with a Works Council because there is a legal obligation to provide information on the general business outlook, employment policy, and financial condition of the enterprise on a regular basis.

However, Article 25 of the Royal Decree of November 27, 1973, provides that additional information (as opposed to information provided periodically, as discussed above) must be given to the Works Council

- Whenever events occur that may have an important effect on the enterprise; and
- Whenever internal decisions are made that may have an important effect on the enterprise.

Article 11 of the collective bargaining agreement of March 9, 1972, provides that, in the event of a merger, acquisition, or other important structural change, the employer must consult with the Works Council on the repercussions on future employment levels prior to any announcement.

The employer must determine an appropriate time for such consultation, taking into account the following principles:

- The information may not adversely affect the prerogatives of the employer on the economic aspects of the decision.
- The information may not interfere with possible ongoing negotiations.
- The information must be given prior to any public announcement or actual implementation of the merger or acquisition.
- The information must be given in a timely manner to allow the employer and its employees sufficient time to discuss the consequences of the decision in the Works Council.

The Works Council must be informed of the economic, technical, and financial bases upon which the reorganization has been decided, as well as the economic, financial, and social consequences thereof, including the consequences to employment within the enterprise, e.g., layoffs.

In addition, union representatives must have access to every possible facility to establish whatever contacts may be necessary to ensure the integration, retraining, or (re)insertion of dismissed or transferred employees.

Committees for Prevention and Safety at Work

Like Works Councils, Committees for Prevention and Protection at Work are regulated by the Laws of September 29, 1948, and August 4, 1996, and must be established by election if certain workforce size requirements, set forth by law and decree, are met.

The functions of the Committee for Prevention and Protection at Work can be summarized as follows:

- Advise on health and safety conditions and on other problems relating to working conditions;
- Approve the appointment and replacement of the head of security and health, and any assistants, as well as the appointment of any temporary replacement for such persons or the content of their functions;
- Look for means to improve the working premises;
- Demand that the labor physician visit the enterprise;
- Propose that medical supervision be extended to cover all or part of the workforce not covered by relevant legal provisions; and
- Participate in the organization and implementation of measures to secure emergency assistance and first aid to injured employees.

Notice Period

The notice period to be observed by an employer in case of dismissal depends on the duration of employment.

Either party can terminate an employment contract of an indefinite period at any time by serving notice on the other party. The reasons for the termination need not be set out, nor must the employer obtain prior or subsequent administrative or judicial approval; however, strict formalities and statutory minimum periods of notice apply. The length of the notice period depends on whether the employee is blue-collar or white-collar. Claeys Formula, a statistical formula applicable to white-collar employees, is a good indicator of the notice period that could be awarded by a labor court.

A contract for an indefinite period can also be terminated at any time by either party with immediate effect and without cause or any other formality. In this case, the notified party is entitled to a lump-sum payment in lieu of notice. This payment is equal to the total remuneration, including all benefits, that would have been paid during the notice period if the contract had been terminated with advanced notice. This is the most common way of terminating a contract in Belgium.

Blue-collar workers are entitled to damages equal to six months' salary if the employer fails to establish that dismissal was fairly based either on economic grounds or on competence or attitude. This rule does not apply to white-collar employees, who may obtain damages for unfair dismissal in only specific circumstances (see Section IV below). However, special procedures must be followed for informing and consulting employees prior to a layoff (see Carrying Out a Workforce Reduction below).

Carrying Out a Workforce Reduction

Information and Consultation Duties

The procedures for informing and consulting employees prior to a layoff (or the closing of an enterprise) are based on a variety of collective bargaining agreements and royal decrees as well as on the Law of February 13, 1998, implementing EEC directive 75/129 on the approximation of the laws of the Member States relating to collective redundancies (amended by the Council Directive 92/56 of June 24, 1992) and Council Directive 98/59 of August 12, 1998, on the approximation of the laws of the Member States relating to collective redundancies.

These rules are applicable to an enterprise employing more than 20 workers. Dismissal is deemed collective when it affects ten workers out of a workforce of 21 to 99, 10 percent of a workforce of 100 to 299, or at least 30 workers of a workforce of 300 or more. Lower thresholds and/or other rules may exist and apply depending on the applicable industry-level collective bargaining agreements.

The rules require an employer (1) to inform and consult with employees' representatives in the Works Council or, in the absence thereof, in the Union Delegation, for the purpose of considering measures to prevent such layoffs or to minimize their consequences and (2) notify the Regional Employment Office of the intent to proceed with a layoff. A 30-day cooling-off period following such notification must be observed before layoffs can take place. This period may be either reduced or extended by another 30 days by the Regional Employment Office.

It should be noted that the Law of December 21, 1994, provides that the King may, by royal decree, subject the layoff of workers to a prior authorization, in execution of the European Union requirements. However, no royal decree has been adopted to that effect.

The rules governing the closing of an enterprise are laid down in the Law of June 28, 1966, and the Royal Decree of September 20, 1967, and apply to enterprises (or autonomous divisions) employing at least 20 employees. Closure is defined as the permanent cessation of the main activity of an enterprise (or of an autonomous division) where the number of employees is reduced to less than one-fourth of the average number employed during the preceding calendar year.

In the event of a layoff resulting from a closure, the layoff procedures precede the implementation of the closure procedures, i.e., the various information and consultation steps required by law for a layoff must be taken before the steps specifically required for closure. However, it is understood that during the information and consultation stage required for a layoff, the employees and their representatives will be informed of the expected closing of the enterprise.

The Law of February 13, 1998, confirmed and emphasized an employer's obligation to inform and consult, regardless of whether the layoff results from a closure, *prior to any final decision making*. This Law sets forth four conditions an employer must satisfy. The employer must be able to produce evidence that it has fulfilled each of these conditions, and the burden of proving compliance lies with the employer. The conditions are as follows:

- The employer must provide the Works Council or, in the absence thereof, the Union Delegation, or, in the absence thereof, the employees themselves, with a written report indicating its intent to carry out a layoff, regardless of whether the layoff is within the framework of a closure, and setting out the full details of the layoff and/or closure. Because this report must be in writing, the report itself can serve as proof of compliance.
- The employer must hold a meeting concerning its intent to carry out a layoff with the Works Council or, in the absence thereof, with the Union Delegation or, in the absence thereof, with the employees themselves. Written notification of the meeting (which may be sent by registered mail) and written minutes of the meeting should qualify as proof of compliance.
- The employees' representatives or, in the absence of such representatives, the employees themselves, must be given the opportunity to ask questions regarding the intended layoff and to formulate arguments and counterproposals. For purposes of evidence and proof, such opportunities should be fully set out in the written minutes of the meeting.
- The employer must study the questions, arguments, and counterproposals of the employee representatives or employees themselves and provide answers, rebuttal, and explanation. Again, for purposes of evidence and proof, the employer's analysis and study should be the subject matter of written minutes of meetings.

Notwithstanding these conditions, the decision to proceed with a layoff and/or closure remains exclusively with the employer.

Once the employer is satisfied that it has complied with the information and consultation procedures and has sufficient evidence thereof, it must provide written notice to the Director of the Regional Employment Office. This notification must confirm that the above four conditions have been fulfilled. In practice, the employer should provide the Director with copies of all relevant reports communicated to employee representatives, notifications to attend meetings, and minutes of such meetings.

On the day of notification to the Director, the employer also must provide the following:

- A copy of the notification to the Works Council or, in the absence thereof, to the Union Delegation;
- A copy of the notification for posting in a visible location on the premises of the enterprise; and
- A copy of the notification sent by registered mail to the employees who will be affected by the layoff and to those whose employment contract has terminated on the day of the notification and of its posting.

In the event of a closure, additional information must be provided to the representatives of the employees (and the Works Council, if any), as well as to the Regional Employment Officer.

Risks of Noncompliance

An employer that does not comply with the above steps exposes itself to the following risks:

- Legal action by the unions, employees, and/or the Social Inspectorate of the Ministry of Labor;
- Criminal penalties[1] or administrative fines;[2]
- Adverse publicity in the national and international press; and
- Difficulties in the implementation of the layoff or closure.

In this regard, employees are protected if an employer fails to comply with proper procedures in a layoff.

These protections apply to employees dismissed within 60 days of qualifying for a layoff and within the subsequent 60-day period. In the case of a closure, these protections apply to employees dismissed within 60 days of qualifying for a layoff, extended until the date of closure (i.e., the first day of the month following the date on which the number of employees decreased to less than 25 percent of the average number of workers employed during the year before the closure).

Within 30 days of the posting of the notification to the Director of the Regional Employment Office, the employee representatives (Works Council or Union Delegation) or, in the absence of such representatives, the employees themselves, may notify the employer of any objections to the employer's compliance with the layoff procedure.

If, within the 30-day period, the employee representatives or the employees have not notified the employer of any objections, a dismissed worker may no longer challenge the employer's compliance with the layoff procedures. Such employees are no longer eligible for special protection against dismissal.

However, if the employee representatives or the employees themselves have made timely objections, any dismissed worker may challenge the employer's compliance with the layoff procedure, provided that the employee notifies the employer of his or her complaint by registered mail within 30 days from the date of dismissal.

An employer faced with an objection regarding the procedure within the 30-day time period must decide whether to proceed with the layoff, in which case it might face claims from dismissed workers, or to begin the procedure again.

In the case of dismissed employees who are in a position to challenge the employer's compliance with the layoff procedure, and who actually do challenge such compliance within the prescribed time period, the Law of February 13, 1998, distinguishes between various situations and grants certain protections based on such distinctions.

Contract Terminated with Notice

For an employee whose contract has been terminated with notice, the notice of termination will be suspended as of the third day following the mailing date of the worker's letter challenging the employer's compliance with layoff procedure, unless the employer produces evidence that the worker's complaint is ill-founded. During the suspension of the notice period, the employer must continue to pay the worker. Suspension of the notice period terminates 60 days after the employer's legally valid notification of the intent to make a layoff to the Director of the Regional Employment Office.

Should an employer be sued for failing to comply with the proper layoff procedure and be ordered to resume the procedure, a legally valid notification of the intent to make a layoff to the Director of the Regional Employment Office could very well take place several months after the initial, invalidated notice and would, in such case, extend the notice suspension period.

During the suspension period, an employee is entitled to terminate the employment contract without notice and/or severance compensation.

Contract Terminated without Notice

An employee whose contract has been terminated without notice must formally request reinstatement in a letter challenging the employer's compliance with the proper layoff procedures.

If the employer cannot produce evidence that the worker's complaint is ill-founded, it must reinstate the worker within 30 days from the third working day of the mailing date of the letter of complaint. In addition to reinstating the worker, the employer must pay the employee his or her salary from the date of dismissal. However, the worker must reimburse the employer for any severance compensation.

If the employer refuses to reinstate the worker, the employer must pay the worker his or her salary from the date of dismissal to 60 days after a legally valid notification of the intent to make a layoff to the Director of the Regional Employment Office.

Should an employer be sued for failing to comply with the proper layoff procedure and ordered to resume the procedure, a legally valid notification to the Director of the Regional Employment Office of an intent to implement a layoff could very well take place several months after the initial invalidated notice and would, in such a case, extend the period during which salary was due.

Negotiating New Employment and Salary Conditions

Collective Bargaining

Employment and salary conditions are set in collective bargaining agreements, which can be negotiated at three levels: the national level, the industry level, or the enterprise level. However, collective bargaining agreements negotiated at the enterprise level may be superseded by agreements reached at the industry or national levels and may not depart from the essential rights set forth in such agreements.

Most collective bargaining agreements are negotiated at the national level and cover working hours, minimum wages, flex-time, job security arrangements, etc. Such agreements are then implemented with further elaboration within the National Labor Council but more often at the industry level within the Joint Committees or Joint Subcommittees.

The content of a collective bargaining agreement can be divided into two categories of provisions: individual provisions and collective provisions. Individual provisions contain rules governing individual employment contracts (wages, holidays, working hours, etc.). Collective provisions relate to collective rights and obligations (welfare, funds, union delegation, etc.).

Although enterprise-level collective bargaining agreements are generally negotiated by the members of the Union Delegation, it is important to note that employees may enter a collective bargaining agreement only through a representative union. Collective bargaining agreements concluded by other parties, e.g., by a union that is not recognized as "representative," are not legally enforceable.

Strikes

Strikes are common in collective negotiations and collective disputes because they are widely considered to be the most efficient way to put pressure on an employer.

The Law of July 17, 1990, enacted the European Social Charter signed in Turin on October 18, 1961. Before the law was enacted, the legitimacy of strikes were determined on a case-by-case basis. Case law now recognizes that employees have a right to strike. Consequently, participation in a strike cannot, as such, be regarded as a breach of contract.

The Belgian Supreme Court has held that employment contracts are suspended during a strike; employees on strike are not entitled to compensation and will be liable for damages caused to the employer and/or to third parties during the strike. This is contrary to the situation where such damage is caused in the course of an employment contract. Article 18 of the Law of July 3, 1978, limits an employee's liability to cases of fraud, serious fault, or minor faults, which occur frequently during strikes.

Participating in a strike does not justify termination of the employment contract without notice or indemnity, regardless of the cause or motive for the strike. Certain "aggravating circumstances" can, however, justify termination for cause, such as violence and vandalism. Likewise, picketing does not justify termination for cause, unless it is accompanied by "aggravating circumstances."

For a number of years, employers tried with some success to stop the "collateral effects" of strikes and third-party picketing by seeking injunctive relief from the President of the Court of First Instance to enforce the right to work of workers who do not participate in a strike, to permit the supply of raw material or the shipping of merchandise, to stop plant occupations, etc. The aggrieved party brings his or her summons for injunctive relief before the President of the Court of First Instance rather than before the President of the Labor Court, on the grounds that private property rights are actually or possibly affected as a "collateral" effect of picketing, violence, plant occupation, etc. The civil courts have generally steered a cautious course in imposing injunctive relief measures in order to avoid interfering with the unabridged right to strike.

The government contemplated limiting this form of injunctive relief at one point in time. Under the proposal, mediation by a civil servant appointed by the Minister of Employment and Labor would be a mandatory precondition to any possible court action. In addition, only the President of the Labor Court would be competent to decide on any form of injunctive relief, it being understood that the labor court might be less sympathetic to the grievances of an employer than a civil court. However, the management and union federations convinced the government not to regulate this issue and are negotiating an agreement that will define the context in which employers may seek redress in court against "collateral damage" caused by the secondary effects of strikes and/or picketing.

SECTION III

My client wishes to sell its existing facility. What restrictions do we need to consider?

In the event of a contractual transfer of (or part of) an enterprise, Collective Bargaining Agreement No. 32bis of June 7, 1985, stipulates that all existing employment contracts of the transferred personnel of the assignor (seller) are transferred to the assignee (buyer).

The notion of transfer of (or part of) an enterprise is defined by Collective Bargaining Agreement No. 32bis as "the transfer of an economic entity which retains its identity, meaning an organized grouping of resources which has the objective of pursuing an economic activity, whether or not this activity is central or ancillary."

Belgian case law regarding Collective Bargaining Agreement No. 32bis is very much in line with the case law of the European Court of Justice regarding underlying EU Directives, which may be relied upon when assessing the possible application of Collective Bargaining Agreement No. 32bis.

The following different elements must therefore be considered in determining whether an outsourcing operation may qualify as a transfer in the sense of the EU Directives and Collective Bargaining Agreement No. 32bis:

- The continuation of the same or similar economic activities (identity of activities element);
- The take-over of assets, material or immaterial, such as machines, equipments, computers, licenses, etc. (assets element); and
- The transfer of (part of) the personnel (human resources element).

The European Court of Justice has ruled that, in certain industries, an enterprise is primarily defined by the activities of its employees who do not require substantial or specific assets to carry out these activities. Therefore, when an activity is characterized by a high degree of expertise of its personnel and when a high percentage of this personnel is taken over, their continued activities may support a finding of identity and continuity of the business and will prevail over the other elements. This means that all rights and obligations of the assignor toward its employees existing on the date of the transfer are automatically transferred to the assignee. Therefore, in case of transfer, all employees may be assigned to the new employer without their consent as an automatic result of the transfer.

The employees are transferred on their existing terms and conditions of employment.

Unilateral modification of the essential elements of the employment contract constitutes a breach of contract, giving the employee the right to claim a severance indemnity. In that regard, a unilateral modification of the place of employment resulting from the transfer (e.g., to another city or country) may constitute such a breach of contract; this issue must be examined in due time in order to anticipate any major drawbacks, such as an illegal layoff, as a result of the transfer.

Furthermore, the assignee must observe the existing collective bargaining agreement applicable within the transferor. The Supreme Court (Hof van Cassatie/ Cour de Cassation) recently decided that when the transfer entails a change of sector or industry, the assignee must offer to the newly acquired employees all advantageous terms and conditions provided for in the collective bargaining agreement of the assignee.

In light of the above, changes in the terms and conditions are possible only if the parties to the employment contract agree to such changes. Certain flexibility may exist with regard to the nonessential terms and conditions, however, depending on the content of the employment contracts.

The purchaser is bound to assume all liability resulting from the existing employment contracts. This includes all vested rights, such as seniority privileges, extra vacation days, and bonuses. However, employees' rights under supplementary pension plans are not automatically transferred from the seller to the buyer by virtue of the transfer itself. One exception exists with respect to supplementary pension plans, which are based on collective bargaining agreements. Moreover, the statement regarding the absence of automatic transfer of the employees' supplementary pension rights must be moderated because it could be argued that the buyer/transferee would, in most hypotheses, be obliged to "do something" vis-à-vis the transferred employees.

The obligations of the assignor toward former employees whose contracts of employment have been terminated before the date of transfer are not transferred to the assignee (e.g., severance allowances still to be paid). The assignor and the assignee are, on the basis of Collective Bargaining Agreement No. 32bis, considered to be joint debtors (employer's liability *in solidum*) for the debts of the assignor on the date of the transfer. Under the provisions of Collective Bargaining Agreement No. 32bis, the assignor must assume all future and existing liabilities for employee wages and benefits at the time of takeover. With regard to liabilities arising from or after the transfer, the buyer will be liable vis-à-vis the transferred employees. Contractual arrangements regarding the liabilities arising from the transfer may be entered into between assignor and assignee, it being understood that the employees are not bound by such agreements. The necessary guarantees must therefore be foreseen in the agreement between the seller and the buyer.

Collective Bargaining Agreement No. 32bis also specifies that the transfer may not be used as a reason for dismissal. The only dismissals allowed are those for serious cause or for economic, technical, or structural reasons. This rule applies to the assignor as well as to the assignee.

In order to avoid a situation in which this rule acts as a deterrent to taking over an enterprise in bad financial condition, it appears that some courts and trade unions will allow employees to be dismissed for economic, technical, or structural reasons before the transfer is agreed upon in certain circumstances, in order to enable a transfer on a basis acceptable to the buyer.

There are information and consultation obligations at Works Council or Union Delegation or employee levels to be complied with prior to the final decision of transfer. In the absence of a Works Council and a union delegation, the employees should be informed. These obligations require that an actual dialogue be established between the employer and the employee representatives regarding the impact on the employment of the transfer envisaged. Typically, the following items must be discussed: (1) the reasons for the transfer envisaged; (2) the legal, economic, and social implications of this transfer for the employees; (3) the measures envisaged in relation to the employees; and (4) the proposed date of the transfer. However, the employee representatives do not have the right to interfere with the transaction as such.

Although no formal timetable exists, it is wise to organize the information and consultation process in a way that allows the employer to demonstrate the existence of a dialogue. Noncompliance with the above information and consultation obligations may trigger criminal or administrative penalties and may form the basis for claims for damages by the employees. In principle, it would likely not prevent the operation from taking place, although such a risk cannot be totally excluded.

SECTION IV

My client wishes to replace its senior manager(s). What restrictions do we need to consider?

Proposed changes to key managerial positions must be assessed carefully. Any intended unilateral modification of an essential employment condition, such as the position itself and/or its responsibilities, may be considered a breach of contract and may entitle the employee to claim the appropriate severance compensation.

Article 25 of the Law of July 3, 1978, provides that any clause in an employment contract whereby the employer reserves the right to unilaterally modify an employment condition is null and void. However, case law reveals, and legal scholars admit, that Article 25 applies to only the essential terms and conditions of an employment contract and not to secondary, nonessential conditions.

Essential terms and conditions of an employment contract include

- The (overall) remuneration;
- The position and the nature of responsibilities; and
- The working time, place of employment, and territory assigned to sales representatives.

The clauses whereby the employer reserves the right to modify nonessential terms and conditions are upheld only if

- The employment contract specifies explicitly that the conditions that may be modified by the employer are considered by the parties as nonessential.
- The modification clause is drafted in such a way that the implementation of a modification will not depend solely on the discretionary decision of the employer. In other words, reference should be made to objective requirements/criteria that, if met, could trigger the employer's decision to modify the contract.
- The implementation of the modification clause is carried out in good faith.

Executive employees who object to some or all of the modifications could claim that the unilateral modifications to the agreed terms and conditions of their employment constitute a constructive dismissal. If they are successful, these employees will be entitled to the amounts due in the event of termination: severance indemnity, possible client indemnity, possible noncompetition indemnity, etc.

In the absence of any immediate reaction by executive employees, it cannot be argued that these employees have, by default, agreed to the modifications. Certain modifications may not be immediately obvious and may therefore go unnoticed for some time. Moreover, the nature of the relationship between the employer and executive employee may prevent the employee from immediately objecting to the modifications. Therefore, in the absence of the explicit consent of the executive employees, the risk that the modifications might be challenged later cannot be totally excluded.

SECTION V

What prohibitions exist against discrimination on a basis of age, race, gender, disability, pregnancy, and other factors? What are the rights of employees, applicants, or former employees who believe that they have been discriminated against?

General Framework

On February 25, 2003, the Belgian Parliament enacted an antidiscrimination law concerning all aspects of "social relations," including employment relations, implementing Council Directive 200/78/EC of November 27, 2000, which establishes a general framework for equal treatment in employment, and Council Directive 2000/43/EC regarding equal treatment of persons regardless of race or ethnic origin.

This law does not set aside the Law of July 30, 1981, prohibiting racial discrimination, or the Law of May 7, 1999, regarding equal treatment of men and women, as discussed later in this section.

The February 25, 2003, law defines the following as possible grounds for discrimination:

- Gender
- Race
- Skin color

- Origin
- National or ethnic descent
- Sexual preference
- Marital status
- Wealth
- Age
- Religion or faith
- Present or future health situation
- Handicap or physical propriety

Referring specifically to employment relations, Article 2, Section 4 of the February 25, 2003, law prohibits every form of direct or indirect discrimination regarding "the conditions of access to employed work, unpaid work, self-employed activities, including criteria of selection and hiring, irrespective of the type of activity and level of professional hierarchy, including possibilities of promotion, conditions of employment and work, including dismissal and remuneration, as well in the private as the public sector."

Forbidden forms of discrimination include

- Direct discrimination
- Indirect discrimination
- Lack of adequate facilities for the handicapped
- Harassment (pestering)
- Discrimination against persons on any grounds (with the exception of "positive discrimination" in favor of disfavored groups or distinctions that are reasonably and objectively justified)

Violations of the February 25, 2003, law are subject to criminal sanctions and to civil remedies, such as injunctive relief.

Victims, unions, representative action groups, and the federal Center for Equal Opportunity and Combating of Racism may bring actions in court. Whistleblowers are protected against dismissal as a form of retaliation.

Equal Treatment

The Law of May 7, 1999, regulates, in one broad sweep, the equal treatment of men and women in Belgium regarding working conditions, access to work and promotion, access to independent professions, and complementary Social Security schemes.

The May 7, 1999, law implements EU Council Directive 96/97 of December 20, 1996, amending Council Directive 86/378 (regarding equal treatment of men and women in enterprises and occupational Social Security schemes), as well as Council Directive 97/80 of December 15, 1997 (concerning the burden of proof in cases of discrimination based on sex).

The May 7, 1999, law does not deal with equal rights to unemployment benefits, health insurance, Social Security–funded pensions, family allowances, or benefits related to work accidents or occupational diseases.

The May 7, 1999, law distinguishes between direct discrimination—based, for example, on pregnancy, which is forbidden per se—and indirect discrimination that may be justified in certain cases. (Certain types of work may require a female employee rather than a male, or vice versa.) Positive forms of discrimination, such as maternity leave, are allowed under the law. For the time being, special protective rules regarding the well-being of women at work remain unchanged. However, the law forbids gender-related stipulations in employment conditions regarding remuneration, working hours, vacations, hiring and firing, etc. All discriminatory clauses in existing contracts, work regulations, etc., are deemed null and void.

Under the May 7, 1999, law, sexual harassment, or "undesired sexual conduct at work," is defined as "each form of verbal, nonverbal, or body language of a sexual nature of which the party who is guilty thereof, knows, or should know diminishes the dignity of men and women at work." Through royal decrees, the King can issue measures to combat and prevent sexual harassment.

In a separate chapter, the May 7, 1999, law requires that complementary Social Security schemes (mostly occupational pensions) be gender-neutral in all respects: access, age, contributions, and benefits.

Under the May 7, 1999, law, labor courts may issue injunctions to compel an employer to end a specific discriminatory policy within given time limits. When in doubt as to whether discrimination actually exists, a court may seek advice from a government committee.

For the first time in Belgium's history, there is now whistleblower protection against dismissal for employees who have complained to the Social Inspectorate or sued their employer regarding gender discrimination and sexual harassment. The burden of proving that dismissal was not linked to the complaint rests with the employer. If the employer does not meet this burden, the whistleblower must be reinstated. The request for reinstatement must be filed within 30 days from the date of dismissal, unless the employee claims constructive dismissal or was terminated for serious cause that subsequently was not upheld in court.

Failure to reinstate can subject the employer to a penalty of six months' remuneration, plus salary from the date of dismissal until the court verdict is handed down. Extraordinary damages also are available if the employee suffered damages greater than the statutory lump-sum indemnity of six months' pay plus the aforementioned salary.

Age Discrimination

Pursuant to the February 13, 1998, law, no applicant responding to a job advertisement may be rejected on the basis of age, unless the very nature of the job justifies an age requirement. Age alone as a reason for refusing to hire or laying off older persons provides an employer no legal protection. Applying maximum age limits for hiring is grounds for penal sanctions, but the victim does not have a right to be hired.

Violence and Harassment

A law was passed on June 11, 2002, for the purpose of "protecting workers against violence, pestering, and undesired sexual conduct at work." This law amended the Law of August 4, 1996, regarding the well-being of workers. The law enjoins all workers, according to their training, the instructions of the employer, and their best judgment, to protect their own safety and health and that of their coworkers by "contributing positively to a prevention policy that is being implemented [by the employer] in the framework of the protection of workers against violence, pestering, and undesired sexual conduct at work, to refrain from each act of violence, pestering, or undesired sexual conduct at work, and to refrain from any illegitimate use of the complaints procedure." The terms "violence at work," "pestering at work," and "undesired sexual conduct at work" are defined by Article 32ter in the Law of August 1996. The law is a combined implementation of (1) EU Framework Directive 89/391, regarding safety and health in the workplace; (2) Directive 2000/43, regarding equal treatment of persons irrespective of race or ethnic origin; and (3) Directive 2000/78, establishing a general framework for equal treatment in employment and occupation.

The definition of undesired sexual conduct at work is contained in Article 5 of the Law of May 7, 1999, on the equal treatment of men and women in employment. The definition of ethnic and racial harassment is contained in Article 2.3 of EC Directive 2000/43. Shop-floor violence is not defined. The term "pestering" is so broadly defined that can it also include racial stereotyping.

Under the new law, as implemented by the Royal Decree of July 11, 2002, a worker who believes he or she is a victim of violence, pestering, or sexual harassment at work has various means of recourse:

- The victim can turn to a "person of trust" or a "prevention advisor" who will attempt to reconcile the parties;
- The victim can file a duly detailed written complaint with either one of the aforementioned persons;
- The victim can file a complaint with the Social Inspectorate;
- The victim can bring a lawsuit against the employer for failing to take preventive or remedial action, seeking injunctive relief and/or damages;
- If the facts qualify as a criminal violation or give rise to civil recourse against the perpetrator, the victim may bring an action before a criminal or civil court.

If a victim brings a lawsuit, the burden of proving that the necessary measures have been taken rests with the employer. In addition, the fact that a victim files a complaint or a suit may not be used by the employer as a reason for dismissal.

Lawsuits to prevent or remedy workplace violence, pestering, or sexual harassment also may be brought by the union or by a special purpose nonprofit action group.

Equal Pay

Article 119 of the EU treaty requires Member States to ensure that men and women receive equal pay for equal work. This EU-wide mandate has been incorporated in Belgian law by Collective Bargaining Agreement No. 25, concluded within the National Labor Council in which the three national confederations of trade unions and all national associations of employers are represented, which was rendered obligatory for all employers and workers by the Royal Decree of December 9, 1975. The text of this collective bargaining agreement must be attached to the work regulations of every Belgian enterprise.

NOTES

1. The Law of June 28, 1966, which relates to indemnification of dismissed workers in the case of closure of an enterprise, as implemented by the Royal Decree of 20 September 1967, provides for the following criminal sanctions in case of noncompliance with the obligation to inform: imprisonment for eight days to one month and/or a fine of €0.64 to €12.39, to be multiplied by (currently) 200. (Fines are multiplied by a factor of 200 to achieve the net fine because the base fines are set at historical levels. The multiplication factor is adjusted periodically by law.)

The Law of December 5, 1968, which relates to collective bargaining agreements and joint committees, provides for criminal sanctions in case of infringements of provisions of collective bargaining agreements (CBAs) made mandatory or generally applicable by royal decree, such as CBA No. 9 and CBA No. 24: imprisonment for eight days to one month and/or a fine of €0.64 to €12.39, to be multiplied by (currently) 200, to be multiplied by the number of workers, with a maximum ceiling of (currently) €247,894.

The Law of September 20, 1948, which organizes the economy and relates, among other matters, to the establishment and functioning of Works Councils, imposes criminal sanctions on the employer that hinders the Works Council in the performance of its mission by, among other things: not providing the Works Council with the information required by the law, its implementing royal decrees, and the CBAs made mandatory or generally applicable by royal decree; providing the information in a manner that is not in accordance with the rules; not carrying out the consultations in accordance with the rules. The sanction imposed by this law is a fine of €2.48, to be multiplied by (currently) 200, to be multiplied by the number of workers, with a maximum ceiling of (currently) €495,787.

2. In case of infringement of the Law of June 28, 1966, which relates to indemnification of dismissed workers in case of closure of the enterprise and the implementation of the Royal Decree of September 20, 1967, an administrative fine of €49.58 to €1,239.47 can be imposed.

In case of an infringement of a collective bargaining agreement made mandatory or generally applicable by royal decree, an administrative fine of €49.58 to €1,239.47 can be imposed, to be multiplied by the number of workers, with a maximum ceiling of €19,831.48.

CHAPTER 2

Labor and Employment Law in Brazil

Isabel C. Franco

Section I

My client wishes to establish a manufacturing facility in Brazil and will need to hire a workforce. What are the key legal issues involved?

Employment Contracts

Under Brazilian labor law, the execution of a written employment contract is not mandatory, although it is common procedure in Brazil. Most Brazilian companies use standard employment contracts that correspond to various categories of employees. The employment relationship is well regulated by statutory law and by collective bargaining agreements, however, so there is little room for negotiation. Overly detailed employment agreements are rare and generally unnecessary.

Employment contracts may be executed for either limited or unlimited periods of time, but are usually executed for an indefinite term. It is recommended that employment agreements executed in Brazil be written in Portuguese to avoid future problems comprehending the provisions of the agreement.

Employment contracts for a fixed term may be executed for specific jobs as established by law, but may not exceed a maximum term of two years. If the employment relationship continues beyond the maximum term, the contract will automatically become an employment contract for an unlimited period of time.

Employers may establish an initial trial period of employment for a maximum term of 90 days. If the employer elects to keep the employee at the end of this trial period, the employment contract then becomes one for an unlimited period of time. If the relationship is terminated, certain legal severance payments are due at that point, such as prorated vacations and a prorated Christmas bonus for the period employed, among others. See comments under Statutory Severance Pay Requirements under Section IV below.

Companies must establish fixed working hours for employees performing back-office activities. Employees in executive positions, and therefore in positions of trust and command, do not have fixed working hours and, consequently, are not entitled to overtime pay. Similarly, employees performing exclusively out-of-office activities, such as traveling salespeople, are also not entitled to overtime pay.

Hiring Managers

Brazilian companies may choose between two options to formalize the recruitment of their managers and board members: (1) execute an employment contract, where the employee is included on the employer's payroll, or (2) pay an emolument as *pró-labore* (a remuneration established by the company's charter and by the quotaholders' determination) in lieu of an employment contract. This second option is utilized in cases where a manager does not have an employment relationship with either the employer or any other company in the same economic group, in Brazil or abroad, and holds shares in the company.

The appointment of board members in joint-stock companies must be made by the major shareholders of the company and the shareholders' commission, or by the shareholders' commission by means of a general meeting, where a board member's emoluments, term of office, and responsibilities will be determined. The termination of a board member's employment will depend on whether the board member is considered an employee of the company. If the board member is considered an employee, termination is similar to that of any other regular employee of the company, but will also require his or her removal from the company's bylaws. If the board member is considered a nonemployee manager, it is only necessary to pay the board member eventual pending amounts (accrued compensation and unpaid vacation) and to remove him or her from the company's bylaws.

Wages and Benefits

Minimum Wage

The minimum wage is unified within Brazil's national territory, set, and periodically adjusted by the Brazilian government. The national minimum wage in Brazil currently is R$350. However, collective bargaining agreements may set higher minimum wages than established by law. Certain professionals, such as physicians, lawyers, engineers, and radiology technicians, set their own minimum wages.

Salaries must be paid monthly in Brazil, up to the fifth business day of the month following the month worked, but salary advances are customarily granted on a biweekly basis. Collective bargaining agreements may include other provisions regarding salary advancements. Salaries must also be paid in Brazilian currency (the *real*). Payment in U.S. dollars or any other foreign currency is prohibited.

It is important to emphasize that salaries in Brazil may not be reduced without union approval. Any change in compensation resulting in a loss to the employee is considered unlawful and entitles the employee to legal redress in the labor courts.

Benefits

There are three categories of employment benefits in Brazil: legal benefits, benefits provided under collective bargaining agreements, and fringe benefits granted gratuitously by an employer. Legal benefits and benefits provided under collective bargaining agreements are mandatory. Fringe benefits are not mandatory, but once granted they may not be revoked.

Legal Benefits

Legal benefits include

- Commute pass (*Vale-Transporte*).
- Profit-sharing or result-participation plans. Granted in accordance with the parameters and percentages established by the employer in its specific participation plan.
- Overtime pay of at least 50 percent over the employee's regular hourly wage.
- Payment for night work. An employee working between the hours of 10 PM and 5 AM is entitled to payment at least 20 percent over his or her regular hourly wage.
- Transference allowance. An employee temporarily transferred to a work site in another city is entitled to extra payment in the amount of at least 25 percent of his or her salary.
- Vacation/bonus. Annual 30-day vacation pay plus a bonus equivalent to one-third of the employee's monthly salary.
- Maternity leave. Paid leave (from Social Security) for 120 days.
- Paternity leave. Five consecutive days as of the child's date of birth.
- 13th salary. A Christmas bonus equal to 1/12 of the salary earned in each month of service during that calendar year.
- Unemployment Security Fund (FGTS). A monthly deposit equivalent to 8.5 percent of an employee's salary in a blocked account opened in the name of the employee with Caixa Econômica Federal (Federal Savings Bank). Eight percent of this contribution is earmarked for the employee, and 0.5 percent is earmarked for the government. Further, in case of dismissal without cause, a fine in the amount of 50 percent of the funds deposited in the employee's FGTS account is due, from which 40 percent is allocated to the employee and 10 percent is allocated to the government.
- Work-related accident or occupational disease insurance. The first 15 days following an employee's accident must be paid by the employer. Thereafter, the employee will receive disbursements from Social Security.
- Thirty days' prior notice for dismissals without cause.

Benefits under Collective Bargaining Agreements

Benefits under collective bargaining agreements vary depending upon the economic category under which the position is classified and the union involved. Common benefits under collective bargaining agreements include enhanced legal benefits, extended prior notice periods, extended maternity leave, and job tenure for employees nearing retirement, among others.

Fringe Benefits

Fringe benefits are not widespread in Brazil. They can include meals, life insurance, medical insurance (also included under collective bargaining agreements), special indemnifications, car allowances to managerial employees, and school tuition, among others.

In addition, fringe benefits are considered part of an employee's salary, upon which the calculation of legal benefits, such as vacations, Christmas bonuses, and FGTS deposits, among others, is made.

Labor Unions

The Brazilian labor union system is comprised of the following:

- Labor unions, which represent all employees and have jurisdiction in certain cases at the municipal, state, and even federal levels;
- Federations at the state level, which encompass all labor unions; and
- Confederations, which encompass all federations in Brazil.

Under Brazilian labor law, labor unions represent all employees of a certain type (e.g., steelworkers, chemists, bank employees), regardless of whether they are actually members of the union. The terms of the collective bargaining agreement apply to all employees of the same type. Union representatives negotiate benefits and work conditions, which are set forth in the collective bargaining agreement, and provide judicial representation in cases where the rights of employees of a particular type are violated or not observed.

Collective Bargaining Agreements

The Consolidated Labor Law contains certain provisions regarding collective bargaining agreements. First, a General Workers' Meeting called pursuant to the union's bylaws must authorize the union to begin bargaining. Bargaining must take place between the representative union of employees and either the representative union of employers or the employer directly. Mediation by the Regional Labor Department is possible in the event that either party refuses to attend the negotiations.

If a settlement is reached, the agreement, or a "collective labor convention," will be drafted and signed by both parties. A copy of the agreement must then be filed with the Regional Labor Office, the employer, and the union office involved (for publicity purposes).

It is not only the classic terms and conditions of employment that are the subject of collective bargaining agreements; the issues under negotiation may extend to unemployment protection, outsourcing, and production modernization, among others. Over the years, the unions have extended their list of issues (which are only indirectly related to working conditions).

Collective labor conventions contain two types of clauses: mandatory clauses and normative clauses.

Mandatory clauses create obligations for the parties to the agreement and, as a rule, deal with such issues as the protection and encouragement of union representation, organization of union activities within a company, and fines resulting from noncompliance with union freedom, among others. Because mandatory clauses do not affect individual employment relationships, they are not generally incorporated into individual employment contracts.

Normative clauses do, however, affect the relationship between employer and employee. Normative clauses may be further classified as salary clauses and social clauses. Salary clauses deal with salary adjustments and increases, bonuses, allowances, payment protection, union salary scales, salary advances, overlapping of functions, weekend pay, leaves of absence, payment for justified absence, etc. Social clauses generally relate to food, transportation, education, life insurance, medical assistance, allowances for disabled children, nursing, pregnancy tenure, return-to-work issues, minors at military service age, and pre-retirement provisions, among others.

SECTION II

My client is acquiring an existing business in Brazil. How do I assess the existing workforce and consider changes?

Due diligence is the most common procedure in which to obtain information on the existing workforce of an existing business in Brazil. During the due diligence period, all documents related to an existing company's workforce are verified, such as employment agreements, payroll records, internal policies, employees' functions and classifications within the company, and granted benefits, among others, in order to identify possible liabilities as well as areas for improvement.

A change in control of the company does not change the employment contracts in a share deal, unless there is a material change in the company's core business or unless the change in control results in the transfer of employees. Accordingly, there is no need to assess the existing workforce because the employees are directly linked to the business, not the company's quotaholders/shareholders.

Asset deals also do not change the employment contracts, and the buyer will be liable for payments under such contracts only if it is proven that the assets transfer caused the seller's extinction or bankruptcy.

Further, changes in the terms and conditions of employment because of a share/asset transfer represent a risk procedure and can be made only if the company changes its core business or if the share/asset transfer results in the transfer of employees. Both situations may change the applicable collective bargaining agreement and, consequently, the benefits the employees are entitled to receive. To be considered lawful, changes that result in a loss to the employee or in unfavorable conditions can be made only if agreed upon by the relevant union, even if made upon the employee's consent.

Carrying Out a Workforce Reduction

There are no specific provisions regarding workforce reductions in Brazil. Further, employers are not legally required to inform the Ministry of Labor or the relevant labor unions of a workforce reduction, unless a collective bargaining agreement provides otherwise. However, best practices dictate that the employer take the following steps:

1. List all the employees that will be dismissed and establish a timetable for the dismissals.
2. Analyze, on a case-by-case basis, all employees enjoying temporary job stability, e.g. pregnant women and other similarly protected positions. In cases of plant closings, court decisions have held that temporary job stability ceases when the employer winds down its operations. The issue is not yet settled, however, so a legal analysis of each case is recommended before establishing any indemnification payments.
3. Analyze employees on leave on a case-by-case basis. Under Brazilian labor law, the employment agreements of employees on leave due to illnesses or occupational disease or accident are suspended and thus, in theory, cannot be terminated.
4. Analyze measures to reduce future risks.

A common procedure undertaken by Brazilian employers is to propose a voluntary dismissal plan to its employees, under which employees are offered a severance package in addition to the severance payments provided by law. There are no specific rules on what the company should offer; rather, it is entirely within the employer's discretion.

Reorganizing the Workforce

Brazilian legislation provides that changes resulting in a loss or in conditions unfavorable to the employee are lawful only if agreed upon by the relevant labor union, regardless of whether the employee consented to such changes. The employee would be entitled to seek legal redress before the Labor Court, which, by way of a remedy, may order retroactive reinstatement of the employee's previous level of pay. In this way, changes in the organization of the workforce, such as downgrading, will be considered null and void.

Statutory Severance Pay Requirements

The statutory severance payments established by law upon the dismissal of senior employees are the same as those for regular employees. The legal obligations on an employer upon termination of employees in Brazil depend on the manner in which the termination occurred.

Termination of Employment Agreements Having a Determinate Term

Early Termination without Cause by Company's Initiative

The legal obligations on an employer upon early termination of an employee without cause include

- Termination payment in the amount of half of the employee's salary from the dismissal date to the end of the employment period provided in the employment agreement;
- Payment of earned salary;
- Payment of 13th salary (or prorated 13th salary, depending on the dismissal date);
- Payment for earned vacations plus 1/3 additional payment (if terminated after one year of service);
- Payment for prorated vacations plus 1/3 additional payment;
- Deposit in employee's FGTS blocked account of the amount (8.5 percent of the employee's pay) corresponding to the termination month;
- Payment of 50 percent fine on the amount deposited in employee's FGTS blocked account;
- Any other benefits provided by collective bargaining agreement.

Early Termination by Employee's Initiative

The legal obligations on an employer upon early resignation of an employee include

- Payment of earned salary;
- Payment of 13th salary (or prorated 13th salary, depending on the dismissal date);
- Payment for earned vacations plus 1/3 additional payment;
- Payment for prorated vacations plus 1/3 additional payment;
- Deposit in employee's FGTS blocked account of the amount (8.5 percent of the employee's pay) corresponding to the termination month;
- Any other benefits provided by collective bargaining agreement.

Termination at the Expiration of the Employment Period Set Forth in the Employment Agreement

The legal obligations on an employer upon termination of the employment period set forth in an employment agreement include

- Payment of earned salary;
- Payment of 13th salary (or prorated 13th salary, depending on the dismissal date);
- Payment for earned vacations plus 1/3 additional payment (if terminated after one year of service);
- Payment for prorated vacations plus 1/3 additional payment;
- Deposit in employee's FGTS blocked account of the amount (8.5 percent of the employee's pay) corresponding to the termination month;
- Any other benefits provided by collective bargaining agreement.

Termination of Employment Agreements for an Indeterminate Term

Termination as a Result of Resignation

The legal obligations on an employer upon the resignation of an employee include

- Payment of earned salary;
- Payment of 13th salary (or prorated 13th salary, depending on the dismissal date);
- Payment for earned vacations plus 1/3 additional payment (if terminated after one year of service);
- Payment for prorated vacations plus 1/3 additional payment (if terminated after one year of service);
- Deposit in employee's FGTS blocked account of the amount (8.5 percent of the employee's pay) corresponding to the termination month;
- Any other benefits provided by collective bargaining agreement.

Termination at Employer's Initiative

The legal obligations on an employer upon termination of an employee include

- Prior notification;
- Payment of earned salary;
- Payment of 13th salary (or prorated 13th salary, depending on the dismissal date);
- Payment for earned vacations plus 1/3 additional payment;
- Payment for prorated vacations plus 1/3 additional payment (if terminated after one year of service);
- Deposit in employee's FGTS blocked account of the amount (8.5 percent of the employee's pay) corresponding to the termination month;
- Payment of 50 percent fine on the amount deposited in employee's FGTS blocked account;
- Any other benefits provided by collective bargaining agreement.

In the event the Company terminates the employment agreement for cause, the company shall give the employee:

- Payment of earned salary;
- Payment for earned vacation plus 1/3 additional payment (if terminated after one year of service);
- Deposit in employee's FGTS blocked account of the amount (8.5 percent of the employee's pay) corresponding to the termination month;
- Any other benefits provided by collective bargaining agreement.

Death of Employee

In the event of an employee's death, the employment agreement shall be considered terminated and the following shall be paid (assuming an agreement for indeterminate period of time):

- Payment of earned salary;
- Payment of 13th salary (or prorated 13th salary, depending on the dismissal date);
- Payment for earned vacations plus 1/3 additional payment (after one year of service);
- Payment for prorated vacations plus 1/3 additional payment;

- Deposit in employee's FGTS blocked account of the amount (8.5 percent of the employee's pay) corresponding to the termination month.

Further, special conditions and payments such as extension of the medical plan, special indemnifications, payment of outplacement services, and sale of the company car used by the senior manager, among others, may be set forth in the senior manager's employment agreement, in the collective bargaining agreement applicable to such a senior manager, or may be a matter of company policy.

Changing the Wage and Benefits Structures

In general, salaries cannot be reduced without the consent of the labor unions.

The prohibition against changes to employee benefits is not applicable to benefits established under a collective bargaining agreement, which do not integrate employment agreements and are mandatory only during the effectiveness period set forth in the agreement.

Consulting with Labor Unions or Works Councils

In acquiring a company in Brazil it is not necessary to consult with the labor unions or with works councils, because unless the company changes its core business there will be no change in the company's relationship with the unions or in the benefits provided under the collective bargaining agreement. If the company does change its core business, it will begin a relationship with the worker's union representing this new category of employees.

Even though ownership of the company has changed, the employer remains the same for purposes of the employment agreements, making it unnecessary to consult the worker's union or any work council.

The same principles apply in asset acquisitions.

SECTION III

My client wishes to sell its existing facility. What restrictions do we need to consider?

Assessing Employment Contracts

A change in the control of a company will not change the employment contracts, unless there is a change in the company's core business or the change in control results in the transfer of employees. However, if retention of employees is not part of the deal, then the seller must verify whether there are any restrictions (e.g., temporary job stability) on laying off employees.

The same principles apply to assets deals; however, the buyer is responsible for payments under such employment contracts only if it is proven that the assets transfer caused the extinction or bankruptcy of the company.

Consulting with Government

It is not necessary to consult the government in the sale of an existing facility.

Consulting with Labor Unions and Works Councils

It is not necessary to consult labor unions or works councils in the sale of an existing facility.

Negotiating with a Buyer: Special Labor Issues

Brazilian labor legislation does not consider a change in the ownership of a company as a corresponding change in the existing employment agreements, regardless of any liability clause included in the acquisition agreement. The buyer will be directly responsible for any liability resulting from the relationship between the seller and its workforce. Therefore, a thorough due diligence procedure assessing potential liability is important during an acquisition. After that, the buyer may opt to

- Include a clause in the purchase agreement establishing that the buyer will have a right of recourse against the seller for any liability resulting from its relationship with its employees up to the closing date;
- Request the seller to deposit in an escrow account an amount equivalent to the estimated labor liabilities, with the right to withdraw the funds to pay such liabilities; or
- Reduce the purchase price to account for the estimated amount of labor liabilities.

If the buyer acquires an ongoing business where not all the employees will be retained, then the seller may dismiss such employees, and the costs of severance may be negotiated and included in the purchase price. In this case, clauses inserted into the purchase agreement indemnifying the buyer against any expenses from lawsuits arising out of the period prior to the acquisition may have interesting results, given that a former employee may sue a company up to two years after his or her dismissal. Consequently, the buyer may have to defend itself in court.

SECTION IV

My client wishes to replace its senior manager(s). What restrictions do we need to consider?

There are no specific legal provisions regarding changes to employees in key managerial positions. The same provisions that apply to the dismissal of regular employees apply to the dismissal of managerial employees. In other words, managerial employees can be dismissed unless they have been granted job protection resulting from

- Work-related disease or accident;
- Pregnancy;

- Impending retirement;
- Sick leave;
- Membership in a specific accident prevention committee; or
- Union representative status.

The above provisions do not apply to nonemployee board members, unless provided in an agreement held between the parties.

Upon dismissal, key managerial employees, in view of their position in the company, may be entitled to special indemnifications, extension of the medical plan, and payment of outplacement services, among others, if provided in their employment agreement or in the employer's policies.

Employment Contracts

See Employment Contracts under Section I above.

Discrimination Issues

There are no specific provisions regarding discrimination in the dismissal of senior managers, but see Section V below.

Statutory Restrictions on Dismissal without Cause

There are no specific statutory restrictions on the dismissal of senior managers; rather, the regular restrictions mentioned above apply when the senior manager has job tenure resulting from

- Professional disease or accident;
- Maternity;
- Impending retirement;
- Sick leave;
- Member of the specific accident prevention committee; or
- Union representative status.

As already emphasized, key managerial employees, in view of their position within the company, or in view of their age, may be entitled to special payments upon their dismissal, as provided by their employment agreement, employer's policies, or collective bargaining agreement.

SECTION V

What prohibitions exist against discrimination on a basis of age, race, gender, disability, pregnancy, and other factors? What are the rights of employees, applicants, or former employees who believe that they have been discriminated against?

Under the Brazilian Constitution, discrimination based on sex, national origin, race, color, marital status, familial status, and age at recruitment or during employment is forbidden.

Further, it is considered a criminal offense to demand a medical certificate, test, or statement regarding sterilization or pregnancy; however, in practice it is difficult to police such questions asked during the interviewing process. In an attempt to regulate discriminatory recruitment practices, the Labor Public Prosecutor's Office has been pressing employers to remove from their applications for employment any requests for information that may be used for discriminatory purposes, such as questions based on religion, race, etc.

Employees, applicants, and former employees who believe that they have been discriminated against have the right to sue the employer, potential employer, or former employer for "moral" and actual damages. There is no specific parameter to fix the amount related to moral damages, which will depend on the employee's claim and the judge's determination of a reasonable amount to be paid. Brazilian jurisprudence provides that indemnification for moral damages be fixed based on the number of years of service the employee provided to the company. Former employees may also be guaranteed the right to return to work as a result of judicial decision.

SECTION VI

On the Horizon: What key labor and employment law developments should an employer doing business in Brazil anticipate occurring in the coming years?

Congress has formed a committee to consider certain proposed amendments to the Brazilian Labor Code; however, this task will no doubt require constitutional and infra-constitutional amendments to allow the flexibility necessary to make such changes in the working conditions in Brazil.

CHAPTER 3

Labor and Employment Law in Canada

Stuart S. Aronovitch
Jonathan L. Dye

Section I

My client wishes to establish a manufacturing facility in Canada and will need to hire a workforce. What are the key legal issues involved?

Employment Contracts: Who Receives Them and What They Should Include

In Canada, the answer to who receives employment contracts is: *everyone.* In fact, under Canadian law, every employee has an employment contract, whether written or not. The written terms can be contained in a formal employment contract, hiring letter, company policy, or collective agreement with a union. The unwritten terms may be imposed by employment standards legislation, implied by the common law,[1] or agreed to verbally by the parties.

While written contracts can create some liability for employers in Canada, the general consensus is that written employment contracts are a good thing, and should be used frequently if they are used properly.[2] Whereas in the United States contractual terms can impinge upon the "at will" nature of the relationship, because Canadian common law requires notice of termination or payment in lieu, contractual terms are most frequently designed to override these common law severance requirements. In other words, employment contracts can assist employers, by limiting their common law liability to employees.[3]

The situation is different in the province of Quebec, a civil law jurisdiction. There, employees cannot contract out of their rights, including those regarding notice of termination or compensation in lieu.[4] Therefore, an employer's ability to limit its liability for severance is restricted in Quebec. To a certain extent, the same is true in the other (common law) jurisdictions of Canada, where it is clear that written contracts cannot provide lesser entitlements than those imposed by the applicable employment standards legislation.[5]

Every jurisdiction in Canada has legislation governing employment standards. Examples include the *Canada Labour Code* (federal), Ontario's Employment Standards Act, 2000, Alberta's *Employment Standards Code,* Quebec's Labour Standards Act, and Nova Scotia's *Labour Standards Code.* Each of these statutes defines minimum standards for matters such as minimum wage, hours of work, and termination. Again, these minimums are mandatory and, if violated in an employment contract, can render the offending clause, if not the whole contract, unenforceable.[6] For example, if a contractual termination clause fails to provide at least the minimum notice period set out in the legislation, the contractual term is void and treated as if it never existed. The common law then applies, not the minimum requirements of the legislation.[7]

In Quebec, this principle is codified in Section 93 of the Quebec Labour Standards Act. As such, both the minimum notice under the Labour Standards Act and the reasonable notice requirement under the *C.C.Q.*,[8] which often exceeds the minimum statutory notice, will apply as a matter of law.

Finally, while implicit in the preceding discussion, employers and their counsel must realize that the minimum statutory severance requirements are exactly that, minimum standards. They do not oust the common law, so complying with the legislation does not mean the employer has met all of its obligations. In the absence of clear and enforceable contractual terms, the employer still needs to comply with the common law. This is why employment contracts can be so valuable in the Canadian context.[9]

There is little that an employment contract must include. The only mandatory issues to deal with are the usual requirements for valid formation of a contract, i.e., an offer, acceptance, and valid consideration. The offer and acceptance do not have to be in writing and the consideration is obvious; the worker will work and the employer will pay.

That said, there are a number of common elements to Canadian employment contracts that employers should think about including. These include

- **Term:** Is this a fixed term contract or an indefinite term? If it is to be a fixed period (e.g., six months, one year, five years), that should be specified in the contract. If no fixed term is specified, it is deemed indefinite. Note also that absent a clause allowing for earlier termination, a fixed-term employment contract will entitle the employee to payment for the whole term, even if dismissed earlier.[10]
- **Job Description:** A defined job description can define the nature or scope of the employee's duties. Most employees also want to know their job title and the basic requirements of the position. However, employers should ensure that the terms regarding position and duties are flexible enough to allow for necessary changes to the employee's responsibilities. Otherwise, a fresh agreement (or an amendment to the old one) will need to be signed, which may require new consideration.
- **Probation:** If a probationary term is desired, it should be included in the contract. The contract should specify the duration of the probation and the compensation, if any, to which the employee is entitled if dismissed during that period. Note that employment standards legislation will often require compensation after relatively short periods of employment, so any probationary clause must be drafted to ensure that it does not offend the legislation, or the clause will be void. Recall also that Quebec has two, not just one, potentially overriding pieces of legislation that set

minimum entitlements upon termination: the Quebec Labour Standards Act and the *C.C.Q.*

- **Remuneration:** Contracts can specify the amounts, types, and frequencies of payments for services. Clauses can be included setting out whether the employee is to be paid by hourly wage, annual salary, commission, or some variation or combination of these. Other clauses can define the amounts and any qualification requirements for things such as bonuses (discretionary or performance) and stock option grants.
- **Benefits:** Employer-provided benefits can be addressed in the contract (whether the employer pays for them in full or not). Typical provisions include those regarding company cars or vehicle allowances; health and dental insurance (above that covered by the applicable government health system); life insurance; vacation; and pension or Registered Retirement Savings Plan (akin to 401(k)) contributions or plans. Employers should be aware that the employment standards legislation typically provides for a minimum vacation allotment and vacation pay. Pension and RRSP plans are also subject to significant tax and other legislation governing their terms and administration. Finally, the employment standards legislation typically requires that benefits be maintained during the statutory minimum notice period upon dismissal.[11]
- **Termination:** A well-drafted termination clause is probably one of the most valuable inclusions an employer can have. Canadian law is relatively generous to employees dismissed without "just cause." Typically, severance in the realm of one month of total compensation (monetary and value of nonmonetary) for each year of service is often used as a rough estimate. However, this is by no means a fixed calculation, and it skews heavily for very short- or long-service employees. If there is a contractual term setting out the employee's entitlement upon dismissal, then that term will govern, so long as the clause and the agreement itself are valid and the clause meets or exceeds the minimum requirements of the applicable employment standards legislation. Some examples may assist:
    - In Ontario and other common law provinces, with a properly drafted termination clause, an employer's liability to a 12-year employee can be reduced from approximately a year of severance to as little as eight weeks.
    - In Quebec, on the other hand, Article 2092 *C.C.Q.* provides a statutory entitlement to reasonable notice of termination that cannot be relinquished by contract. In addition, under Section 124 of the Labour Standards Act, all employees in Quebec (other than senior management) with two or more continuous years of service with an employer can challenge the employer's reason for their dismissal as being without "just and sufficient cause." In other words, in Quebec, most employees fired without just and sufficient cause can be reinstated, with compensation for lost salary and additional damages in certain circumstances. Reinstatement is normally unavailable, however, where the termination is imposed for legitimate economic reasons (e.g., restructuring).

- **Restrictive Covenants:** Employers may want to include contractual terms such as a noncompetition or nonsolicitation clause. While such terms, particularly the former, have become increasingly more difficult to sustain and enforce in Canada, they nonetheless can be invaluable if properly drafted. Fiduciary duties, the duties of confidentiality and fidelity, and some statutory obligations placed upon employees will protect the employer to an extent, but contractual terms can be very helpful to augment these rights.[12]
- **Ownership of Developments/Intellectual Property:** Terms specifying the employer's ownership and rights to inventions and other employee works can be essential, particularly in creative industries and positions.
- **Governing Law/Choice of Venue/Arbitration:** Foreign-based employers may want to define which jurisdiction's law applies, and where any legal dispute is to occur. While the contract cannot oust applicable legislation, it can oust Canadian common law.[13] Employers may also wish to insert an arbitration clause, particularly if confidentiality in disputes with employees is desirable.

Hiring Managerial Employees

Hiring a manager is not too legally different from hiring any other employee in Canada. Managers' employment cannot, by definition, be covered by a collective agreement. However, the legalities of their employment contracts are not significantly different from those of other nonunion employees. Managers may fall within certain exemptions to some statutory employment standards (discussed in Section IV below), but this generally has very little effect on the hiring decision.[14]

That said, there are, of course, certain clauses that are more likely to be included in an executive's contract. For example, more complex pay and benefit packages may require a more detailed contract. Executives are also more likely to want to have fixed severance packages defined by written agreement. Other potential terms include[15]

- **Duties and Performance:** Job descriptions are rare. These terms are generally defined broadly to encompass all reasonable duties, and often define some means of measuring successful performance.
- **Nonsalary Compensation/Benefits:** Detailed systems for defining entitlement to and calculation of bonuses, stock options, or other "phantom" ownership plans should be clearly set out in the contract or schedules. Other typical benefits include "top-hat" insurance and pension plans, Registered Compensation Agreements, and provisions for the reduction of income tax payable. Related clauses defining what happens to these items upon dismissal is also essential.

This latter issue arises frequently, particularly for U.S. employers applying their benefit plans to their employees in Canada. The question often arises whether the benefit-plan language is sufficient to get around the Canadian "notice of termination or pay in lieu" principle. For example, many foreign companies with employees based in Canada grant stock options to their employees. The option plans (often the same one as used by company's home jurisdiction) frequently make little or no reference to what would happen to options if employment was terminated. Most simply state that the options would expire "upon termination of employment." This may seem straightforward enough, but Canadian common law means that things are not so simple.[16]

In *Veer v. Dover Corp. (Canada) Ltd.*,[17] the Ontario Court of Appeal considered just this issue. The court interpreted the word "termination" in the option plan to mean "termination according to law," and reasoned that the parties would not have intended a wrongful termination to end the employee's option rights. Therefore, the court ruled that during the common law reasonable-notice period (in Mr. Veer's case, 24 months) the employee was able to exercise his rights under the stock option agreement. The court confirmed that parties to a stock option agreement could expressly agree to a different result (i.e., contract out), but the bar to do so was high.[18]

The *Veer* principle is not limited to stock options. Cases involving an employee's right to commissions, bonuses, and other benefits during the notice period have regularly adopted and applied the theory. Contractual terms therefore need to be very carefully drafted in order to limit the compensation to which an employee is entitled upon termination without just cause.[19] Even still, in Quebec such clauses may be nullified if a court finds them "abusive," such as where the terms of the contract were imposed by the employer and were not negotiable.[20]

- **Perks:** Like other benefits, these items can be included in the executive employment contract and can include items like company cars, chauffeurs, paid expense accounts, fax/Internet/cell phone usage, and club memberships. Again, provisions should be included to deal with what happens to these benefits upon dismissal.
- **Golden Parachutes:** Just a fancy name for an enhanced severance package, these clauses generally apply to dismissals that occur because of a change in control at the most senior managerial or ownership levels of a company. These clauses are both an incentive for a desirable executive to join a company and an incentive for that executive to act in the company's best interests. The employer can also include terms to mitigate the size of the parachute (e.g., by paying a smaller lump sum rather than a larger amount over time, or by reducing the liability if the executive gets a new job elsewhere). Absent such mitigation terms, however, the executive is generally entitled to the full amount, though the converse is true in Quebec, where mitigation is the presumption.

A parachute clause is generally triggered by some "change of control event," followed by the dismissal of the executive or a resignation following a significant change in the executive's terms of employment (i.e., a "constructive" dismissal). The "change of control event" can be whatever the parties define it to be, but generally will be some event that changes the identity, for practical purposes, of the owner and/or directing minds of the corporation. Such events can include the replacement of a majority of the board of directors; a change in majority shareholder(s); bankruptcy or insolvency of the corporation; de-listing from a stock exchange; or replacement of the employee's boss.

There are also statutory considerations that apply to the creation of a golden parachute. Under the Canada Business Corporations Act and similar provincial statutes, the corporate articles, agreements, and bylaws may affect the company's ability to implement certain parachutes. These same statutes have disclosure requirements for executives that must be observed. Finally, statutory and fiduciary obligations exist that require any parachute to be in the best interests of the corporation.

Labor Unions and Collective Agreements

We are presuming for the purpose of this section that the company in question is opening a new (i.e., not yet in existence) manufacturing facility. As such, it is unlikely that there will be any labor union or collective agreement applicable. While certain businesses in Canada may be unionized by virtue of their industry (e.g., film production or construction), that is very rarely the case.

For the vast majority of businesses, the workplace becomes unionized only after an organizing drive and a union is certified as bargaining agent for the bargaining unit of employees in question. Certification usually occurs as a result of a vote in favor of a union (by a majority of eligible employees that vote) or, in some jurisdictions, where the labor relations board imposes the union because it has determined that there is sufficient union support and a "fair" vote has not occurred and/or cannot occur, because of unfair labor practices by the employer. There are also means by which the employees can "decertify" their union, but this is not a frequent occurrence. The key principle in any certification or decertification process is that the employees are to be free to make their own decision, without undue influence or threats (explicit or implicit) by the employer.

Once a union is in place, a first collective bargaining agreement (CBA) will need to be negotiated.[21] It, and all subsequent CBAs, will have a fixed duration. Once signed, the CBA runs its course unless the parties amend it by agreement. Strikes or lockouts are illegal while a CBA is in effect. Once it expires, however, strikes and lockouts can result.

SECTION II[22]

My client is acquiring an existing business in Canada. How do I assess the existing workforce and consider changes?

Assessing the workforce of an existing business is always a smart idea for a potential purchaser of a Canadian business because, depending how the deal is structured, a buyer may be taking on, or may be asked by the seller to take on, considerable liabilities. As such, there are three key questions to ask from the buyer's perspective:

1. Is this a share purchase or an asset purchase?
2. If it is an asset purchase, do I, the buyer, want to hire any of the vendor's employees?

3. If I do want to hire some of the vendor's employees, will it be on their current terms of employment with the vendor, or will I want them to work under new terms?

Share Purchase versus Asset Purchase

As a matter of Canadian common law, contracts of employment are not assignable. In other words, if there is a sale of business that alters the identity of the employer (i.e., an asset sale, as opposed to a share sale), the vendor cannot "sell" its employees' contracts to the purchaser. In a share purchase, on the other hand, the corporation being sold does not change, only its owner. As such, the employment relationships between the corporation being sold and its employees are unaffected. In this fashion, the entire corporation, including its employees, are effectively sold to the new owner, and the corporation retains all of its liabilities to its employees.

In an asset sale, an employee of the vendor cannot be forced to accept new employment with the purchaser. If the employees are dismissed as a result of the sale (e.g., if the business closes or the job is gone because the company sold all of its assets), the liability for any severance obligations owing to the employees remains with the vendor. However, if the purchaser offers to hire the vendor's employees in the same positions and on the same terms, the employees will be able to mitigate their "damages" fully by working for the purchaser, thus removing the vendor's obligation at common law, though not necessarily its statutory obligations.

The Impact of Employment Standards Legislation

The common law described above with respect to an asset sale has effectively been altered by employment standards legislation. Most Canadian jurisdictions have a "successor employer" concept, which automatically transfers the employee's statutory entitlements to the purchaser. If the purchaser "buys" all or part of a business and hires the employees of the vendor within a certain defined time, the employees carry with them all of their accumulated service with the vendor and all of their statutory entitlements. In other words, the purchaser essentially hires the employees "as is, where is" for statutory purposes. If the purchaser does not hire the vendor's employee, however, the vendor retains any liability if the employee loses his or her job because of the sale.

While employees' length of service is definitely "carried over" for statutory purposes when they join the purchaser following a sale of business, the same is not so clear at common law. Again, traditionally an asset sale terminates the employment contract with the vendor, and a new contract, with fresh service, could be entered into with the purchaser. However, recent case law suggests that Canadian courts will take prior service with the vendor into account when assessing an employee's entitlements under his or her employment with the purchaser. While this might not be a "one-for-one" acknowledgement of service, Canadian courts have recognized that the purchaser is most often hiring the employee because of his or her experience with the vendor, and not as a "fresh" employee.[23]

As a result, absent clear contractual terms defining their entitlements, the employee could be entitled to such things as enhanced vacation, pension benefits based on the total service with both vendor and purchaser, and greater common law severance entitlements.

The situation is somewhat different in the province of Quebec, where the *C.C.Q.* has dealt specifically with the consequences of the sale of a business on employment contracts. Under Article 2097, a contract of employment is not terminated by a sale of the enterprise or any change in its legal structure. It is binding on the successor employer in any event, and bridges the employee's service if the employee continues to work for the purchaser without agreeing to different terms and conditions of employment.[24]

In conclusion then, from the purchaser's standpoint, it may be desirable to reduce the sale price (or arrange some form of purchase price "holdback" or other financial mechanism) by the amount of any additional severance obligations (statutory, contractual, or common law) being carried over as a result of hiring the vendor's people. It is also extremely important for the purchaser to enter into employment contracts with the vendor's employees it will be taking on, to avoid assuming unintended obligations.

Carrying Out a Workforce Reduction

Carrying out a workforce reduction means providing affected employees with notice or pay in lieu, in the amounts defined by common law or their employment contracts, though these last need to be at least as generous as the legislated minimum, as discussed above. If more than a small number of employees will be dismissed, the legislation in most jurisdictions contains "mass termination" provisions that may apply. Where there will be a relatively significant number of dismissals over a short space of time, there are enhanced statutory severance obligations, and may also be additional notification, disclosure, and employee transition assistance obligations upon the employer. For example, in Ontario, if between 50 and 199 employees are dismissed within a four-week period, every qualifying employee becomes entitled to at least eight weeks' notice or pay in lieu, regardless of length of service. The employer must also notify and provide certain information to the provincial Ministry of Labour before giving notice to employees (or the notice to employees is ineffective), must post the notification to the Ministry in the workplace, and must work with the Ministry in the transition. If the number of employees dismissed is between 200 and 499, the global notice period is 12 weeks. For dismissals numbering 500 or more, the global notice period is 16 weeks. Again, these periods are mandatory and can oust contractual terms that do not meet their minimums.[25]

Role of Labor Unions in Sales of Business or Workforce Reductions

The situation with unionized employees during a sale of the business is relatively simple. If it is a share purchase, nothing changes as the employer does not change. If it is an asset purchase, the "successor employer" provisions of all federal and provincial labor relations legislation are quite similar, and essentially mandate that the bargaining unit and the collective agreement transfer automatically and intact with the business. In other words, the purchaser gets the unionized employees and the collective agreement "as is, where is."

There are questions that may arise when part of a business is sold and only some of the employees in the bargaining unit logically transfer with it. Much will depend here on the scope of what is being transferred and whether the elements acquired by the purchaser are themselves sufficient to be carried on as a going concern. An analysis of this issue is beyond the scope of this chapter. However, as a general principle, the purchaser will still inherit the union (i.e., the bargaining-unit employees that do transfer will still be unionized and the collective agreement will still apply). The issue of what and who transfers may ultimately be a question of negotiation between the corporate parties and with the union, and can be the subject of litigation before the applicable labor relations board.

As for workforce reductions, the simple answer is that unionized employees in Canada can be dismissed only for "just cause." That generally requires a significant act of misconduct after the imposition of progressive discipline. Unionized employees are therefore more likely to be temporarily laid off if the employer has immediate downsizing needs. The exception is where the employer is permanently closing the facility. In that case, there is a general recognition that the employees will never be recalled from layoff, and they are then paid whatever is required by the applicable employment standards legislation upon termination of employment (or any greater amount required by the collective agreement).

Reorganizing the Workforce

In Canadian employment law, where there is a "significant" change in the terms of employment, affected employees may be held to have been "constructively" dismissed. They are then entitled to the same severance package they would receive if they had been fired outright.

This concept can obviously have a major impact upon an employer's ability to reorganize its workforce, whether as a result of a purchase or sale of the business or otherwise. It can therefore be of tremendous assistance if the applicable employment contracts contain provisions explicitly allowing the employer some flexibility to make the types of changes it needs or wants to be able to make. On the other hand, an employment contract with very rigid terms may actually make it more difficult for later changes to occur. Of course, it is always open to the parties to agree to changes. Potential purchasers are therefore well advised to learn what each, or at least key, employees' terms of employment are when doing their "due diligence." In a share purchase, this lets the purchaser know what they are taking on, even if it cannot be changed. In an asset purchase, the purchaser has the additional option of picking which employees it wants to take on, and hiring them with different terms of employment than existed with the vendor. Of course, as noted above, the vendor will often want to prevent the purchaser from hiring employees on reduced terms, as this may leave the vendor with some liability even after the employees join the purchaser.

Reorganizing a unionized workforce, as noted above, is legally simpler but practically more complicated. The employer's ability to alter jobs, wages, benefits, and other terms of employment will be as narrow or as broad as the relevant terms of the collective agreement. If the desired changes are not within management's powers under that agreement, then they cannot be made without the union's consent. It is also clearly prohibited under Canadian labor laws for the employer to try to negotiate changes with individual employees directly. Negotiation of changes with the union is therefore mandatory unless the collective agreement allows the changes to be made. If the ability to make particular changes is unclear under the collective agreement, they will have to be negotiated or a grievance and ultimately arbitration is virtually assured.

SECTION III

My client wishes to sell its existing facility. What restrictions do we need to consider?

For the vendor of an existing facility in Canada, the legal framework for dealing with its employees is the same as that facing the purchaser described in the preceding section. Of course the perspective is precisely reversed.

For the reasons given above, it will obviously make a difference if the transaction is a share sale, rather than an asset sale. Again, in a share sale, the whole corporation, including the employees, is sold and the seller will retain only those liabilities delineated under the purchase and sale agreement.

In an asset sale, on the other hand, the vendor keeps all of the business' liabilities to its employees unless the employees become employed by the purchaser. This must happen within the period defined by statute for the deemed transfer of statutory rights to occur. For common law purposes, the vendor's liabilities are eliminated only if the purchaser hires the employees on the same or better terms and conditions. If the terms are lesser, the employees may still pursue the vendor for the difference.

From the vendor's standpoint, therefore, to reduce its liability to employees it is essential to have the purchaser agree to hire as many of the vendor's employees as possible upon the sale. Vendors may also want to give their employees as much advance notice of termination as possible leading up to the closing of the transaction, as this will reduce the eventual liability to employees, particularly those who will not be hired by the purchaser and will lose their jobs with the vendor.

SECTION IV

My client wishes to replace its senior manager(s). What restrictions do we need to consider?

While the decisions regarding the retention or dismissal of key managerial employees may be more individualized than those for the majority of the workforce, whether before a sale or following a purchase, as noted above, Canadian legal principles applicable to the dismissal of managers are no different than for other nonunion personnel. It should be noted, though, that members of management (in Quebec, senior management) do not benefit from many of the statutory minimum standards that may protect other employees generally. (See Carrying Out a Workforce Reduction in Section II.)

The first consideration for all employees is the terms of their employment contract. That document will govern with respect to the terms of employment addressed therein (assuming it is otherwise enforceable). Aside from that, common law and employment standards legislation apply.

Employers wishing to change a manager's terms of employment (or any other employee's, for that matter) will also have to consider the potential for a constructive dismissal. As discussed above, where there is a "significant" change in the terms of employment for a nonunion employee (including a manager), that person may be held to have been constructively dismissed. The employee is then entitled to the same severance package that would be received if he or she had been fired outright. Amongst the changes that can be seen as "significant" are demotions, reductions in compensation or changes from fixed to variable compensation, removal of benefits, removal of duties, and changes of location of work.

Another related legal concept that often surprises employers, and that has particular application to many managers (particularly those with long service), is that of "loss of substratum." Just as a "negative" change can amount to a constructive dismissal, a "positive" change can have unintended effects. In particular, if an employee's terms of employment have changed significantly since his or her employment agreement was entered into, Canadian courts are prepared to find that the contract's terms should no longer be binding.

For example, a chief financial officer who signed an employment contract when she joined the company as a junior accounting clerk 15 years ago may no longer be bound by the termination provisions of that contract if she is dismissed, particularly if those terms call for a very low severance package. Canadian courts could find that the parties never intended the less generous terms to apply to a more senior position or lengthy service, and common law severance requirements would then apply.[26]

SECTION V

What prohibitions exist against discrimination on a basis of age, race, gender, disability, pregnancy, and other factors? What are the rights of employees, applicants, or former employees who believe that they have been discriminated against?

Prohibited Grounds of Discrimination

Prohibitions against discrimination in work-related areas are governed by "human rights" legislation, which has been implemented in every Canadian jurisdiction. As with any legislation, there are some variations amongst the different statutes, but the general principle applicable to this discussion is that it is unlawful for an employer to discriminate against an employee or job applicant on the basis of a number of enumerated classifications. These generally include, again with some variation, sex/gender, age, marital status, family status, sexual orientation, creed/religion, nationality, color, physical or mental disability/handicap, political beliefs, and ancestry. Less pervasive classifications that apply in some jurisdictions include civil status, language, social origin/condition, source of income, citizenship, and criminal record.

Direct and Indirect Discrimination

At their most basic, these laws mean that an employer cannot refuse to employ or to continue employing an individual on any of the prohibited grounds. Both direct and indirect discrimination are covered. Direct discrimination occurs when an employer policy or action discriminates on its face.[27] For example, if someone is denied a promotion because of his or her race, direct discrimination has occurred.

Indirect discrimination occurs when an employer policy or practice is neutral on its face, but its effect is discriminatory against one of the enumerated classifications. In other words, because of some special characteristic of the group or an individual, obligations, penalties, or restrictive conditions are imposed on that person or group that are not imposed on other members of the workforce.[28] There need not be any intent to discriminate, so long as the effect is discriminatory. An example of indirect discrimination is when company policy requires employees to wear a certain type of hat even though a specific headgear is required by their religion.

The Duty to Accommodate

Human rights legislation also imposes a "duty to accommodate" upon employers. At its most basic, the duty imposes a legal obligation upon employers to facilitate an employee's ability to participate in the workforce and maintain his or her employment status and rights. The duty arises when an employee needs the employer to change a usual business practice, and the employee's need is created by his or her membership in one of the established classes.[29]

Current principles of the duty to accommodate require that performance standards, whenever possible, be set so as to include employees that require accommodation, rather than setting them at different levels, and then making individual exceptions for employees that require accommodation.[30] This, so the theory goes, helps prevent damage to the dignity and self-esteem of the employee requiring accommodation by making it so that he or she is not being treated differently, but rather is meeting the same standards as other workers.[31]

The employee has the first obligation to communicate his or her need for accommodation. If there is no need expressed, no accommodation can be expected. The exceptions to this are where the employee cannot express the need (e.g., some psychological disabilities), or where the need can be prevented by proactive steps (e.g., preventing workplace injuries that create disabilities). Employees are also required to cooperate and take some active steps in providing information and documentation about their need and their preferences and possible suggestions as to how to accommodate that need. Finally, and most frequently overlooked, is the employee's obligation to assist in developing and implementing reasonable means of accommodation. Specifically, the employee has an obligation to cooperate and facilitate all accommodation assessments and initiatives in a timely manner.[32] The employee is similarly required to be reasonable in conduct; i.e., he or she must act reasonably and try to minimize the disruptive effect of the disability on the workplace.[33]

From the employer's side, there is an obligation to initiate assessments once the need has been communicated. The employer is to analyze all of the accommodation options but in doing so must communicate with the employee and any union representative. Finally, of course, the employer is responsible for implementing the accommodation.[34]

Where there is a union, its obligations are almost a hybrid of the other two parties.' First, the union obviously represents the employee's interests, but also speaks for other members of the bargaining unit. The union can, and is expected to, provide reasonable input and be cooperative in the development and implementation of reasonable initiatives and means of accommodation.[35]

BFORs and Undue Hardship

An employer's actions cannot be discriminatory if the employer can show that they are based on a bona fide occupational requirement.[36] Under the human rights legislation, this bona fide occupational requirement or qualification (BFOR or BFOQ) can exist only if the employee's needs cannot be accommodated without "undue hardship."[37]

The Supreme Court of Canada's now-famous decision in *Meiorin*[38] held that in order for an employer to establish a BFOQ, it must prove three facts:

1. The employer adopted the requirement in question for a purpose rationally connected to the performance of the particular employee's job;
2. The employer adopted that requirement in an honest and good faith belief that it was necessary to the fulfillment of that legitimate work-related purpose; and
3. The requirement is reasonably necessary to the accomplishment of the legitimate work-related purpose. To prove reasonable necessity, it must be shown to be impossible to accommodate individual employees sharing the characteristics of the claimant without imposing undue hardship on the employer.

It should be noted that the term "reasonably necessary" is a misnomer. Without the undue-hardship criterion, for a requirement to be "reasonably necessary" to accomplish a purpose it would not have to be essential, but only objectively helpful in accomplishing the purpose without doing excessive harm (in this case, to the employee's dignity and self-esteem) in the process. As it stands, however, the principle is in fact reversed. The requirement must really be so essential to the accomplishment of the business purpose that it makes accommodation impossible. Taken to its extreme, as in the Ontario Human Rights Commission's policies, the only legitimate business purpose that can meet the test for undue hardship is the very survival of the business itself.[39] This has not historically been the case in the courts or with arbitrators, but the impact of the *Meiorin* standard is still taking shape.[40]

Complaints and Remedies

Human rights legislation is generally enforced by a human rights commission in most Canadian jurisdictions. When employees feel that they have been discriminated against or that their human rights have otherwise been violated, they can file a complaint with the applicable commission. It is also possible in many jurisdictions for others, or the commission itself, to initiate a complaint. Employers are also often able to ask the commission to provide input or opinions about whether a particular intended practice or policy may violate the legislation.

Once a complaint has been filed, the general procedure is for a human rights officer to conduct an investigation. These officers have extremely broad powers and are commonly able to require the production of documents, interview potential witnesses, and enter an employer's premises to do these things. In practice, however, many complaints are referred to mediation or some other form of preinvestigation settlement discussions (which may be voluntary or mandatory, depending on the system) before a full-fledged investigation occurs. This is particularly true where the incident complained of is likely to be isolated rather than company-wide. A settlement process may also occur after an investigation is complete.

If no settlement is reached, the investigating officer makes findings and can refer the matter to a board of inquiry for a full hearing. Generally, the employer, the complainant, and the commission will be parties to the hearing. The board of inquiry will hear all of the evidence and render its decision. Depending on the applicable legislation, there may be rights of appeal, or the parties may have to resort to judicial review.

The Canadian courts have adopted a "hands off" approach to human rights jurisdiction. Specifically, the Supreme Court of Canada has ruled that where the human rights legislation is a complete code of adjudication for these sorts of complaints, recourse is to be had to the commission and board of inquiry procedures, not the courts. The Court in that case rejected the concept of a human rights tort.[41] On the other hand, the Supreme Court recently confirmed that the requirements of human rights legislation create implicit terms in a collective agreement and, as such, the determination of human rights issues is within the jurisdiction of a labor arbitrator.[42]

As for remedies, should a board of inquiry find in favor of the complainant, in all jurisdictions the board may make any order necessary to stop and to rectify the discrimination (i.e., cease and desist orders). As part of this, the board may order that an employee be reinstated if he or she was fired for a discriminatory reason. Orders can also require payment of monetary compensation, or steps to bring the company into compliance, such as implementing policies or conducting education seminars for individuals, all management, or employees in general.[43] Many jurisdictions also allow awards akin to punitive damages or damages for loss of self-respect or dignity. However, these are typically capped at figures far lower than similar types of awards in the United States.[44]

Psychological Harassment

The human rights statutes typically prohibit different forms of harassment based on protected grounds or characteristics. This includes sexual and psychological harassment where it relates to a protected class.[45]

Quebec has gone a step beyond this by specifically introducing new legislation prohibiting psychological harassment in the workplace. This was included in the Quebec Labour Standards Act and came into force on June 1, 2004.

Under Section 81.18, psychological harassment is defined as "any vexatious behaviour in the form of repeated and hostile or unwanted conduct, verbal comments, actions or gestures, that affects an employee's dignity or psychological or physical integrity and that results in a harmful work environment for the employee." This section provides further that "[a] single serious incidence of such behavior that has a lasting harmful effect on an employee may also constitute psychological harassment."

Employers who are covered by the Act must take reasonable action to prevent psychological harassment and, whenever they become aware of such behavior, put a stop to it (Section 81.19). This is an obligation of means and not of result, such that an employer can be expected only to take reasonable measures to deal with the situation.

Quebec's Labour Relations Commission has jurisdiction to hear complaints relating to psychological harassment and possesses vast remedial powers in this regard. For example, in addition to ordering an employer to reinstate an employee with full back-pay, the Commission may order that the employer take reasonable action to put a stop to the harassment, pay punitive damages, and pay for the psychological support needed by the victimized employee for a reasonable period of time determined by the Commission.

It should be noted that these provisions apply in both the nonunionized and unionized settings and are deemed to be an integral part of every collective agreement, with the relevant powers being attributed to a grievance arbitrator.

NOTES

1. Or the civil law in the Province of Quebec.
2. *See generally* J. Dye, *Canadian Employment Law: What American Lawyers Should Know,* 46:3 For the Defense 30 (2004) [hereinafter *Canadian Employment Law*].
3. *Id.* at 32.
4. Arts. 2091, 2092 Civil Code of Quebec [hereinafter C.C.Q.].
5. *Canadian Employment Law, supra* note 2, at 32.
6. Machtinger v. HOJ Industries Ltd., [1992] 1 S.C.R. 986.
7. *Canadian Employment Law, supra* note 2 at 32.
8. Art. 2091 C.C.Q.
9. *Canadian Employment Law, supra* note 2, at 32.
10. In Quebec, such entitlement would be subject to the employee's duty to mitigate.
11. This is not the case under the Quebec Labour Standards Act.
12. In the province of Quebec, employees at all levels are subject to a duty of loyalty and confidentiality that continues for a reasonable period following termination of employment. High-level employees may be subject, as well, to a more intense fiduciary duty.

13. As mentioned, in Quebec the parties to a contract cannot contract out of the reasonable notice entitlement stipulated at Art. 2091 C.C.Q., nor any other public order provision. This limitation may apply in the case of choice of jurisdiction clauses. *See* Art, 3118 C.C.Q.

14. With fewer protections accorded by statute, there are fewer mandatory terms of employment, so the parties are freer to enter into whatever terms they wish upon hiring.

15. R.S. ECHLIN & C. THOMLINSON, FOR BETTER OR FOR WORSE: A PRACTICAL GUIDE TO CANADIAN EMPLOYMENT LAW (1996), at 64–73.

16. *Canadian Employment Law, supra* note 2, at 31.

17. (1999), 45 C.C.E.L. (2d) 183 (Ont. C.A.). *See also* Gryba v. Moneta Porcupine Mines Ltd. (2000), 5 C.C.E.L. (3d) 43 (Ont. C.A.), *leave to appeal to S.C.C. refused,* [2001] S.C.C.A. No. 92.

18. *Canadian Employment Law, supra* note 2, at 31–32.

19. *Id.*

20. *See notably* Arts. 1379 and 1437 C.C.Q.

21. There are varying rules across the country dealing with what happens if the parties cannot reach a first agreement. These are beyond the scope of this chapter, but businesses moving into Canada may want to check the rules of their intended jurisdiction if unionization is a common trend in their industry or in the area in which they intend to locate.

22. *See generally Canadian Employment Law, supra* note 2, at 34.

23. *See, e.g.,* Addison v. M. Loeb Ltd. (1986), 11 C.C.E.L. 100 (Ont. C.A.); Sorel v. Tomenson Saunders Whitehead (1987), 16 C.C.E.L. 223 (B.C.C.A.).

24. Some tribunals have even held that the effect of this provision is to preclude a vendor from terminating the employee in order to permit the purchaser to take on only those employees it wishes to keep or to otherwise limit future severance costs. However, this interpretation of Article 2097 has been controversial. Further, this provision, coupled with Section 124 of the Labour Standards Act, has been used to reinstate employees who were terminated prior to the sale of the business. The relevant tribunals have recognized, however, that employers (including purchasers of a business) do retain the right to terminate employees for legitimate economic or organizational reasons. This is the same after the sale of a business as it is in day-to-day management.

25. Similar provisions are included in the Quebec Labour Standards Act, although the applicable thresholds are different. Where between 10 and 99 employees are terminated in a period of two consecutive months, the required notice is eight weeks. The notice period is increased to 12 weeks where the number of employees affected by the dismissal is between 100 and 299, and to 16 weeks where the number of affected employees is 300 or more.

26. In the province of Quebec, an employee could, in addition to such arguments, rely on Art. 2092 C.C.Q. to set aside termination provisions that are not reasonable at the time of termination.

27. Ontario (Human Rights Commission) v. Simpson-Sears Ltd. (1985), 23 D.L.R. (4th) 321 (S.C.C.).

28. *Id.*

29. J. Dye, *The Duty to Accommodate, BFOQ's and Undue Hardship,* in HUMAN RIGHTS IN THE WORKPLACE (Ontario Bar Association, 2004), ch. 2, at 1 [hereinafter *The Duty to Accommodate*].

30. British Columbia (Public Service Employee Relations Comm.) v. B.C.G.E.U., [1999] 3 S.C.R. 2 [hereinafter *Meiorin*].

31. *The Duty to Accommodate, supra* note 29, at 2.

32. *Bower Inc.* (1999), 82 L.A.C. (4th) 263.

33. *The Duty to Accommodate, supra* note 29, at 6–7.

34. *Id.* at 7.

35. *Id.*

36. Canadian Human Rights Act [hereinafter CHRA] § 15(1)(a). Similar provisions exist in the provincial legislation.

37. CHRA § 15(2), and similar provisions in the provincial legislation.

38. *Meiorin, supra* note 30.

39. *Canadian Employment Law, supra* note 2, at 33.

40. *The Duty to Accommodate, supra* note 29, at 11–12.

41. Seneca College of Applied Arts and Technology v. Bhadauria, [1981] 2 S.C.R. 181. *See also Canadian Employment Law, supra* note 2, at 33.

42. Parry Sound (District) Social Services Administration Board v. O.P.S.E.U., Local 324, [2003] 2 S.C.R. 157.

43. *Canadian Employment Law, supra* note 2, at 33.

44. E.g., tens of thousands of dollars instead of millions.

45. Arguments are made with increasing frequency that psychological harassment of any sort in the workplace triggers both workers' compensation and occupational health and safety legislation.

CHAPTER 4

Labor and Employment Law in China

Qi (Adam) Li
Hong Zhang

The labor law regime in the People's Republic of China (PRC) is complicated and somewhat uncertain. Although the fundamental piece of the labor law puzzle in China is the *Labor Law of PRC* (the *Labor Law*), numerous releases circulated by the Ministry of Labor and Social Security (MLSS), as well as local regulations, have played and will continue to play an important role in filling the gaps between the *Labor Law* and the ever-changing world. The body of labor law in China is constantly evolving.

SECTION I

My client wishes to establish a manufacturing facility in China and will need to hire a workforce. What are the key legal issues involved?

Employment Contracts

Who Receives the Contract

Where an employment relationship exists between an employer and an employee, Article 16 of the *Labor Law* requires that an employment contract be signed.

There is no statutory test to determine whether there is an employment relationship. Rather, it is generally accepted that if a person is on the payroll of another, then an employment relationship likely exists between them. However, the absence of a payroll record does not necessarily mean that there is no employment relationship. If one regularly provides services to another in exchange for compensation, particularly in a facility controlled by the latter, then an employment relationship likely exists.

In the PRC, an employer typically enters into an employment contract with each employee. Since 1994, however, the PRC government has encouraged the use of collective employment contracts where both the employer and the employees bargain the terms of the contract through their representatives. All employees are bound by the terms of a collective employment contract, regardless of whether they have signed it. However, a collective employment contract does not necessarily prevent an employee from signing an individual employment contract with the employer, provided that the terms of the contract are no less advantageous to the employee than the terms of the collective employment contract.

Collective bargaining is a relatively new concept under PRC law. It is not yet popular practice.

It must be noted that only an incorporated company or entity (e.g., a branch of a bank) may hire a workforce directly. Representative offices must hire a workforce through human resource (HR) agencies in China.

What Employment Contracts Must Include

The mandatory provisions of an employment contract under Article 19 of the *Labor Law* include

- The term of the employment contract;
- A job description;
- A description of the work environment;
- Remuneration;
- Disciplinary provisions;
- Preconditions for the termination of the contract; and
- Liability provisions in the event of a breach of the contract.

In addition to the above seven mandatory provisions, the following terms should also be included in collective employment contracts: (1) working hours; (2) resting rights and vacations; (3) insurance and benefits; and (4) procedures to revise, rescind, or terminate the contract.

Although the above terms are referred to as "mandatory provisions," their absence in an employment contract does not necessarily render the contract illegal or invalid. Rather, a court or tribunal will incorporate "implied terms" into the contract, often drawing from current prevailing practice to interpret the contract.

In addition, some statutory provisions are not mandatory in employment contracts, but rather function as a matter of law. For example, all labor disputes must be arbitrated by local labor arbitration tribunals, but the tribunal's decision is not final. Either party may litigate the matter in court.

Special Provisions on Noncompetition and Confidentiality

Although their use is still only emerging, noncompetition and confidentiality provisions are more frequently incorporated in employment contracts, especially contracts for managerial positions.

- Noncompetition periods included in employment contracts may not exceed three years from the date of termination of the employment contract.
- Employees who breach a confidentiality provision under an employment contract likely will be liable for damages. Further, employers using confi-

dential information obtained as a result of a breach of contract shall, pursuant to Article 20 of the *Law of the PRC against Unfair Competition,* also be liable for the losses arising out of the breach.

Legal Consequences If an Employee Does Not Receive an Employment Contract

If there is no written employment contract between an employer and employee, the employment relationship, and by extension the protection afforded by it under the *Labor Law,* is questionable. Under some circumstances, however, an employee may claim the rights that exist under an employment contract if he or she can establish the existence of a de facto labor relationship. Once a de facto labor relationship is established, the employee is afforded the procedural privileges and substantive protections provided under the *Labor Law.*

Hiring Managerial Employees

Under PRC law, there is no material difference between hiring managerial employees and hiring nonmanagerial employees. In practice, "confidential undertakings" and "noncompetition" provisions are included in employment contracts.

The law in China contains special provisions on the qualifications required for managerial positions. Careful consideration should be given to those who have a criminal history, who have run an insolvent company, who own or have interest in a competing business, who are public servants, or who have substantial personal liabilities.

In addition, the law provides for overtime compensation for all employees, except those on irregular work schedules. Employers often prefer that irregular work schedules be incorporated in managers' employment contracts in particular to accommodate the necessary flexibility the company often must offer to managerial employees.

Wages and Benefits

Employer's Rights

An employer has the right to determine salary packages and how it will distribute salary.

Minimum Wage Standard

Once an employment relationship has been established, an employer is required by law to pay the employee at or above minimum wage. The minimum wage is set by local government after consulting trade unions and employers' associations (chambers of commerce), and varies among the different regions in the PRC. The minimum wage excludes overtime payments, allowances, benefits, and social insurance.

Social Insurance

Employers must participate in the various insurance schemes in the PRC. Both the employer and the employee must contribute their respective required portions to local social insurance funds. In addition, as stipulated in Article 73 of the *Labor Law*, employees must participate in pension, medical insurance, work-related injury insurance, unemployment insurance, and maternity insurance plans as long as they are available in the relevant locales.

Labor Unions

Any employee has the right to join a labor union pursuant to the *Labor Union Law of the PRC* (the *Labor Union Law*). The reality, however, is that in companies in which unions have formed, all employees are likely union members. Employers undertake no obligation to organize a trade union for their employees.

Rights of Labor Unions

If an employer elects to unilaterally terminate an employment contract prior to the expiration of its term, the employer is required in many provinces and cities to inform the labor union of the reason for the termination in advance. There have been cases where failure to inform resulted in a nullification of the termination decision.

Rights of Labor Union Officials

- A union chairman or vice chairman may not be transferred to another position before the expiration of his or her tenure. If a transfer is desirable, approval must be secured from the union.
- When an employee is appointed as the chairman or the vice chairman of a labor union, his or her employment contract is automatically extended until he or she is removed from the chairmanship.

Collective Bargaining

Labor unions may sign a collective employment contract with an employer on behalf of all the employees. At present, collective employment contracts are not required by law. However, if a labor union requests an employer to negotiate a collective bargaining contract, the employer may not refuse the request.

A collective employment contract need not cover all aspects of employment, and it need not apply to every employee in the company or bar the employer from entering into individual employment contracts with certain employees. Collective employment contracts serve as a default benchmark to prevent any individual employment contract from providing terms less advantageous to any employee than those in the collective contract.

Where no union exists, employee representatives can still opt for collective employment contracts if the employer agrees to the terms. There are strict rules on quorum and approval procedures, however.

Collective employment contracts are subject to substantive review by the government. However, these contracts will take effect 15 days after the fully executed contract is filed with the Office of Administrations of Labor if that office does not object to the contract's provisions within that time.

SECTION II

My client is acquiring an existing business in China. How do I assess the existing workforce and consider changes?

As a general matter, if an existing company is state-owned or formerly state-owned, there likely is some arrangement with the employees on the number of years of employment they have accumulated, which likely means obligations with respect to insurance and benefits on the part of the existing company. Due diligence on the company's insurance and benefits payment history is highly recommended for this reason. It is not unusual for a company to have failed to pay all insurance and benefits owed, thereby exposing the acquiring company to hidden liabilities.

Making Changes to Key Managerial Positions

Current labor laws and regulations do not prohibit an employer from making changes to key managerial positions. However, employers should be aware of the terms under which it may discharge management, and must calculate the cost of a possible breach of these terms under the employment contract. See the discussion in Section IV below.

Terminating Employment Contracts

Employers must comply with the following rules, unless the employment contracts provide otherwise:

- Early termination of an employment contract by mutual agreement or upon the occurrence of a termination event stipulated in the contract is permitted, provided that the employer compensates the dismissed employee.
- Under Article 25 of the *Labor Law*, an employer may terminate an employment contract without the employee's consent in the following circumstances:
  - The employee failed to prove his or her qualifications to hold the position during a probationary period;
  - The employee has seriously violated labor discipline rules prescribed by law, regulation, or company policy;
  - The employee has caused substantial losses to the employer due to gross negligence or malpractice; or
  - The employee has been charged with a criminal offense.
- Under Article 26 of the *Labor Law*, an employer may terminate an employment contract with 30 days' prior written notice to the employee in the

following circumstances, provided that the employer compensates the dismissed employee:

- The employee was on sick leave or on leave for a non-work-related injury and is unable to undertake the original assignment or the new assignment specifically arranged by the employer;
- The employee was not qualified for the job and, after having been trained by the employer, is still not qualified; or
- The circumstances upon which the employment contract was entered into have materially changed such that the original contract can no longer be carried out, and the parties are unable to agree on terms for future employment.

If due under the above circumstances, financial compensation must be paid in accordance with the *Measures on Financial Compensation for Breach and Rescission of Labor Contracts* (Ministry of Labor Doc. No. 481 (1994)). Essentially, for each year of employment the employer must pay one month's salary as severance, capped at 12 months' salary. However, employers are required to pay more than the cap in certain circumstances.

If an employer has failed to make severance payments to its employee upon rescission of the employment contract, the employer must pay the employee damages up to as much as 50 percent over the amount of the unpaid severance payment on top of the severance payment itself.

Carrying Out a Workforce Reduction

It typically is very difficult to carry out a workforce reduction during a merger where the Chinese entity is the surviving entity. However, the following list sets forth situations that justify a workforce reduction under Article 27 of the *Labor Law:*

- Where an enterprise is on the verge of bankruptcy and has been ordered by the People's Court to undergo reorganization within the statutorily prescribed period; or
- Where the business operations of the enterprise have suffered hardship that reaches the threshold defined by the local government as a "distressed enterprise."

If a workforce reduction is justified by either of the above events, the employer must disclose all relevant information to the labor unions or all its employees, and must file this information with the local administration of labor and Social Security.

Even in a workforce reduction, the following employees may not be laid off under Article 5 of the *Regulation for the Reduction in Personnel by Enterprise for Economic Reasons:*

- Those with occupational diseases or work-related disability;
- Those suffering from illness or injury during their prescribed medical treatment and recuperation period; and
- Female employees during pregnancy, maternity leave, or nursing period.

If an employer wishes to add to its workforce within six months of a reduction, the employees terminated as part of the original reduction have priority in hiring. The employer must also file all relevant information about its recruitment with the local administration of labor and Social Security.

Reorganizing the Workforce

There are no particular regulatory provisions on reorganizing a workforce. If reorganization triggers the termination of employment agreements, then the requirements discussed above apply. If reorganization involves changing its employees' positions, then the employer must carefully review the terms of the original employment contracts.

Changing the Wage and Benefits Structures

The PRC imposes minimum wage requirements on employers. In addition, the current benefits structure in the PRC typically includes various types of social insurance, pension plans, and other benefits. The types of benefits available vary from location to location, but some benefits are mandatory and may not be changed. However, if wage and benefits structures are clearly defined in employees' original employment contracts, then an employer may negotiate with its employees to change them.

It is also worth noting that although many employees, particularly managerial employees, wish to receive stock options from their employers, they are technically impossible under current PRC law. More and more foreign employers are providing stock options of their foreign parent or affiliated companies.

Consulting with Labor Unions or Works Councils

There is no statutory requirement to consult labor unions or works councils prior to or during a merger with an existing company. However, as discussed above, a labor union's blessing may be necessary in some areas.

SECTION III

My client wishes to sell its existing facility. What restrictions do we need to consider?

Assessing Employment Contracts

The sale of an existing facility does not necessarily trigger changes in employment unless the sale involves a transfer of the seller's employees to the buyer. Under the *Labor Law,* employment contracts are not assignable by either the employee or the employer. Therefore, a seller might have to terminate its employees' contracts in order to permit them to enter into new employment contracts with the buyer.

The concept of employment at will does not exist in China; therefore, if an employer elects to terminate a contract with an employee prior to the expiration of its term, all the restrictions discussed above, as stipulated in Articles 24 through 28 of the *Labor Law*, apply.

Early termination in these instances would also trigger compensation issues, which are discussed in Terminating Employment Contracts under Section II above.

Consulting with Government

Generally, there is no requirement to consult with the government before terminating an employment contract, unless the employer is a state-owned enterprise.

Consulting with Labor Unions or Works Councils

An employer assumes no legal obligation to consult with labor unions or works councils if it wishes to sell its facility. See Consulting with Labor Unions or Works Counsels under Section II above.

Negotiating with a Buyer: Special Labor Issues

In the sale of a facility, employees may be very much concerned about the continuance of their insurance and benefits. Many benefits are cumulative based upon the number of years employed, and termination of employment contracts (which will end the accumulation of the number of years employed) may adversely affect the employees. Therefore, as the seller, the employer will often raise these issues and hope that the buyer continues the accumulated employee benefits. Buyers, for their part, will investigate whether all the insurance and benefits payable by the seller have been paid in full. Buyers typically will ask for indemnification for any unpaid amount and may seek governmental action for the seller's failure to pay.

SECTION IV

My client wishes to replace its senior manager(s). What restrictions do we need to consider?

As previously discussed, replacement of senior managers entails no more issues than replacement of regular employees. An employer may choose to either change the position of the manager-employee or terminate the employment contract altogether.

Although changing a position is, in theory, an option for senior managers, the senior manager position often is clearly defined in the employment contract. Thus, changing that position is not possible without breaching the employment contract.

Even if the position is not clearly defined in the employment contract, an employer may not be able to demote the senior manager's position, as the court is likely to conclude that the manager was hired for the senior management position, and that implication would be read into the employment contract.

As a result, replacing a senior manager often triggers termination, and all the above-described restrictions apply.

SECTION V

What prohibitions exist against discrimination on a basis of age, race, gender, disability, pregnancy, and other factors? What are the rights of employees, applicants, or former employees who believe that they have been discriminated against?

Under Articles 12 and 13 of the *Labor Law,* employees shall not be discriminated against on the grounds of nationality, race, gender, or religious belief. In particular, women shall enjoy equal employment rights to those of men.

Under PRC law, no one may be legally employed if under 16 years of age. In addition, there are restrictions on employing children between the ages of 16 and 18. Such children may not work in mine shafts, for example, or with poisonous or harmful substances or engage in physical labor of the fourth degree of intensity as prescribed by law.

Discrimination against female employees is prohibited under the *Labor Law.* Specifically, female employees may not be dismissed during pregnancy, maternity leave, or postnatal nursing, even if the following occurs:

- The employee returned from sick leave or leave for a non-work-related injury and is unable to undertake the original assignment or the new assignment specifically arranged by the employer for the employee;
- The employee was not qualified for the job and, after having been trained by the employer, is still not qualified;
- The circumstances under which the employment contract was entered into have changed such that the original contract cannot be carried out, and the parties are unable to agree on terms for future employment; or
- There has been a reduction of the workforce for economic reasons.

SECTION VI

On the Horizon: What key labor and employment law developments should an employer doing business in China anticipate occurring in the coming years?

There have been no modifications to the *Labor Law* since 1995. Nevertheless, the law has evolved and sometimes is not interpreted to the letter.

The *Law of Labor Contract* and *Law of Social Insurance* are still in draft form. The draft of the *Law of Labor Contract* has not yet been released but likely will focus on the effects of various forms of contracts. It is believed that oral agreements will have the same effect as written agreements under this new draft.

CHAPTER 5

Labor and Employment Law in France

Salli A. Swartz

Although there are a few exceptions, the general rule is that employees who are employed by a French entity and who perform their duties in France will be subject to and will benefit from the provisions of French labor law.

Employees who are employed by a foreign company but who perform their duties in France may also be subject to certain provisions of French labor law, in particular those provisions that are "public order provisions," depending upon other elements of their particular situation such as where they are paid and in which country they contribute to obligatory Social Security regimes.

In addition to the provisions of the French Labor Code, the terms of the national collective bargaining agreements that are applicable to the activity of the company concerned will apply; to the extent they are more favorable to the employee, they will supersede the provisions of the French Labor Code. This is usually the case. Likewise, the terms of the employee's employment contract, if more favorable to the employee than the Labor Code and the applicable national collective bargaining agreement, will supersede the provisions of the Labor Code and the national collective bargaining agreement.

National collective bargaining agreements will apply to newly formed companies if such companies are in a sector that has a collective bargaining agreement. If a company is not in a sector that has a collective bargaining agreement, the company can choose to apply the terms of a national collective bargaining agreement applicable to a sector that is similar to the activity of the newly formed company. A newly formed company that fails to adhere to any collective bargaining agreement may have difficulty recruiting, as new hires will want to benefit from the generally more favorable terms of a collective bargaining agreement.

SECTION I

My client wishes to establish a manufacturing facility in France and will need to hire a workforce. What are the key legal issues involved?

French Employment Contracts

French law does not permit "at will" employment, and there are only two types of employment in France: indefinite-term and fixed-term employment. Although offer letters are used, they are not the usual practice, and contracts (whether indefinite or fixed term) are almost always signed. The official version of an employment contract must be signed by both parties in the French language.

Indefinite-Term Employment

Indefinite-term employment contracts are the norm. As the name suggests, these contracts do not have a term or duration. Moreover, they typically provide for the following terms, most of which are required either by French labor law or by the provisions of the applicable collective bargaining agreement.

Trial Period

The length of the trial period will depend upon the type of position (worker, clerical, nonmanagement, management, etc.). The different durations for trial periods can be found in the Labor Code, but they are sometimes extended by the applicable national collective bargaining agreement or by contract. Typically, a clerical position will have a one-month trial period and a management position will have three to six months.

During the trial period, the employer and the employee may terminate the employment contract for any reason whatsoever with no legal consequences and no indemnities being payable.

Job Duties

French employment contracts detail with great specificity the obligations of the employee, although no law or regulation requires this. The reason for this practice is to protect both parties in the case of dismissal. It is therefore advisable to have a complete description of the employee's duties in the contract.

Remuneration

Basic Salary. The employment contract should state the annual gross remuneration of the employee and specify that it is payable in monthly installments. French companies pay salaries on a monthly, not weekly, basis. Although the law is silent on this issue, most collective bargaining agreements provide for employees to be paid on a 13-month basis, meaning that the gross annual remuneration is paid in 13 equal installments. The 12th and 13th months are usually paid together at the end of December of each year. Before offering anyone employment in France, this point should be verified. In no event should the salary be expressed in monthly terms, since this could cause problems when discussing the 13th-month remuneration issue.

Commissions and Bonuses. If commissions are an integral part of the employee's salary, their method of calculation, accrual, and payment should be very specifically detailed in the employment contract in order to avoid any misunderstandings. Issues such as whether commissions are due to the employee when the sale is made or when the monies are actually received by the employer and what happens to commissions payable on sales made before the employee leaves the company but that the employer receives after the employee has left the company need to be addressed.

The basic salary of an employee and the method of calculating commissions cannot be modified by the employer unilaterally without the agreement of the employee, even if the result is that the employee's remuneration may be increased. The employee must agree to the modification; otherwise, the French courts could hold that there has been a substantial and material modification of the employment terms that have not been agreed upon by the employee and qualify the act as a constructive dismissal of the employee at the employer's cost, with all of the resulting financial consequences.

Bonuses, if provided in the employment contract or if given to the employee on a regular annual basis for several years, will be considered by the French courts to be an integral part of the employee's remuneration and therefore due to the employee. Thus, when drafting bonus clauses, it should be very clear that these may be given by the employer on a fully optional basis. When considered to be part of the salary, bonuses are deemed to be acquired advantages and cannot be eliminated by the employer at will.

Social Security and Other Withholdings

The employer is obligated to withhold and then pay to the appropriate French administrative entities obligatory French Social Security and other contributions. The amounts of such withholdings will vary depending upon the salary and level of the employee, but generally such amounts range from 15 percent to 28 percent of the employee's gross salary. The contributions cover health care, unemployment, and retirement benefits.

In addition to the amounts withheld from the employee's salary, the employer is also obligated to contribute to the same government managed funds as the employee. The employer's contribution again will depend upon the level of the employee's job, but as a general rule, the obligatory employer contributory regimes amount to approximately 48 percent to 52 percent of the employee's gross remuneration.

Working Week and Vacations

The official French working week has been fixed by law at 35 hours. This legislation requires the payment of overtime or compensatory time off unless the employment contract specifically provides otherwise. Top-level managerial employees can be excluded entirely from the 35-hour-week legislation, but this requires careful wording in the employment agreement (as well as the employee's agreement thereto). Before attempting to draft any exclusion to the 35-hour-work week legislation, an employer should obtain legal advice as the legislation is complex and noncompliance can cost more than the cost of legal advice.

French law grants all employees a minimum of five weeks' paid vacation per year. In addition, employees in companies that negotiated a reduction in the work week from 39 to 35 hours may have several additional weeks' vacation. Furthermore, employees are entitled to 11 official legal holidays, including New Year's Day, Labor Day (May 1), WWII Victory Day (May 15), All Saints Day (November 1), Armistice Day (November 15), and Christmas Day (December 25).

Notice Period

The employment agreement should provide for the duration of the notice to be given by either party to terminate the contract. The term of the notice period will usually mirror the trial period, but its term cannot be reviewed.

Other Benefits

Additional Health Insurance. Although not obligatory, many companies will offer a group plan for additional health insurance to increase the amounts reimbursed to the employee under the general Social Security plan. The cost of the additional insurance is shared by the employee and employer and the employee's share is withheld from his or her monthly salary.

The type of plan and its cost should be mentioned in the employment contract.

Transportation. For companies that are located in the greater Parisian region (*Ile de France*), the employer must share the cost of a monthly public transportation ticket equally with the employee. The employee's share is deducted from his or her monthly salary. This may be mentioned in the employment contract for purposes of clarity, but as a general rule, since it is obligatory, most French contracts do not mention it.

Meals. For companies that employ more than 25 employees who habitually eat their meals on the premises, the employer must either make cooking facilities and a place to eat available to the employees (such as a company-run cafeteria, or kitchen with microwave, sink, utensils, etc.) or the employer must share in the cost of meal tickets that the employer will purchase and then remit to the employee, usually on a monthly basis. The employee's share of the meal tickets is deducted from his or her salary.

Expenses. If the employee will be reimbursed for expenses incurred while carrying out his or her functions, the employment contract should specify what type of expenses will be reimbursed, the documentary proof of expenses that will be required to obtain reimbursement, and the method of reimbursement (e.g., monthly by check, quarterly by bank transfer).

Automobile. If an automobile is put at the disposition of the employee, the employment contract will need to specify what expenses will be paid by the employer (insurance and maintenance, for example), what expenses will be shared (gasoline, for example, for personal use), and what expenses, if any, will be borne solely by the employee. If the personal use of the car by the employee is authorized, the details of such use should be detailed in the contract (use on vacations, for example).

Housing. If a housing allowance is included in the employee's compensation package, the amount of the allowance should be specified. Moreover, the employment contract should also detail which party will pay for telephone and utilities.

Taxation of Advantages in Kind. It should be noted that when an advantage in kind is granted to an employee, such as the use of a company car or company-paid housing, Social Security contributions are payable on the monetary value of the advantages and the employee's salary is grossed up to include the monetary value of such in-kind advantages for tax purposes. When the benefit is monetary, such as housing or education allowance, such amounts will be subject to Social Security contributions and taxation as part of the employee's compensation package. Whether in kind or monetary in nature, the advantage will be indicated on the employee's pay slip.

Fixed-Term Employment

Fixed-term employment is highly regulated in France and it can only be used temporarily and for certain reasons that are defined by legislation. Such reasons are currently the following:

- To replace an employee who is out of work (for example, to replace someone who is on maternity, sick, or vacation leave);
- To replace an employee who has left, pending the elimination of the job itself;
- To replace an employee who has resigned pending the arrival of a new employee who has been hired pursuant to an indefinite-term contract;
- To assure habitual seasonal work, such as agricultural harvesting work (for example, as the harvesting of grapes in the autumn) or tourist activities;
- To effectuate a specific mission, such as a financial audit.

Fixed-term contracts may also be concluded when the company's main activity is, by nature, temporary, such as jobs relating to theatrical or musical performances, certain teaching, educational, or cultural activities (such as the biannual couture fashion shows), or construction work.

When such contracts are justified, their duration must be indicated in the contract and such durations are restricted as follows:

- The maximum duration is 24 months when the purpose of the contract is to transfer an employee abroad, or when an employee has resigned and the job will be eliminated or to assure an exceptional export order;

- The maximum duration is 18 months when the purpose of the contract is to accomplish a specific and temporary task;
- The maximum duration is nine months when the purpose of the contract is to replace an employee who has left when his or her replacement (hired under an indefinite-term contract) has not yet arrived, or to accomplish urgent work to assure the security of the workplace;
- The maximum duration is three months when the purpose of the contract is to assure the accomplishment of a temporary increase in activity.

Aside from the duration of the contract itself, the only other differences between a fixed-term and indefinite-term contract are as follows:

- Upon the expiration of the term of the contract, the employer must pay an indemnity to the employee at the expiration of the contract. The amount of such indemnity is currently 10 percent of the total gross amount of remuneration paid to the employee for the duration of his or her employment.
- Unless the parties agree otherwise, the contract may not be terminated by either party during its term unless the employer can prove the gross negligence of the employee or if a case of force majeure arises.

All of the other provisions relating to Social Security contributions, vacation, working hours, and other benefits as described above also apply to fixed-term employment contracts.

Employing Non-French Citizens

Residency and Working Papers

First and foremost, all non–European Union citizens must obtain the proper residency and working papers in order to live and work in France. This process can take several months and must be started from the country of domicile of the employee and the parent company.

The French require non–European Union citizens to obtain a visa to enter France in order to file the paperwork requesting a residency permit (*carte de séjour*) with the right to work. The paperwork is filed with the French embassy or consulate closest to the parent company's offices. It is illegal to enter France with the intention of working and residing without first filing a request for and obtaining the necessary residency and working papers.

Spouses who accompany expatriated employees will receive a residency permit but will not be granted the right to work in France, unless they have individually applied and can justify a valid job offer from a company established in France (or from a foreign company that wants to promote its business or do a market study for its products in France). Minor children will be given residency permits.

A non-EU person hired to hold the office of president or manager of a French company can be appointed without having to obtain a commercial card if such person is a national of a country that is a member of the Organization for Economic Cooperation and Development and will neither reside nor work in

France. However, if the person intends to work and reside in France, he or she will have to obtain the necessary residency and working papers.

Social Security Contributions

Many countries have entered into bilateral treaties with France providing that the employee need not contribute to the French regimes if the employee is contributing to them in his or her home country. However, in order to qualify for this exception, documents are always required and in the case of the United States, the proper form can be obtained from the United States Social Security Office upon justification of the request.

Taxes

If the employee is domiciled in France (living in the country for more than 183 days per calendar year or has family ties to France, i.e., if the employee's spouse and children are living with him or her in France), the French authorities could consider that the employee is a French resident for tax purposes and that person will have to file and pay taxes in France. If the employee is also a U.S. citizen (or a green card holder), that person should also file in the United States, but will receive a tax credit for taxes paid in France.

Most countries have concluded bilateral tax treaties with France to avoid or diminish double taxation.

Expatriate Employment Contracts

To the extent the employee will be managing or working for a French legal entity and living in France, certain provisions of French labor law will apply irrespective of whether the person has a French contract, a U.S. or English contract, or no contract at all. This means that the employee can request and should obtain the same type of benefits as if he or she was employed by a non-foreign-owned French company. These benefits will prevail over anything to the contrary written in any employment contract concluded by the parent company and the employee. Such benefits include the vacations, maternity (and paternity) leave, dismissal procedures, and indemnities payable thereunder, to name a few.

Some benefits may be waived, but those that are considered to be of public order cannot be waived; these include anti-dismissal protection for pregnant women and maternity leave.

Thus it would be wise, in order to avoid any future disputes, to clear the air when expatriating an employee and to suspend his or her current employment contract and negotiate and conclude a contract that will be applicable to the employee when employed in France. Countless lawsuits and bitter "divorces" will be avoided if this issue is resolved before the employee is expatriated.

The other issues that should be taken into consideration are home leave, relocation and moving expenses, tax issues, school expenses, and a housing allowance, to name a few.

SECTION II

My client is merging with an existing company in France. How do I assess the existing workforce and consider changes? My client wishes to sell its existing facility. What restrictions do we need to consider?

The laws and regulations discussed in this section apply to both share and asset sales.

Before the Merger or Sale

Under French law, whenever a major reorganization, a sale of a major part or all of the assets or shares, or the merger of a French company is planned, management of that company (or both companies if both companies are French) must consult and inform the labor representatives of the French company. In companies having more than 50 employees, the organ that must be consulted is the Workers Committee (*Comité d'Entreprise*). The unions are represented through the members of the Workers Committee and need not be consulted separately. In companies that do not have a Workers Committee, the personnel representatives must be consulted. Personnel Representatives should be elected in companies that have at least ten employees.

The consultation process involves a minimum of two separate meetings. The purpose of the first consultation with the Workers Committee is to present and explain the envisaged operation. The purpose of the second consultation with the Workers Committee is to detail and explain any effect it may have on employment. If the effect on employment will result in dismissals, this will require the drafting by management and the approval by the Workers Committee of a social plan.

Although the premerger consultations with the Workers Committee or the personnel representatives cannot prevent the merger or sale from occurring, the consultation procedure can slow down the operation and there may be calls for strikes. The Workers Committee (or the Personnel Representatives) of both the acquiring and the to-be-acquired companies must be consulted before the merger becomes final. Consultations with the appropriate labor representatives of both companies often will be a condition precedent to the effective date of the merger or sale.

Reduction of Workforce

Under both European and French law, all employees employed by the absorbed company or who work in the sold division or business are automatically transferred to the absorbing or purchasing company by operation of law. Thus, unless the absorbed company undertakes to reduce its workforce before the merger, all of its salaried employees will automatically become employees of the absorbing company upon the effective date of the merger or sale. If the purchasing company is located in an EU country, the above will apply to both the selling and purchasing entity. In share transfers, since only the identities of the shareholders change, the status of the employee remains the same.

The reduction of the workforce is not simple, as an employer cannot easily dismiss employees in France. The requirements set forth below apply to all employees, including management-level employees and board members who are also employees, but not to board members who are not employees of the company.

Only two legal justifications exist to dismiss employees: a real and serious cause (i.e., a professional reason concerning the employee) or an economic reason. Economic reasons must be proved through financial evidence. If the employer wishes to dismiss one or more employees for real and serious cause, the employer will have to follow a highly regulated procedure and be in a position to prove the cause (fault, negligence, disagreement with strategy, to name a few). The procedure, whether for economic or personal reasons, provides for notice, a predismissal meeting, and a reasoned dismissal letter. Each step has certain time periods that must be respected. An employer cannot dismiss an employee in a matter of hours in France.

The failure to justify adequate reasons for dismissing an employee or the failure to respect the proper procedure could cause the labor courts to hold that the dismissal was not lawful, in which case the employer will be ordered to pay damages to the employee in addition to whatever other amounts may be owed to the employee, such as salary during the notice period, a dismissal indemnity as required by law or the national collective bargaining agreement, and accrued but not taken vacation days. The amount of damages will depend upon the seniority of the employee and can amount to several years of salary for those who have been employed for many years. The minimum payable in the event of nonrespect of the procedure is six months.

Employees rarely resign in France because if they do so, they are not entitled to unemployment benefits. The amount and duration of unemployment benefits varies, but can range (according to the legislation in effect upon the writing of this chapter) from 57 percent to 80 percent of the dismissed employee's salary for up to two years.

In workforce reductions following a merger or sale, the usual justification is economic reasons since it is difficult to justify the dismissal of more than a few employees for professional reasons. Under French law, dismissals for economic reasons can be justified only if the employer can prove one or several of the following: financial difficulties, changes in technology that result in a reduction in the workforce and that are necessary to preserve the competitive nature of the company, and the restructuring of the company in order to maintain its competitive nature.

Companies that wish to dismiss more than ten employees over a 30-day period and companies that have Workers Committees must prepare a social plan. It must include the following:

- Justification for the reasons for the dismissals (i.e., technological, economic, financial, structural);
- The number of dismissals envisioned and the types of positions concerned by the dismissals;

- The criteria for the choice of which employees will be dismissed;
- The proposed timing of the dismissals;
- The possibility to reduce the number of hours worked in order to preserve employment in the event the company has not already complied with the regulations concerning the 35-hour work week;
- The efforts that have been and will be made to find jobs for the employees to be dismissed, including the provision of outplacement opportunities; and
- The financial package(s) offered to the employees.

The criteria for the choice of who will be dismissed must be objective so as to avoid the employer making "arbitrary" choices, although one of the criteria can be job performance. Usually, the criteria chosen are seniority with the company, age, number of family members who are supported by the employee, and type of job (for example, if people in a certain job category are being replaced by machines, or if an entire department or branch of the company is being eliminated). The employer may choose the criteria that will apply and may apply then in any order.

The precise dismissal procedures to be followed will vary and will depend upon the number of dismissals to be made within any 30-day period as well as the total number of employees employed by the employer. The procedure to dismiss less than ten employees over less than 30 days in a company that employs less than 50 employees and that does not have any personnel or union representatives is less complex than the one that will apply to the dismissal of more than ten employees in 30 days or more in a company that employs more than 50 employees.

To take the most complex example, in a company that employs more than 50 employees (and thus has a Workers Committee) and that wants to reduce its workforce by more than ten employees over a period of 30 days, the following procedure must be followed (failing which the dismissals could be declared illegal by the courts):

First Meeting of the Workers Committee

Management must convene a meeting of the Workers Committee and present to the Workers Committee the draft social plan that covers the issues set forth above. The purpose of the first meeting is for management to explain the draft social plan and to answer questions. During this meeting, the members of the Workers Committee may object to all or certain parts of the draft social plan and may make a number of suggestions and requests to management such as the addition of elements to the package that is being offered (for example, the payment of moving expenses if the employee finds another job and needs to move).

The Workers Committee has the right to appoint an independent expert (who is usually an accountant) to assist it in evaluating the justification for the reasons for the suggested dismissals (i.e., the economic or financial or technological basis for the reduction in the workforce). The employer is responsible for the payment of the expert's fees and cannot object to the appointment of such an expert. Moreover, the employer must make available to the expert the same documents that it must make available to the statutory auditor. The expert may visit the premises and interview employees.

The draft social plan must also be remitted to the Labor Inspector, who is responsible for ensuring that the proper procedure is being followed and that the draft social plan is a responsible one in light of job preservation and avoidance of unemployment in the geographic region for which he or she is responsible.

Minutes of all of the meetings of the Workers Committees are drafted and signed by the representatives of the Workers Committee and management. The minutes should reflect the discussions that occurred and should note any suggestions and objections raised by the Workers Committee.

Expert Report and Second Meeting of the Workers Committee

If no expert has been appointed, the second meeting of the Workers Committee can take place 15 days after the date of the first meeting if the number of dismissals is less than 100 people. The second meeting should take place 21 days after the date of the first meeting if the number of dismissals exceeds 100 people or 28 days after the date of the first meeting if the number of dismissals exceeds 250 people.

If an expert is appointed (which is generally the case), instead of two obligatory meetings of the Workers Committee, there will be three. The expert will have between 15 and 21 days from the date of the first meeting of the Workers Committee to remit his or her report. This report must be distributed to the members of the Workers Committee and to the management at least eight days before the second meeting of the Workers Committee.

Management must make available to the expert the same financial documents as those that are available to the statutory auditors.

The Second or Third Meeting

During the second meeting if no expert has been appointed, or the third meeting if one has been appointed, management and the Workers Committee are supposed to agree on the content of the finalized social plan, including the amount and scope of the package(s) offered, the type of efforts that will be made to find jobs for the dismissed employees, the criteria by which the employees will be chosen, and the timing of the dismissals.

The Workers Committee needs to sign off on the definitive social plan through written minutes. If management and the Workers Committee do not agree, the minutes should reflect the Workers Committee's objections to the draft social plan and its suggestions. Further meetings can be convened and held in order to continue the negotiations.

Moreover, the Labor Inspector, with whom the minutes of each meeting must be filed, can intervene and make suggestions in order to get the parties to agree.

If no agreement is reached and the draft social plan is not approved, management cannot proceed with the dismissals legally. No dismissals may occur before the social plan is finalized and approved by the Workers Committee. If dismissals do occur before the social plan is approved, the employees can usually obtain a court order reinstating them.

If and when the social plan is approved by the Workers Committee, it must be filed in its finalized and approved form with the Labor Inspector and the Departmental Labor Administration. The social plan is then binding on the employer and the employees can no longer object to its being put into place.

Harmonizing Employee Benefits Postmerger

Establishing Uniform Benefits at French Legal Entity

The major issue in postmerger situations (aside from dismissals rendered necessary following the reorganization of the workforce) is the harmonization of employee benefits.

If the benefits afforded by the company that is absorbed are more favorable than those granted to the employees of the absorbing company, there will be a problem since acquired advantages cannot be reduced or eliminated by employers without the employees' agreement. It is irrelevant whether the acquired advantages are granted by a national collective bargaining agreement or by virtue of contractual provisions.

This situation will undoubtedly come up during the obligatory consultations with the Workers Committees of the two companies and should be addressed at that time. It is also a financial factor that must be considered when a merger is being discussed within the two companies concerned.

When the employees of the absorbed company have less favorable benefits than the employees of the absorbing company, then the employees of the absorbed company will automatically benefit from the acquired advantages granted by the absorbing company to its employees.

The only way to minimize the generalization of the most advantageous benefits to all employees (i.e., those of both the absorbed and absorbing companies) is to negotiate with the employees through the Workers Committee or the Personnel Representatives. Such negotiations can take place either before or after the merger, but as stated above, it is more than likely that they will occur during the premerger obligatory consultations with the Workers Committee or the Personnel Representatives.

Establishing Benefits That Are Uniform with the Parent Company

There is no prohibition against granting employees of a French legal entity the same benefits as those enjoyed by the employees of the parent company. However, in light of the obligatory nature of many benefits that must be granted to employees of a French legal entity and the difficulty of eliminating advantages that are enjoyed by employees of a French company, management of the parent company should take great care when examining the issue of benefit grants.

For example, stock-option plans are treated very differently by the French tax and Social Security authorities than they are in the United States.

Without getting into all of the details of the differences, it should be noted that as a general matter, most U.S. companies need to create a separate French stock-option plan or subplan in order to comply with a certain number of French requirements, such as vesting periods. Moreover, the tax treatment of stock options under current French tax law makes such plans less of an incentive for hiring and retaining key employees than U.S. plans do. Although this may change, U.S. management should not assume that the creation of a stock-option plan for French employees will be an important incentive for France-based employees, although there may be certain individual situations when French stock options could make sense.

Internal regulations and policies of the U.S. company, such as ethics reporting, drug testing, privacy of e-mail, and the like as well as legal regulations, such as the Foreign Corrupt Practices Act, the Equal Employment Opportunity Commission, and other regulations that may apply to employees of a foreign-based subsidiary of a U.S. company may not be capable of direct "as is" application to employees of a French subsidiary.

The first problem with such an approach is that any attempt by an employer to effect a unilateral modification of an employee's contractual terms after the employment contract is signed, if significant, may be lawfully rejected by the employee. Thus, the introduction of constraints such as obligatory drug testing after the employment contract is concluded could result in the constructive dismissal at the employer's cost of an employee who refuses to accept the modification.

The second problem is that many internal policies are culturally unacceptable in France. One that comes to mind is the reporting of employees who are not respecting a regulation (whistleblowing). Although this does occur in France, institutionalizing the practice may not be acceptable in a French business environment.

The third problem is that some internal policies are not required because they are already provided by French law. This would be the case, for example, for both sexual and moral harassment in the workplace, which is prohibited by French law, as well as racial or gender discrimination.

Thus, French counsel cannot simply translate internal policies or regulations in an attempt to have them apply prima facie to employees of French subsidiaries of U.S. companies.

To avoid these issues, it is advisable to have the texts of internal policies and regulations reviewed by French counsel in order to ascertain which parts of them may be applied to employees in France and the most effective legal manner to render them applicable to such employees. It is always better to examine this issue before any employees are hired so that such internal policies and regulations can be adapted to French law and attached to the French employment agreements.

SECTION III

What prohibitions exist against discrimination on a basis of age, race, gender, disability, pregnancy, and other factors? What are the rights of employees, applicants, or former employees who believe that they have been discriminated against?

French law No. 2002-73, of January 17, 2002, which incorporated several European Directives issued in 1978, 2000, and 2002, prohibits discrimination on the basis of union membership, age, gender, race, religion, nationality, ethnic origin, family situation, health, sexual orientation, physical appearance, handicapped status, morals, political opinions, family name, or pregnancy,

Discrimination on the basis of union membership is punishable by fine and/or imprisonment of up to €3,750 for a first offense and up to €7,500 and one year of imprisonment for repeated offenses (Article L-412-2 of the Labor Code).

Discrimination of any type on the basis of pregnancy is sanctioned by Article L-122-25 of the Labor Code, and the labor courts can and will award appropriate damages for violations. Such discrimination is also punishable under the penal code by a fine of a maximum of €1,500 and up to €3,000 in the case of repeated violations.

In addition, discrimination in hiring or dismissing on the basis of gender, race, religion, ethnic origin, nationality, family situation, age, handicapped status, morals, or health situation are sanctioned usually by damages, two years' imprisonment, and a fine of up to €30,000 (Article 225-2 of the Penal Code). Thus, a provision that prohibited the hiring of children of employees was held to be discriminatory and a violation of Article 225-2 of the Penal Code because it was discrimination on the basis of family situation.

Discrimination against employees who have been the subject of, or refused to be the subject of, or were witnesses to, or were whistleblowers concerning sexual or moral harassment are sanctioned by the same Article of the Penal Code Section and Articles L 122-46 and L 122-49 of the Labor Code.

SECTION IV

On the Horizon: What key labor and employment law developments should an employer doing business in France anticipate occurring in the coming years?

The most pressing and major issue for French politicians is whether or not the French government will loosen the restrictive labor laws and regulations to allow for a more fluid and flexible labor market. Such reforms could affect the 35-hour work week and the cost of the Social Security system, and thus the level of obligatory contributions both by employees and employers. The right to strike is also being examined for public services in order to require a longer period of notice of such strikes and the maintenance of a minimum service.

CHAPTER 6

Labor and Employment Law in Germany

THOMAS MÜLLER-BONANNI

SECTION I

My client wishes to establish a manufacturing facility in Germany and will need to hire a workforce. What are the key legal issues involved?

German Labor and Employment Laws: Whom They Apply To

Germany's labor and employment laws apply to all employees. Whether or not a person qualifies as an employee is a question of fact and does not depend on the signing of a written contract of employment.

The crucial test is whether the person in question (1) works for another person or legal entity (2) for remuneration and (3) subject to the other person's or legal entity's instructions as to the time, place, and content of the services that are to be provided. Based on this test, the vast majority of persons who are employees from a commonsense point of view also qualify as employees from a legal point of view. By contrast, independent consultants (*Berater*), commercial agents (*Handelsvertreter*), and board members (*Geschäftsführer, Vorstände*) are considered to be self-employed and therefore do not enjoy the protection of Germany's mandatory labor and employment laws.

Staff handbooks are relatively uncommon in Germany since most issues that are typically dealt with in staff handbooks are subject to co-determination of the works council (*Betriebsrat*) and are therefore dealt with in works agreements (*Betriebsvereinbarungen*) (for more details, see Works Councils below).

Employment Contracts: Who Receives Them and What They Must Include

There is no legal duty to provide employees with a written contract of employment. However, under the Act on the Evidencing of Employment Conditions (*Nachweisgesetz*) implementing the European Council Directive No. 91/533/EC, all employees are entitled to a written statement of the main terms and conditions of employment within one month of the start date of their employment.

Most employers discharge their corresponding obligation in a formal contract of employment that provides the following relevant information:

- Name and address of employer and employee;
- Start date;
- If fixed-term contract, term of employment;
- Place of work;
- Brief description of the services that are to be provided;
- Rate and dates of remuneration;
- Hours of work;
- Holidays;
- Notice periods; and
- Reference to the applicable collective bargaining agreements (*Tarifverträge*) and works agreements (*Betriebsvereinbarungen*), if any.

Where the employer is bound by collective bargaining agreements or works agreements that cover these issues, it is possible simply to refer to those agreements instead of listing the aforementioned terms and conditions of employment. Employment contracts for blue-collar workers will typically make use of this option and therefore tend to be rather short whereas employment contracts for white-collar employees will normally be more detailed and include additional provisions (e.g., on bonuses, intellectual property, confidentiality, and restrictive covenants).

Protection against Termination

Employees who have been employed for more than six months enjoy protection against termination under the Unfair Dismissal Act (*Kündigungsschutzgesetz*), provided that the relevant establishment (i.e., the shop or the site, as opposed to the legal entity) employs more than ten employees on a regular basis. Under the Unfair Dismissal Act, the employer cannot terminate the employment contract by way of notice unless there is (at least) one of the three statutorily defined reasons for termination (breach of contract, incapacity, and redundancy). Where the employer's notice is lacking the necessary justification under the Unfair Dismissal Act it is void and therefore will not terminate the employment contract. It is thus not possible to employ staff "at will" in Germany (for managerial employees, see Hiring Managerial Employees below).

Fixed-Term Contracts

In order to avoid the inflexibilities of the Unfair Dismissal Act, many companies employ newly hired staff on the basis of fixed-term employment contracts before signing an employment contract for an indefinite period of time. Fixed-term employment contracts can be entered into for a maximum term of up to two years without any justification being required. It is also possible to sign a fixed-term employment contract for a shorter period of time (e.g., six months) and to extend the term of the contract for up to three times within the maximum term of two years. Fixed-term contracts for more than two years can be entered into if there are objective reasons justifying the term (e.g., a project) although experience shows that such reasons are often difficult to prove in practice.

Hiring Managerial Employees

Board Members

Most of Germany's labor and employment laws (in particular the Unfair Dismissal Act) do not apply to members of the management board (*Geschäftsführer, Vorstände*) although corporate law may provide them with a certain level of protection depending on the type of company in which they are board members.

- *Geschäftsführer.* The appointment of a member of the management board of a *Gesellschaft mit beschränkter Haftung/GmbH,* that is, the manager's board membership, can be revoked by the company's shareholders at any time without any justification being required. The board member's employment contract, by contrast, is distinct and separate from his or her board membership and can be terminated only in accordance with the contractually agreed-upon terms and conditions. Typically, a notice period of six to twelve months will have been agreed upon so that the company must continue paying the *Geschäftsführer* during that period of time. The concept of payment in lieu of notice is unknown in German employment law but the company may send the *Geschäftsführer* on garden leave once his or her appointment to the board has been revoked.
- *Vorstand.* Revoking the appointment of a member of the management board of an *Aktiengesellschaft/AG* prior to the expiration of the management board member's term requires that there be objective reasons. Even where there are sufficient reasons to revoke the board membership of the *Vorstand,* however, this does not automatically allow the company to terminate the *Vorstand*'s employment contract. Rather, as board members of an *Aktiengesellschaft* are normally employed on the basis of a fixed-term contract (maximum term: five years) their employment cannot be terminated prematurely unless they are in breach of contractual duties. In practice it is therefore common to agree on a voluntary resignation of the *Vorstand* and a pay-out of the contractually agreed-upon remuneration during the remainder of the contract term in one lump sum (potentially reduced by interests and other earnings that the *Vorstand* may have during that period of time).

Other Managerial Employees

All other managerial employees enjoy basically the same protection and benefits as regular staff with three important exceptions. Firstly, the works council (*Betriebsrat*) is not in charge of so-called *leitende Angestellte* (typically the senior management immediately below board level). Secondly, labor unions normally do not negotiate wages (although sometimes other terms and conditions of employment) for senior and mid-level management. Thirdly, managers who have the power to either hire or dismiss staff without having to seek third-party consent can be terminated "at will" (although they are entitled to a statutory severance payment if terminated without objective reasons within the meaning of the Unfair Dismissal Act; See Statutory Severance Pay Requirements under Section IV below). In practice, however, this power is rarely granted, so managerial employees normally enjoy the same protection against termination under the Unfair Dismissal Act as regular staff (see Fixed-Term Contracts above).

Wages and Benefits

General

Wages and benefits vary considerably among industries and depending on whether or not the company is subject to a collective bargaining agreement (*Tarifvertrag*) (see Labor Unions below). However, some terms and conditions can be said to be standard across the economy.

Hours

Most industries work between 35 and 40 hours per week. Senior managers normally work longer in accordance with business needs.

Wages

There is currently no minimum wage in Germany although there is a political debate on whether to introduce one.

Collective bargaining agreements establish minimum terms and conditions of employment only for those companies that are bound to such agreements. It is noteworthy that, unlike in other jurisdictions, collective bargaining agreements cannot establish a maximum wage and that many companies pay wages above the collectively agreed-upon pay scales.

Regular staff will typically receive overtime pay in excess of the basic hourly pay rate, whereas middle and senior management will normally not receive overtime pay.

Vacation

The Federal Vacation Act (*Bundesurlaubsgesetz*) provides for a minimum of 24 days of paid leave of absence per year based on a six-day week (20 days based on a five-day week). In most industries, 28 to 30 days' paid leave of absence per year based on a five-day week are common. Those days are in addition to public holidays (the number of which varies from state to state).

Other Benefits

Medical and unemployment insurance are covered by compulsory state plans, the costs of which are shared on an equal basis between the employer and the employee. Company plans are therefore uncommon.

There is also a compulsory state pension plan, which works along the same principles. Since the benefits under this plan are largely perceived to be insufficient, however, many companies offer additional, employer-sponsored plans.

Labor Unions

German labor unions negotiate collective bargaining agreements on wages, hours, and other terms and conditions of employment. They do not involve themselves in operational questions such as the hiring or dismissal of staff, the beginning and the end of daily working hours, etc., since this is the responsibility of the works council (*Betriebsrat*).

Collective bargaining agreements (*Tarifverträge*) are normally negotiated at industry level between an employer's association and the competent labor union. This is because most unions have organized themselves along industry lines (*Industriever-bandsprinzip*). For example, there are labor unions for the metal industry (*IG Metall*), the services industry (*ver.di*), and the mining, chemicals, and energy industry (*IGBCE*). Collective bargaining agreements made between an individual employer and the relevant trade union (*Firmentarifvertrag*) are possible but do not cover as many companies as the existing industry-wide collective bargaining agreements.

In accordance with the organizational structure of labor unions, collective bargaining agreements are normally made for all employees of a given establishment (i.e., the shop or the site). For example, in an establishment that belongs to the metal industry, the collective bargaining agreements signed with the metalworker's union will also apply to the sales staff who, considered on a stand-alone basis, would belong to the services industry.

Labor unions do not have to "organize" a company in order to sign collective bargaining agreements on behalf of the company's staff. They are competent to sign collective bargaining agreements for all companies within their industry sector as a matter of law. However, a collective bargaining agreement will become binding on the employer and the employee only if the employer is a member of the employers' association that signed the collective bargaining agreement (or if the employer itself signed the collective bargaining agreement) and the employee is a member of the relevant labor union. In practice, however, companies that are bound to a collective bargaining agreement normally pay all employees in accordance with the relevant agreement regardless of whether they are a labor union member in order to ensure that employees do not have any additional incentive to join the labor union.

Labor unions have a number of auxiliary competences such as the right to initiate works council elections or to advise and support the members of the works council. Also, in companies that are subject to the co-determination laws (*Mitbestimmungsgesetze*), a certain fraction of the employee seats on the company's supervisory board are reserved for union members.

Works Councils

A works council (*Betriebsrat*) can be elected in every establishment (the shop or the site, as opposed to the legal entity) with at least five employees. The works council is distinct from the labor union in that, inter alia, its members must belong to the staff of the relevant establishment (although many works council members are also members of the labor union).

Where a company (i.e., the legal entity) consists of more than one establishment, the works councils of the various establishments may choose to establish a company works council (*Gesamtbetriebsrat*). Within a group of affiliated companies, a group works council (*Konzernbetriebsrat*) can be established at the level of the ultimate (German) parent company if certain conditions are satisfied. The rationale of the works council, company works council, and group works council concept is to establish employee representation bodies at every level at which decisions with a potential impact on the interests of the workforce are being taken.

Company works councils and group works councils do not have other or even additional competencies than "regular" works councils. Rather, they have the same rights and duties but are competent in matters that cannot be dealt with at the next lowest level of employee representation. For example, if the employer intends to introduce a company-wide, uniform shift model (as opposed to a shift model at the level of one establishment only), this will come within the jurisdiction of the company works council (and not within the jurisdiction of the various local works councils). It is important to note, though, that where the company works council or the group works council is competent for a given matter it will represent the employees of all establishments/group companies irrespective of whether there is a local works council in the establishment/group company in which the employee works.

Works councils have a wide variety of rights ranging from information to consultation and co-determination. Where the works council has a co-determination right, the employer cannot take the relevant measure without the works council's consent. This applies to ordering overtime work, for example. If the works council and the employer cannot reach an agreement, either side may call for the creation of a mediation board (*Einigungsstelle*) consisting of an equal number of employees' and employer's representatives and a neutral chairman (typically a labor judge). The mediation board will then decide the matter with binding effect for both the employer and the works council.

In a number of areas the works council does not have a co-determination right within the strict meaning of the word but ignoring the works council's rights will nevertheless have grave consequences. Most importantly, the works council must be heard and provided with certain information before notice of dismissal is given to employees who come within its jurisdiction. Failure to hear the works council or possessing incomplete information will make the notice letter void. Also, the works council must be heard and provided with certain information before new employees are hired. Noncompliance with that procedure entitles the works council to seek a court injunction against the employment of the relevant employee.

Dealing with a works council that uses its full range of powers can be time-consuming and costly. However, most companies that have works councils do not experience major difficulties in their day-to-day operations.

SECTION II

My client is acquiring an existing business in Germany. How do I assess the existing workforce and consider changes?

Basic Principles

Share Deals

Share transactions (i.e., the sale and purchase of the shares of the target company) have no impact on the existing employment contracts. In particular, the change in share ownership as such does not entitle the company to terminate the existing employment contracts. Just like prior to the transaction, the termination of employment contracts is possible only in accordance with the rules of the Unfair Dismissal Act (see Protection against Termination above). A change in share ownership also does not trigger any protective rights for the benefit of the affected workforce (for information and consultation requirements with employee representatives, see Consulting with Labor Unions or Works Councils below). The employing company remains subject to the same protective labor and employment laws and continues enjoying the same legal flexibilities as it did prior to the share transfer.

Share transactions may affect certain claims or rights of employees that are contingent on the employer company belonging to a particular group of affiliated companies. For example, the employees of the target company may lose share options that have been issued by the parent company; bonus plans that relate to group-wide performance targets may have to be adjusted.

Asset Deals

In the event of an asset deal (i.e., a sale and purchase of some or all of the assets of the employer company) the existing employment contracts will transfer across to the purchaser by operation of law if the asset transfer satisfies the criteria of a (partial) transfer of undertaking within the meaning of the European Acquired Rights Directive No. 2001/23/EC and Section 613(a) of the German Civil Code, which implements the Acquired Rights Directive in Germany. If the sale of assets does not satisfy the criteria of a (partial) transfer of undertaking, the existing employment contracts will stay behind with the seller.

Whether or not a transfer of assets qualifies as a (partial) transfer of undertaking will be determined by the German courts on the basis of seven criteria: (1) the type of undertaking or business concerned, (2) whether tangible assets are transferred, (3) the value of intangible assets at the time of transfer, (4) whether the majority of employees are taken over by the new employer, (5) whether customers are transferred, (6) the degree of similarity between activities carried on before and after the alleged transfer, and (7) the period, if any, during which those activities are suspended. This test will not be applied in a checklist-like manner. Instead, one or more lacking criteria may be compensated for by other criteria. Ultimately, the courts will look at all facts of the case at hand. This may make it sometimes difficult to predict whether a particular transaction qualifies as a transfer of undertaking. However, some general principles may serve as guidelines:

- In an asset-based business (e.g., manufacturing) a (partial) transfer of undertaking will not occur unless the principal assets that are necessary to run the business (or a part of it) are transferred. Therefore, the sale of a single piece of equipment (e.g., a certain machine) normally will not trigger a transfer of undertaking.
- By contrast, in labor-based businesses (e.g., cleaning services), a (partial) transfer of undertaking may occur where the buyer offers employment to a significant part (in terms of number and qualification) of the seller's staff. For example, if the buyer of a cleaning business were to offer employment to 80 percent of the seller's staff it is likely that a transfer of undertaking would be triggered, and the buyer would also be obliged to take over the remaining 20 percent of the seller's staff—even if the buyer does not take over any significant assets.
- The outsourcing of activities that are being completed in-house does not constitute a transfer of undertaking if neither assets nor staff are being transferred to the service provider.

In the event that an asset transfer qualifies as a transfer of undertaking, the employment contracts of all employees pertaining to the relevant entity will transfer across to the buyer by operation of law with all rights and duties. For example, the buyer will have to recognize the transferring employees' lengths of services spent with the seller and will have to pay the same salaries as the seller. On the other hand, the seller and the buyer may alter the transferring employees' terms and conditions of employment or even terminate staff in accordance with the generally applicable labor and employment laws. Section 613(a) of the Civil Code contains only very few limitations in this respect. The most important are

- A transfer of undertaking as such is not a valid reason for the termination of employment (but the seller or the buyer may make staff redundant in the context of a transfer of undertaking); and
- Detrimental amendments to the transferring employees' terms and conditions of employment (e.g., a salary decrease) require objective reasons (e.g., if without the salary decrease employees would have to be dismissed) even if the employees consent (different rules apply where alterations of the transferring employees' terms and conditions of employment are approved by the labor union or the works council).

In the course of a (partial) transfer of undertaking the buyer will also become liable to pay the company pension, if any, of the transferring staff (however, not of pensioners and employees who left the company with a vested pension right prior to the transfer) including past service obligations. This will have to be taken into account when determining the purchase price for the transferring assets.

Making Changes to Key Managerial Positions

Board Members

A share transaction has no effect on either board membership or the underlying employment contracts of the existing board members. Termination of board membership and the existing employment contracts by the buyer follows the rules set out under Board Members above and Section IV below.

The same is basically true for asset transactions although, in this case, termination of the board membership and the employment contracts of the existing board members will be the responsibility of the seller. This is because Section 613(a) of the Civil Code does not apply to board members, which means that they will not transfer across to the buyer (but will remain employed with the seller company).

Strategically it is advisable for the buyer (in both share transactions and asset transactions) to seek agreement on the future role of the existing board members at an early stage of the transaction so as to avoid potential conflicts of interests. Where the buyer does not want to retain one or more board members it is customary to sign termination agreements with those board members that allow them to resign "voluntarily" rather than to revoke their board membership and to give notice of termination for their employment contracts (on the size of severance packages, see Board Members above and Statutory Severance Pay Requirements below). It may be sensible to pay special bonuses to departing board members in order to motivate them to continue working to the best of their abilities through the transaction.

Due diligence should have determined whether there are change of control clauses in place that entitle board members to special payments or early resignation from their positions.

Other Managerial Employees

Section 613(a) of the Civil Code *does* apply to all other (i.e., below board level) managerial employees; upon an asset transaction that qualifies as a transfer of undertaking, their employment contract will transfer across to the buyer. A share transaction leaves the employment contracts of the managerial employees below board level unaffected since the employer company remains the same. In either case (share transactions and asset transactions) termination of employment follows the rules set out in Other Managerial Employees in Section I above. This means, in particular, that termination of employment is lawful only in line with the rules of the Unfair Dismissal Act. A change to the existing management structure that makes one or more managerial employees redundant may provide such objective reasons. By contrast, a change in ownership as such is not an objective reason that allows the buyer to terminate managerial employees (see also Section IV below).

Carrying Out a Workforce Reduction

Unfair Dismissal Act

Under the Unfair Dismissal Act the employer cannot terminate an employee unless at least one of the statutorily defined reasons for termination exists (see

Fixed-Term Contracts above). Redundancy is a statutorily recognized reason for termination and the employer is free to decide on the size of its workforce. In particular, there is no obligation on the employer to demonstrate economic difficulties before making staff redundant.

On the other hand, where part of the workforce is redundant, the employer cannot simply terminate the redundant employees but must make a selection among comparable employees on the basis of "social criteria" (i.e., age, seniority, family status, and disabilities). Employees are comparable in this sense if (1) they are on the same level of hierarchy, (2) the employment contract of the redundant employee allows the employer to transfer the redundant employee to the less protected employee's position, and (3) the redundant employee is qualified for the other employee's position. For example, where redundant employee A is 45 years of age, has been with the company for 20 years, is married, has two minor children, and is comparable to employee B who is 30 years of age, has been with the company for five years, and is single with no children, the employer can terminate only employee B. There is some flexibility in the selection process allowing the employer to preserve the current age structure of the workforce and to retain employees with key qualifications. Moreover, the selection process does not have to be observed when signing termination agreements with employees (but only where the employer gives notice of termination).

The above principles apply to both share transactions and asset transactions.

Works Council Involvement

The works council must be informed and consulted regarding each individual employee before notice of termination is given. Failure to comply with that procedure will render the notice letter void. On the other hand, an objection by the works council to a particular dismissal does not affect the validity of the notice letter. The obligation to inform and consult with the works council is of purely procedural nature.

Prior to a mass dismissal the employer will have to negotiate a compromise of interests (*Interessenausgleich*) and a social plan (*Sozialplan*) with the works council (for the definition of mass dismissals see Consulting with Government under Section III below). The compromise of interests will contain an agreement with the works council on the number of employees who are to be dismissed, the process, and the timing. The social plan will provide severance payments and other measures, as appropriate, aiming at mitigating the adverse effects that employees suffer because of the redundancies. Severance payments are in addition to the applicable notice period (normally four weeks to seven months depending on the employee's seniority) and will typically be calculated on the basis of the following formula

$$\text{age} \times \text{seniority} \times \text{gross monthly salary} \; / \; x = \text{severance payment}$$

where x is subject to negotiations with the works council and may be staggered for different groups of employees (e.g., for different age groups, to take account of their risk of unemployment).

Strictly speaking, the employer must only *try* to reach an agreement with the works council on a compromise of interests (but must not actually sign such agreement) prior to giving notice of dismissal. However, the negotiation process is relatively formalized and may take several months (there is no time limit). Where the redundant staff cannot be employed in a meaningful manner during the negotiations with the works council this may be a considerable cost factor. Disobeying the negotiation requirement may sometimes be a valid strategy as it does not render the dismissals void but only gives rise to a right for the affected employees to sue for a redundancy award. Such a redundancy award will be fixed by the labor courts and may amount to up to 12 months' or even 18 months' pay depending on the employee's age and company seniority (see Statutory Severance Pay Requirements under Section IV below). It is therefore normally preferable to offer adequate redundancy packages in the negotiations with the works council on a social plan so as to induce the works council to sign a compromise of interests quickly.

Reorganizing the Workforce

Employment contracts will normally be flexible enough to allow the employer to implement smaller changes of the job location (e.g., within the same city) or job responsibilities (e.g., exchanging one or two of several of the employee's responsibilities for other responsibilities). More radical changes (e.g., a relocation to a different part of the country; an exchange of all of the employee's job responsibilities for other responsibilities) will often require the employer to give notice of termination while simultaneously offering continued employment with altered terms and conditions of employment (*Änderungskündigung*). Since the employer will have to justify this type of dismissal under the Unfair Dismissal Act, it is not used very frequently.

Depending on how significantly the current organizational structures are to be changed, a reorganization of the workforce may trigger an obligation to negotiate a compromise of interests (*Interessenausgleich*) and a social plan (*Sozialplan*) with the works council (see Works Council Involvement under Section II above). For example, if the employer intends to switch from a horizontal organizational structure to a vertical business unit structure it will have to negotiate with the works council an agreement on if, when, and how this change is to be implemented (compromise of interests) and an agreement on how any adverse effects employees may suffer because of the change will be mitigated (social plan). Most of the procedural considerations outlined under Carrying Out a Workforce Reduction under Section II above in connection with mass dismissals apply mutatis mutandis.

The above principles apply to both share transactions and asset transactions.

Changing the Wage and Benefits Structure

Due diligence should have determined to what extent wages and benefits are flexible. Typical ways to make wages and benefits flexible are the granting of benefits on a voluntary or a revocable basis. Where a benefit has been granted on a voluntary basis (e.g., a Christmas bonus) the employer is free to decide anew every year whether or not to pay the benefit. Where a benefit has been granted on a revocable basis, the employer is basically under an obligation to pay that benefit but may stop doing so in future years provided that (1) there are objective reasons (e.g., economic difficulties of the company), and (2) the employer exercises its discretion in an equitable manner. Another way of making benefits flexible is to grant them for a fixed period of time only (bonus plans and stock option plans are often introduced for one or several years only and followed by new plans once the old plan has expired). The courts are reluctant to accept arrangements that make more than approximately 20 percent of the employee's overall compensation package subject to unilateral changes by the employer.

Where employees have a contractual right to a certain benefit, the employer must give notice of termination and, at the same time, offer continued employment at altered terms and conditions (*Änderungskündigung*) in order to dispense with the benefit. Given that this type of notice must satisfy the criteria of the Unfair Dismissal Act and can be challenged in court, this route of action is often impractical. In no event does the buyer's interest in harmonizing terms and conditions of employment following a transfer of undertaking justify such dismissals. Notice of termination (combined with an offer of continued employment at altered terms and conditions) aimed at reducing the employee's base salary (as opposed to fringe benefits) will be possible only in a near insolvency situation.

Where certain benefits have been granted on the basis of a works agreement (*Betriebsvereinbarung*) made with the works council they can be altered (even to the employees' detriment) by way of a new works agreement. This is an instrument that is used frequently following a transfer of undertaking for purposes of harmonizing terms and conditions of employment.

Special rules apply to occupational pension plans. Broadly speaking, the claims of pensioners, employees who have left the company with a vested right to a company pension, and the accrued rights of active employees (past benefit obligations) can be reduced only in quite extreme situations (e.g., to avoid insolvency), whereas future earnings can be reduced or even stopped depending on the reasons for such alteration. These rules apply also to agreements made with the works council.

The above principles apply to both share transactions and asset transactions.

Consulting with Labor Unions or Works Councils

Share Transactions

Local works councils have no information or consultation rights with respect to share transactions, as their co-determination rights are directed against the employer company and the sale of the shares of the employer company takes place at shareholder level. It is best practice, though, to inform the works council in advance of a change in share ownership. Normally, this information will be provided shortly before the sale and purchase agreement on the employer company's shares is signed. Where there is an economic committee (*Wirtschaftsausschuss*) (a special employee representation body in charge of economic affairs that can be established in companies with more than 100 employees), there is a legal duty to inform the economic committee of changes in the share ownership of the employer company. Arguably, this information can be provided after the signing of the sale and purchase agreement but, again, it is best practice to do so shortly before signing. There is no obligation to make available to employee representatives a copy of the sale and purchase agreement.

Where there is an European Works Council (*Europäischer Betriebsrat*), there may be an obligation to inform and consult with the European Works Council depending on the agreement establishing the European Works Council.

Asset Transactions

Regarding asset transactions, a distinction must be made between the sale of the entirety of an establishment (*Betrieb*) (i.e., the shop, the site) and parts of an establishment. Upon a sale of an establishment in its entirety the economic committee (and, if there is no economic committee, arguably the works council) must be informed and consulted with in good time prior to the sale, but the employer company does not need the economic committee's or the works council's consent to sign or complete the transaction. By contrast, where only part of an establishment is sold, there will normally be an obligation to negotiate a compromise of interests (*Interessenausgleich*) and a social plan (*Sozialplan*) with the works council before the transaction can be completed. The negotiation procedure is comparable to that on mass dismissals (see Works Council Involvement under Section II above). There are strategies to avoid this consequence, although a description of these would go beyond the scope of this chapter.

Additionally, Section 613(a) of the Civil Code obliges the seller and the buyer to inform the transferring employees in advance of a (partial) transfer of undertaking of (1) the time of the transfer, (2) the reasons for the transfer, (3) the legal, economic, and social consequences of the transfer, and (4) any measures that the buyer intends to take with respect to the transferring workforce. This information must be provided in writing to every transferring employee.

Labor Unions

Labor unions have no information or consultation rights on either share transactions or asset transactions.

SECTION III

My client wishes to sell its existing facility. What restrictions do we need to consider?

Assessing Employment Contracts

The key issues the buyer will normally look at in its due diligence exercise are

- The number of employees, in particular whether there are "hidden" employment contracts (freelancers or agency workers who are in reality employees of the seller company);
- The size of the seller's pension obligations. In particular the buyer will review whether there is an underfunding of the seller's pension obligations.

This is an issue not only in share transactions but also in asset transactions as, under Section 613(a) of the Civil Code, the buyer will assume liability for all pension obligations vis-à-vis the transferring employees by operation of law (but not for pensioners and employees who have left the company with a vested pension right prior to the transfer of undertaking);
- Restructuring obstacles such as an agreement with the works council that rules out dismissals on grounds of redundancies for a certain period of time (such agreements can sometimes be found where the company has recently undergone a restructuring);
- Change of control clauses in the employment contracts of management-level employees that entitle them to certain payments or give them a right to terminate their employment early;
- Any liability relating to the time prior to the transfer (e.g., unpaid wages or Social Security, liability from illegal discrimination).

In the sale and purchase agreement, the seller will normally have to warrant that only a certain number of employees will transfer across to the buyer and will have to indemnify the buyer against the costs of additional employees transferring across. It is also customary that the seller indemnifies the buyer against liabilities relating to the time up until the transfer of undertaking (unless the buyer accepts disclosure in the due diligence exercise as sufficient). Whether or not the seller will be able to resist a purchase price reduction because of an existing underfunding of its occupational pension plans will depend on the circumstances of the case. Sellers should bear in mind in this context that, where pension obligations are totally unfunded (as is customary in Germany), the company's balance sheet will not show the actual size of the company's liability but, because of tax law, only lower figures. The buyer will therefore often insist that an actuary calculates the company's full liability under U.S. generally accepted accounting principles (GAAP) or international financial reporting standards (IFRS).

Consulting with Government

Labor and employment law does not establish obligations to consult with government in the context of corporate transactions. There is an obligation, though, to notify the labor authorities in advance of a mass dismissal under the European Mass Dismissal Directive No. 75/194/EC and Section 17 of the Unfair Dismissal Act, which implements the Mass Dismissal Directive in Germany. A mass dismissal will occur where, within a period of 30 calendar days,

- In establishments (i.e., the shop or the site, as opposed to the legal entity) with more than 20 but fewer than 60 employees, more than five employees are dismissed;
- In establishments with at least 60 but fewer than 500 employees, 10 percent of the workforce or more than 25 employees (whichever is smaller) are dismissed;
- In establishments with at least 500 employees, at least 30 employees are dismissed.

Consulting with Labor Unions or Works Councils

The information and consultation requirements mirror those applicable on the acquisition of an existing business (see Consulting with Labor Unions or Works Councils under Section II above).

Negotiating with a Buyer: Special Labor Issues

Where a transaction triggers co-determination rights of the works council (see Consulting with Labor Unions or Works Councils under Section II above) it is important duly to coordinate the negotiations with the works council and with the buyer. The buyer will often make it a condition precedent to closing that the negotiations with the works council have been completed. If the works council learns that such a condition exists, however, it will have additional leverage in the negotiations with the seller.

In addition, the seller will have to negotiate with the buyer various warranties and indemnifications in the sale and purchase agreement as outlined under Assessing Employment Contracts under Section III above.

SECTION IV

My client wishes to replace its senior manager(s). What restrictions do we need to consider?

Employment Contracts

The cost of terminating members of senior management depends on whether they are board members or "normal" employees (see Hiring Managerial Employees under Section I above).

Board members do not enjoy protection against termination under the Unfair Dismissal Act. The cost of terminating their employment will therefore depend on the contractually agreed-upon terms. Board members of a *Gesellschaft mit beschränkter Haftung* (*GmbH*) will normally have a notice period of six to 12 months so that the company must either continue paying the board member during that period of time (on payment in lieu of notice, see Hiring Managerial Employees under Section I above). Board members of an *Aktiengesellschaft* (*AG*) are typically employed on the basis of fixed-term contracts with a maximum term of five years. In a separation scenario the company will often agree with the board member on "voluntary" resignation and pay out the remainder of the contract term (see Hiring Managerial Employees under Section I above). It is important to note that board membership is distinct from the underlying employment contract. In a *GmbH*, board membership can be revoked at any time without any justification being required whereas in an *AG* a revocation of the board membership requires objective reasons (see Hiring Managerial Employees under Section I above).

Managerial employees below board level do enjoy protection against termination under the Unfair Dismissal Act (see Hiring Managerial Employees under

Section I above). Notice of dismissal is therefore unlawful (and void) unless the employer company can demonstrate the existence of at least one of the statutorily defined objective reasons for termination (see Fixed-Term Contracts under Section I above). It is possible, though, to sign a termination agreement provided that the employee consents. Normal severance packages agreed upon in termination agreements range between 0.5 to 1.0 monthly remunerations (including all benefits) for every year of employment. Those payments are in addition to the applicable notice period.

Discrimination Issues

Discrimination issues will be dealt with in Section V below.

Statutory Severance Pay Requirements

Employees

German law does not provide statutory severance payments. Within the scope of application of the Unfair Dismissal Act notice of dismissal is either lawful, in which event the employer's notice letter will terminate the employment contract without any obligation on the employer to make a severance payment, or unlawful and therefore void, in which event the employment contract will continue.

There are only two exceptions to this rule: (1) social plans (*Sozialpläne*) negotiated with the works council (see Carrying Out a Workforce Reduction under Section II above) and (2) certain situations in unfair dismissal litigation. More specifically, where the employer's notice is lacking the necessary justification under the Unfair Dismissal Act (and is therefore void) but there are objective reasons not to continue the employment contract, the court may dissolve the employment contract and order the employer to make a severance payment. Such severance payments are generally capped at 12 monthly remunerations (including all benefits). If the employee is at least 50 years of age and has been with the company for at least 15 years, severance payments are capped at 15 monthly remunerations (including all benefits); where the employee is at least 55 years of age and has been with the company for at least 20 years, a cap of 18 monthly salaries (including all benefits) applies. It is important to emphasize that the courts rarely make use of their power to dissolve an employment contract as the Unfair Dismissal Act is aimed primarily at continued employment.

Yet other rules apply to managerial employees who have either the power to hire or dismiss staff without having to seek third-party consent (a power that is rarely granted in practice). If the employer company requests that the court dissolve the employment contract of such an employee, the court must grant the employer's motion irrespective of whether there are objective reasons for termination and order a severance payment to be made (within the aforementioned financial limits).

Board Members

Board members do not fall within the scope of application of the Unfair Dismissal Act and are therefore not entitled to statutory severance payments. Exceptions to this rule apply only where a board member is also an employee of the company (a situation that may arise in some circumstances).

Statutory Restrictions on Dismissal without Cause

Outside the scope of application of the Unfair Dismissal Act, the employer does not need objective reasons to terminate an employment contract. By contrast, within the scope of application of the Act, the employer cannot terminate the employment contract unless (at least) one of the statutorily defined reasons for termination exists (see Protection against Termination in Section I above). It is not possible to terminate an employment contract in breach of the Unfair Dismissal Act. If the employer's notice is lacking the necessary justification under the Act it is void and will therefore not terminate the employment contract.

SECTION V

What prohibitions exist against discrimination on a basis of age, race, gender, disability, pregnancy, and other factors? What are the rights of employees, applicants, or former employees who believe that they have been discriminated against?

General Principle of Equal Treatment

Under the general principle of equal treatment the employer must not treat employees in similar situations differently without justifying reason. For example, absent justifying reasons, it is unlawful to set up a company pension plan for the benefit of white-collar employees but not for blue-collar workers. Violations of the general principle of equal treatment will entitle those employees who have been discriminated against to the same benefits as have been granted to all other employees. In the aforementioned example, blue-collar workers also would be entitled to a company pension in accordance with the plan established for white-collar employees unless the employer can demonstrate objective reasons for the exclusion of blue-collar workers from the company pension plan.

Gender Discrimination

In addition to the general principle of equal treatment, Section 611(a) of the German Civil Code prohibits discriminations against a (prospective) employee on the basis of his or her gender. In particular, Section 611(a) of the Civil Code prohibits gender discrimination in connection with the establishment of an employment relationship, professional promotions, employment-related instructions, and the termination of the employment relationship.

Employees who have been discriminated against on the basis of their gender are entitled to an equitable monetary award. The size of such awards is unpredictable, though, since there are only very few court precedents. In addition to the monetary award, where the employee has been unlawfully excluded from a certain benefit he or she will be entitled to that benefit. Where the employee has become subject to unlawful detrimental measures by the employer (e.g., a demotion), the relevant measure will be considered void.

Special rules apply where a (prospective) employee applies for a vacancy. In this situation the best qualified applicant who has been discriminated against will be entitled to an equitable monetary award (the size of which remains unclear in the law) but not to instatement to the vacant position. All other employees are entitled to a maximum of three months' pay (as they would have received in the vacant position).

Antidiscrimination Act

Germany currently has no comprehensive antidiscrimination laws but there is draft legislation pending for an Antidiscrimination Act. The current draft prohibits discriminations on the basis of race, ethnic origin, gender, religion or belief, disability, sexual orientation, and age. It obliges the employer to take certain organizational measures in order to avoid unlawful discrimination, such as a duty to provide training to employees. Under the draft Act, employees who have been discriminated against are entitled to damages and to an additional award to compensate for harm and suffering. The details of the Antidiscrimination Act are still under heavy political debate.

SECTION VI

On the Horizon: What key labor and employment law developments should an employer doing business in Germany anticipate occurring in the coming years?

It is widely felt that Germany's labor market is overregulated. Current proposals for deregulation focus primarily on three areas: (1) unfair dismissal, (2) collective bargaining agreements, and (3) employee representation on the supervisory board.

More specifically, proposals have been made to raise the threshold figure as of which the Unfair Dismissal Act applies (currently, as of ten employees). It has also been proposed to allow employers to deviate from applicable collective bargaining agreements provided that the works council and/or a certain quorum of the workforce consent. Finally, there are moves to reduce the number of employee representatives on the supervisory board of large companies. Currently, companies that employ more than 500 employees or more than 2,000 employees must reserve one third or one half of the seats on the company's supervisory board (*Aufsichtsrat*) for employee representatives (provided that other conditions are satisfied). Proposals for legislative reform aim at reducing this number to a maximum of one third of the seats on the company's supervisory board. None of the aforementioned proposals have reached the stage of draft legislation yet.

CHAPTER 7

Labor and Employment Law in Italy

Alberto Maggi
Silvia Tozzoli

SECTION I

My client wishes to establish a manufacturing facility in Italy and will need to hire a workforce. What are the key legal issues involved?

A company wishing to hire employees in Italy has various options to choose from: It may enter into the standard full-time, open-ended employment contract, or it may establish one of the so-called "flexible" employment relationships (e.g., fixed-term contracts, part-time contracts, agency work, special contracts with young people, and job-sharing contracts).

The mosaic of rules applicable to the employment relationship has been developed by both the law and national collective labor agreements. In principle, collective agreements are legally binding only if the employer and the employee actually concerned join the signatory employers association or trade union. But because collective agreements often set minimum standards to which labor courts routinely defer when implementing general employment laws, in practice these labor agreements enjoy a general application to all companies operating in the covered sector(s).

The Employment Contract

Form and Notice Obligations

Italian law does not provide for a specific form of employment contract (but see below for the trial period clause and flexible contracts). This means that no written document is required, and employment relationships can be established in whatever way the parties agree.

According to standard practice, an offer letter is normally provided. The content of such a letter is rather simple: a reference to the relevant provisions of the governing law, the applicable national collective labor agreement, and any additional agreement that may be entered into at company level.

Pursuant to a legislative decree of 1997,[1] however, the employer is bound to provide each new employee with the most important information relating to his/her employment: starting date, duration, trial period, salary, tasks to be performed, working time, holidays, and notice period. Such information can be included in the offer letter or in a separate written statement to be sent within 30 days from hiring. If this deadline is not respected, the employer can be issued an order by the provincial labor office and, in case of noncompliance, is subject to a fine.

On the date of hiring, a communication must be filed with the provincial labor office and with the Social Security authorities. Failure to comply in a timely manner will subject the employer to a fine.

In the Italian system, there is no general obligation to give notice of new hires to trade unions or work councils at company level. Certain collective agreements, however, provide for an obligation of this kind, especially in the case of employees hired under flexible contracts.

Trial Period

Employment agreements can be subject to a trial period, the maximum duration of which is established by national collective labor agreements and normally depends on the employee's professional level, but in no case exceeds six months. During this period, either party to the employment relationship can terminate the agreement without the need to give notice or provide a specific justification.

To be valid, the trial period clause must be inserted in writing in the employment agreement and accepted by the employee before or on the effective date of employment.

Terms and Conditions of Employment

The parties are free to determine the terms and conditions regulating the employment relationship. A number of statutory provisions, however, fix a mandatory minimum standard for specific aspects of the employment relationship. If the individual agreement contains clauses that are below these minimum standards, they will be considered null and void and the employee shall be entitled to have the legal standards enforced.

As far as pay is concerned, Article 36 of the Italian Constitution states that employees are entitled to receive a fair remuneration for the work performed and that, in any case, such remuneration must be adequate for workers to maintain themselves and their families.

In the absence of national legislation setting a minimum salary, the fairness and adequacy of the remuneration is determined by labor courts with reference to the level of salary determined by collective agreements for each category of employees.

In addition to the normal salary, determined as above, Italian law also provides for a mandatory severance pay, *trattamento di fine rapporto* (TFR), which is due in case of termination of the employment relationship, even if for reason of resignation, expiration of a fixed-term contract, or dismissal for gross misconduct. The amount of the TFR is equal to approximately one month's salary multiplied by the years of employment with the company, and is allocated in the company's financial statements throughout the entire term of employment. The accrued amount is revaluated with the application of an interest rate in line with the rate of inflation.

With regard to working time, since the adoption of two reforms in 1997[2] and 2003,[3] the standard working time has been fixed at 40 hours per week. Collective agreements, including those entered into at a company level, may, however, establish a shorter working time, and define the working time by reference to annual averages.

Work performed in excess of such limits is classified as overtime, which is allowed only if the employee agrees and is compensated in addition to the normal salary.

The maximum weekly working time, including overtime, may also be established by collective agreements. If no collective agreement is applicable, the law provides that the average weekly working time, considering a "reference period" of at least four months, shall not exceed 48 hours.

The Italian Constitution also guarantees each employee an annual vacation of not less than four weeks.[4] Such a right cannot be waived, nor, during the employment, can the holiday entitlement be exchanged for payment. Only upon termination of the employment contract is the employee paid for any accrued holidays.

Mandatory leaves and time off are provided for by the law in a number of cases. Of these, it is worth mentioning (1) maternity leave (the period of five months, running from two months before to three months after the birth of the child or, alternatively, from one month before to four months after the birth, during which the employee must abstain from performing any working activity); (2) marriage leave (the duration of which is determined by collective agreements and is usually 15 days); (3) time off for medical and health reasons (provided for by the law in a number of cases); (4) time off for union representatives (which depend on the size of the company and can be paid or unpaid).

In case of absence due to sickness, Italian employees are entitled, pursuant to Article 2110 of the Civil Code, to keep their position for a certain period of time (so-called *periodo di comporto*). This period is a suspension of the contract with job protection: The employer cannot dismiss the employee. During the *periodo di comporto,* the employees shall receive all or part of their salary and have their *periodo di comporto* calculated for seniority and Social Security purposes. National collective labor agreements provide for the length of such period and the rate of salary to be paid. When no national collective labor agreement applies, the *periodo di comporto* is determined by labor courts.

Fixed-Term Contracts

Fixed-term employment is now allowed whenever justified by technical, organizational, or productive reasons, or by the need to replace other employees. Fixed-term agreements cannot be entered into in certain circumstances (among others, to replace workers on strike and in companies putting in place collective dismissals). Moreover, it is left to national bargaining agreements to determine quantitative restrictions when resorting to fixed-term employment agreements. Where such requirements and prohibitions are not complied with, the agreement will be considered open-term.

The duration of fixed-term agreements must be set forth in writing (unless the term is shorter than 12 days). Otherwise, the agreement shall be deemed an open-term agreement. The employer must deliver a copy of such written document to the employee specifying the objective circumstances that made it necessary to resort to a fixed-term agreement.

Part-Time Contracts

Part-time contracts are defined as individual contracts that establish working hours less than the standard working time of 40 hours per week provided for by the law or the time established by national labor collective agreements. The contract can take different forms, depending on whether the reduction of hours is established in relation to daily hours; the performance of the working activity is carried out on a full-time basis, but for limited periods in the course of the week, month, or year; or the working activity is carried out according to a combination of the two. Fixed-term employment agreements may also be part-time.

The part-time contract must be in writing, and notice must be provided within 30 days to the provincial labor office.[5] In addition, the duration and time schedule of the work activity must be precisely indicated in terms of day, week, month, and year. For each of these provisions, the decree provides for specific sanctions, including the transformation of the part-time contract into a full-time employment relationship.

In the presence of specific organizational needs, the employer is entitled to request part-timers to perform additional work, i.e., work performed in excess of the working hours contemplated in the schedule agreed between the parties and in any case not exceeding the full-time limit.

Job On-Call and Job-Sharing Contracts

In a recent major reform of labor legislation,[6] two types of contracts widely used abroad are now admissible also in Italy: job on-call and job-sharing contracts. Specific rules apply, which should be considered carefully.

Training Employment Contracts

Training employment contracts are intended to facilitate the entrance into the labor market of young or disadvantaged people, who will also benefit from the training to be provided in the performance of the contract. Training contracts are divided into apprenticeships and "entrance" contracts. Specific rules apply, which should be considered carefully.

Employment Agencies

Two types of contractual relationships emerge from employment agencies: One is the contract between the employer and the agency; the other is the contract between the agency and the employee supplied. Both contracts shall be drawn up in writing subject to the penalty of nullity, and both shall contain specific elements required by law.

Contracts between employers and agencies may be for a fixed term or for an indefinite period of time (so-called staff leasing). Both types are subject to specific rules, which should be considered carefully.

Executives (Dirigenti)

Dirigenti are considered the highest level of employees, and they are defined as the alter ego of the employer, in charge of directing the whole enterprise or an important or autonomous branch thereof, operating with full autonomy under the general direction of the employer. *Dirigenti* are organized in separate trade unions from those of other employees and have separate national collective labor agreements.

Although *dirigenti* are usually members of the company's board of directors, the director relationship is different from the employment contract.

The legal regime applicable to employment contracts with *dirigenti* differs, in some aspects, from the general regime described above. In particular, *dirigenti* are excluded from the application of the legislation governing dismissals (discussed below). They are not subject to the legal provisions limiting working time, and they can be freely hired under fixed-term contracts for a duration of up to five years: the requirement of technical, organizational, productive, or replacement reasons does not in fact apply to them.

Among the clauses that are often inserted in the individual employment contract with *dirigenti* are those aimed at ensuring employee retention. To that purpose, firms often make use of noncompetition covenants or stock option and incentives schemes. Article 2125 of the Italian Civil Code provides that post-employment noncompetition covenants may be deemed valid and enforceable only if they (1) are specified in writing; (2) set forth a specific consideration in favor of the employee; (3) have a limited scope and geographical extent; and (4) have a term not exceeding five years (three years for non-*dirigenti*). The employer has the right to request compensation for the damage it has suffered due to a breach of the noncompetition covenant. Such damages are often predetermined in a liquidated damages clause included in the covenant.

Stock option and incentives schemes are often deployed as an instrument to ensure a certain degree of stability to the employment relationship. In particular, long-term vesting periods may serve the purpose of retaining managers.

Under certain circumstances, benefits deriving from such plans are subject to a favorable tax and Social Security regime. There is, however, the risk that said benefits could be taken into account in the determination of the severance pay and the pay for unjustified dismissal, as labor courts have not yet adopted a clear position on the question.

Social and Mandatory Insurance Policy

Social Security Contributions: INPS

Social Security contributions for pensions, unemployment, and family allowances are paid to the National Institution for Social Security (*Istituto Nazionale della Previdenza Sociale,* INPS) by the employer.

Family allowances, in particular, are paid by the Social Security authorities to those employees having dependent relatives and earning an income below a certain threshold.

The total amount of Social Security contributions are 40 to 45 percent of salary, of which the employer pays 30 to 35 percent.

Mandatory Insurance Policy: INAIL

Employees are covered for risks deriving from the work activity, including death and permanent or temporary disability, by a mandatory insurance policy managed by the National Insurance Institute for Accidents at Work (Istituto Nazionale Assicurazione Infortuni sul Lavoro, INAIL) and fully paid by the employer. The amount of the relevant premium varies according to the type of activity carried out by the employer.

SECTION II

My client is acquiring an existing business in Italy. How do I assess the existing workforce and consider changes?

Workforce Assessment and Purchaser's Obligations

Assessing the Workforce: Transfer of Shares versus Transfer of Assets

Where the acquisition of an Italian business is effectuated by a transfer of shares, the employment relationships in force will not be affected, and they will transfer unchanged to the new employer (see also Share Transfer under Section III below). The same principle applies when a transfer of assets occurs, in that the entire workforce will be transferred to the purchaser by operation of law (see Transfer of Business (or Part Thereof) under Section III below).

Where only a portion of the assets are transferred, however, the seller and the purchaser will retain a certain freedom in determining exactly which activities are to be transferred. Thus, between them, they are able to manage which employees will continue with the transferee and which will remain with the transferor.

In any case, both the transferor and the transferee will have to comply with a number of notification and consultation obligations (see Transfer of Business (or Part Thereof) under Section III below).

Obligations to the Employees in Case of a Transfer of Assets

The purchaser shall be jointly liable with the seller for the employees' rights and credits at the date of transfer, irrespective of whether or not they have been recorded on the company's books.

Moreover, the purchaser will be bound to the terms and conditions set forth by collective agreements entered into by the seller applied until their expiration, unless they are replaced by collective agreements entered into by the purchaser at the same level (see also Transfer of Business (or Part Thereof) under Section III below).

Changing Terms and Conditions of Employment

In Italy the employers' power to unilaterally modify the employment terms and conditions originally agreed upon with their employees is significantly limited by Article 2103 of the Civil Code.

According to this rule, "employees must be assigned the duties for which they have been hired or those duties corresponding to the higher category that they may have subsequently attained or duties equivalent to the duties last performed, without any reduction in their remuneration. . . . Any agreement in breach of the above shall be null and void."

The above general principle aims first of all at avoiding the so-called "disqualification" of employees. Disqualification can occur either when an employee is assigned duties that correspond to a lower professional level (as described in the national collective labor agreement) or when the new duties may be considered lower in relation to the employee's know-how, professional background, and career prospects. Therefore, a correct assessment of the new duties to be assigned to an employee implies a detailed analysis of the entire job situation, with reference to the facts at hand.

The above provisions aim at protecting the level of remuneration earned by the employee. They forbid the employer from unilaterally reducing the employees' aggregate remuneration.

In addition to such general protection afforded by the law to all employees, special provisions are contained in the collective labor agreements applicable to *dirigenti*. According to these provisions, if the *dirigente*'s activity within the firm is changed in such a way as to affect his or her position and role, the *dirigente* will be entitled to resign and receive severance pay equal to the pay in lieu of notice, amounting to a certain number of monthly salaries.

Given the wide scope of the above rules, the ability to vary, either unilaterally or by mutual consent, the tasks and role of personnel is somewhat limited. There are, however, some instruments that may be deployed in order to reach this goal.

First, it is permissible for the employer and employee to agree on the termination of the existing employment and the commencement of a new relationship governed by different terms and conditions. This is a pattern usually followed when employment under new conditions is the only alternative to the employee's dismissal or to the transfer to a distant business unit; in such cases, employees are often ready to give their consent to the above solution. The agreement must be drafted in such a way as to contain all the appropriate waivers.

Second, in the context of a procedure of collective dismissal (see CIG (Cassa Integrazione Guadagni) Programs below), the law allows the employer and the trade unions to enter into a collective agreement providing for the possibility to derogate from Article 2103 if this represents the only alternative to dismissals.

Changing the Place of Work: Transfer and Reassignment

Pursuant to Article 2103 of the Italian Civil Code, the employer is allowed to unilaterally transfer the employee to another workplace only if there are technical, organizational, or productive reasons for doing so. These reasons must apply not only with reference to the original workplace, but also with reference to the new one. For example, in the event of a transfer determined by the elimination of a certain duty in the original job, the employer also has to prove that the same function has become necessary in the new destination.

Although the law does not provide for any economic entitlement to the transferred employee, most collective agreements provide for transfer allowances and/or for reimbursement of travel and moving expenses.

In the event of transfer involving a group of employees (so-called "collective transfer"), collective agreements generally require the employer to inform trade unions of the reasons for the expected measure.

Reducing the Workforce: Individual Dismissals

Grounds for Lawful Dismissal

Dismissal of employees is subject to stringent restrictions. Employers may not dismiss employees at will, and dismissals merely for cost savings are prohibited. Employees may be lawfully dismissed only when there is a "just cause" or "justified grounds."

Notice of the dismissal must be in writing and must indicate the reasons on which it is based. Moreover, whenever a dismissal is due to the employee's conduct, the employer must follow a specific disciplinary procedure set forth by law in order to give the employee the opportunity to accurately defend his or her position.

Rights of Employees

Upon termination of employment, employees are entitled to (1) payment of the TFR (see Terms and Conditions of Employment in Section I above); (2) some minor termination payments (pay in lieu of unused holidays and mandatory time off, accrued 13th monthly salary (an extra month's pay), and so on); and (3) a notice period (the duration of which varies according to the employee's seniority and professional level and is established in the applicable national collective labor agreement). If the employer exempts the employees from working during the notice period, the employees must receive a corresponding payment in lieu of notice, which is equal to the normal salary (less Social Security deductions) that would have been paid during the notice period.

The TFR and termination payments are always due in any case of dismissal, while the notice period payment is not due in the event of dismissal (1) for "just cause," (2) during the trial period (see Trial Period under Section I above), and (3) upon expiration of a fixed-term contract (see Fixed-Term Contracts under Section I above).

An employer that is staffed with more than 15 employees per production unit or more than 60 employees in total may be required to reinstate an unfairly dismissed employee in his or her previous position and pay the employee damages amounting to the salary accrued between the date of dismissal and the date of reinstatement (with a minimum of five monthly salaries). Without prejudice to the right to the damages, the employee may elect to waive the reinstatement and receive an additional 15 monthly salary payments, regardless of seniority.

Employers staffed with fewer than 15 employees are exempt from the obligation to reinstate unfairly dismissed employees (except in cases of discriminatory dismissal) but may be ordered to pay damages in an amount ranging from two and a half to six monthly salary payments. This maximum amount can be increased to up to 10 or 14 monthly salary payments for employees with seniority longer than 10 and 20 years, respectively.

Reducing the Workforce: Collective Dismissals

Whenever an employer staffed with more than 15 employees intends to dismiss, for reorganization or termination of business, at least five employees in the same province within a period of 120 days, the legal provisions regulating collective dismissals apply.

The provisions do not extend to *dirigenti*. However, pursuant to a national bargaining agreement,[7] *dirigenti* of companies in the industrial sector who are dismissed within the context of a collective dismissal procedure due to the employer's restructuring, reorganization, conversion, or economic crisis acknowledged by a Ministry of Labor decree are entitled to receive the statutory termination payments, an indemnity in lieu of notice, and an additional indemnity (equal to the economic rights (salary, etc.) that the executive would have been entitiled to during the notice period, had he or she actually performed his or her functions), which can be further increased on the basis of the *dirigente*'s age.

Procedure to Be Followed

Before implementing a collective dismissal, employers are asked to complete the following procedure, within the maximum duration of 75 days (37.5 days if the dismissal involves fewer than ten employees).

First, the employer must give a written notice of its intention to commence a collective dismissal to the Works Council and to the appropriate trade unions, with copy to the provincial labor office, indicating, among other details, the reasons for the dismissal, the number and qualifications of the normal staff and of those to be made redundant, and the date on which the proposed dismissal will be effective.

The works council and/or the trade unions may request a consultation phase. This phase will start no later than seven days following the written notice and shall last no longer than 45 days. If the consultation reveals that it is not possible to avoid the dismissal, the parties shall examine the possible adoption of social measures aimed at retraining and finding new employment for the dismissed workers.

If no agreement is reached with the trade unions within 45 days, the parties will attempt to reach an agreement through mediation at the provincial labor office. The duration of this "administrative" phase shall not exceed 30 days.

Once an agreement has been reached or the administrative phase has been completed, a written notice of dismissal is delivered to the individual employees concerned. Name, age, place of residence, and employment position of the dismissed employees, as well as the criteria followed for their selection, are communicated to the regional employment office, to the regional agency for employment, and to the unions.

Selection Criteria

The criteria to be used for selecting the employees to be dismissed should preferably be agreed upon with the trade unions, taking into account the employer's technical and production-related needs.

Should no agreement be reached with the trade unions, in selecting the employees to be dismissed reference must be made to the following statutory criteria: (1) technical and production-related needs of the employer, (2) employees' family conditions, and (3) employees' seniority.

Employer's Costs

Dismissed employees are entitled to be listed in the so-called "mobility lists." Such lists facilitate the employees' re-employment, because other employers choosing employees from such lists will benefit from certain advantages in terms of Social Security charges.

Moreover, for a certain period of time (the length of which depends on the employees' age and location), employees included in such lists shall receive a "mobility treatment" from INPS.

Employers contribute towards the cost of such treatment through (1) regular monthly payments levied on all companies that can benefit from CIGS procedures (explained next) and (2) a specific contribution applicable to employers implementing collective dismissal procedures.

CIG (Cassa Integrazione Guadagni) Programs

The CIG (*Cassa Integrazione Guadagni*) is a special public fund aimed at guaranteeing a minimum income to employees who have been suspended from work as a consequence of their employer's decision to interrupt or reduce the activity. In practice, the existence of the CIG fund allows the employer not to have to terminate the employment agreements in force, while awaiting the future resumption of the working activity.

Within the framework of the CIG, the law differentiates between CIGO (*Cassa Integrazione Guadagni Ordinaria*) and CIGS (*Cassa Integrazione Guadagni Straordinaria*) programs.

CIGO programs are used when the resumption of the working activity is certain, and particularly in the case of (1) relatively short reductions or suspensions of the working activity or (2) negative market conditions that are only temporary.

CIGS programs are used when working activity is suspended because of particularly complex and long-lasting circumstances having a considerable social impact. As CIGS programs are aimed at protecting not only the employer and employees' interests but also the more general interests of the development and recovery of the national economy, the CIGS fund is financed both by employers and the government.

CIGS programs can be used by employers[8] facing any of the following circumstances: (1) restructuring, reorganization, or conversion needs, (2) business crisis, or (3) bankruptcy or other insolvency procedures. Special rules apply, which should be considered carefully.

Works Council or Trade Union Consultation

In Italy, the presence of works councils or trade unions in the workplace is not mandatory. Even where a company works council has been established within the firm, no general right of notification and consultation is provided for by the law beyond that described above.

However, most collective agreements impose quite broad obligations on the employer to consult with the company works council in cases of decisions that have a general effect on employees—including reorganizations, changes in work patterns, and collective transfers.

Should the company also have established a European Works Council, additional notification and consultation requirements may apply.

SECTION III

My client wishes to sell its existing facility. What restrictions do we need to consider?

Whenever a transfer of ownership of a company takes place, the employment agreements existing at the time of the transfer survive and continue with the purchaser. This means that the relevant terms and conditions cannot be modified as a consequence of the transaction, and that the transaction cannot in itself constitute grounds for dismissing employees. Such a general rule is valid both in the case of a transfer of shares and in a transfer of assets.

Share Transfer

In the case of a share transfer, the above effect ensues from the fact that the identity of the employer, and therefore one of the parties to the employment agreements, remains unchanged. The seller and the purchaser are not subject by law to any particular pre-closing notification or consultation requirement; there may exist, however, a specific obligation in the applicable collective agreement or the internal practice of the company.

In any event, it would be advisable to give advance notice of the share transfer to the applicable trade unions.

Transfer of Business (or Part Thereof)

In the case of a transfer of assets, the employees pertaining to the business are transferred to the purchaser by operation of law, irrespective of the seller's and the purchaser's intentions, pursuant to Article 2112 of the Italian Civil Code (which implemented the EC Acquired Rights Directive[9]).

According to Article 2112, as recently amended, an asset transfer includes any transaction that, following a contractual transfer or merger, causes a change in the ownership of an economic business activity organized for the purpose of producing goods or services, for profit or not, that existed prior to the transfer and maintains its identity after the transfer, irrespective of the agreement or the resolution pursuant to which the transfer took place.

Employees' Rights

Should the sale operation fall within the above definition of transfer of a business or a portion thereof, then the relevant employment relationships pass over to the transferee by operation of law, without need for the employees' consent. Employees cannot object to such transfer of their employment. Employees whose working conditions have been substantially changed as an effect of the transfer may, however, resign without giving notice or receiving severance pay. Moreover, the seller and the purchaser are jointly liable for the employees' rights and credits existing at the date of the transfer.

The employees may, however, discharge the seller from such joint liability, according to a specific and official waiver procedure. However, the purchaser remains jointly liable for all credits accrued by the employees prior to the transfer, irrespective of whether the purchaser was aware of such credits or whether they were indicated in the seller's books.

The law also requires the purchaser to fulfill the economic and legal conditions set forth in the collective agreements (entered into at both a national and company level) applied by the seller until their expiration, unless they are replaced by other collective agreements applied by the purchaser, but only when they have been entered into at the same level (i.e., national, local, or company).

Article 2112 provides that an employee whose position has suffered a material change (not necessarily a detriment) due to the transfer shall be allowed to resign with cause within three months from date of transfer, with severance pay equal to the payment in lieu of the notice period that he or she would have received in the case of dismissal.

Notification and Consultation Obligations

In the case of a transfer of business, the seller and the purchaser are also required to fulfill certain notification/consultation obligations vis-à-vis the trade unions.

Whenever an asset transfer involves more than 15 employees, the seller and the purchaser must give advance notice in writing to their internal union representatives (works councils), as well as to their respective external unions, which must be received on the date that the parties reach a binding agreement or 25 days prior to the date on which the contractual instrument providing for the transfer is executed, whichever is earlier.[10] Specific rules apply to the content and procedure of such notice. Failure to comply with the consultation requirement may be regarded as "anti-union conduct" for the purposes of Article 28 of Law No. 300/70.

SECTION IV

My client wishes to replace its senior manager(s). What restrictions do we need to consider?

The dismissal of *dirigenti* is not regulated as is termination of lower-level employees. *Dirigenti* may be dismissed at will provided that a notice period is granted (a notice period is not necessary in case of termination for just cause).

However, the national collective labor agreements applicable to *dirigenti* in the main business sectors have introduced a principle whereby *dirigenti* are entitled to compensation for damages in the event their dismissal is not duly justified by their conduct or the circumstances of the business.

Rights upon Termination

Upon dismissal, *dirigenti* are entitled to certain statutory termination payments and rights. The following are always applicable where the employment relationship is terminated (except when dismissal is for just cause):

- **TFR** (severance payment): The amount of the TFR varies depending on salary and length of service, and is progressively accrued in the employer's financial statements during the term of employment. The TFR is equal to approximately one month's salary per year of service (see also Terms and Conditions of Employment under Section I above).
- **Other minor termination payments:** In addition, other minor payments are payable upon termination. These consist of portions of the 13th and

14th monthly salaries accrued at the time of termination, and payment for accrued holidays.

- **Notice period or equivalent indemnity:** The length of the notice period depends on the *dirigente*'s seniority, and generally ranges from a minimum of six to a maximum of 12 months.

The notice period starts running from the first day of the month following the notice of dismissal. During this period, if the *dirigente* becomes ill, the notice period will be suspended. Nor may the *dirigente* take holidays during this period.

A *dirigente* who is totally or partially exempt from working during the notice period must receive a corresponding payment in lieu of notice, which is subject to Social Security deductions.

When calculating the payment in lieu of notice, the *dirigente*'s total gross salary (including the incidence of fringe benefits and bonuses if paid on a regular basis) must be considered.

Finally, according to some collective agreements, in the case of dismissal, the *dirigente* is entitled to request that the employer provide external outplacement service. The relevant costs shall be paid directly by the employer to the outplacement agency but are deducted from the *dirigente*'s termination payments.

Remedies against Dismissal

A dismissed *dirigente* who believes the dismissal is not justified may either (1) commence a labor dispute before the labor court, or (2) commence the arbitration procedure provided for in national collective agreements.

If the court or the arbitration panel agrees that dismissal is unjustified, the *dirigente* will be awarded compensation for damages suffered as a result of the unjustified dismissal. This generally ranges from a minimum of monthly salary payments equal to the *dirigente*'s notice period to a maximum of 22 salary payments. Generally, this additional indemnity, on which no Social Security deductions are taken, is increased even more if the *dirigente* is between 53 and 64 years old and the length of service exceeds 10 years, to a maximum of about 30 monthly salary payments.

Companies are required to reinstate *dirigenti* only if they have been dismissed for discriminatory reasons.

Possible Amicable Settlement

In Italy, as the above discussion may illustrate, *dirigenti* are rarely dismissed outright, owing to the considerable liabilities that can result. Rather, it is customary to try to reach an amicable settlement providing for the termination of the employment relationship upon mutual consent, against payment of a certain sum of money to the *dirigente,* who in turn waives the right to bring any kind of action or claim in the future against the employer in connection with the employment or termination.

This cost-effective solution permits avoidance of the risks deriving from a dismissal and is used very frequently.

The amount paid as an incentive for the termination is not subject to Social Security deductions, and indeed benefits from a slightly lower tax rate, which is further reduced if the *dirigente* is a male over age 55 or a female over age 50.

SECTION V

What prohibitions exist against discrimination on a basis of age, race, gender, disability, pregnancy, and other factors? What are the rights of employees, applicants, or former employees who believe that they have been discriminated against?

Sexual Discrimination

Although prohibition of discrimination is a principle of the Italian constitution, no legal provisions ensuring the actual implementation of the principle existed for many years. Not until 1977 was legislation enacted to guarantee the equality of treatment between women and men during the employment relationship.[11] This legislation prohibits any discrimination between women and men in all aspects of the employment relationship (recruitment, promotion, vocational training, and so on) and provides that working women are entitled to the same wages as their male counterparts performing comparable jobs.

Nevertheless, this regulation has been inadequate for the purposes of removing the structural causes of discrimination. For this reason, the Italian legislature enacted a new law in 1991.[12] The law introduces affirmative actions, i.e., positive measures designed to remove obstacles to equal opportunities for women and men in the workplace.

The 1991 law provides a definition of direct and indirect discrimination. Direct discrimination occurs when a person is treated less favorably than others because of gender. Indirect discrimination occurs when a condition or a requirement that is formally applied to all employees has an adverse impact on certain employees and is not essential for the development of the working activities.

A definition of sexual harassment is provided for in EU Directive No. 73 of 2002, which also contains the provisions regulating this subject matter. However, Italian law lacks a specific legal definition of sexual harassment, and therefore reference is made to the European source.

Pursuant to the directive, "sexual harassment means unwanted conduct of a sexual nature or other conduct based on sex affecting the dignity of men and women at work. This can include unwelcome physical, verbal or nonverbal conduct." Such conduct becomes unwanted, insensitive, or offensive when it "creates an intimidating, hostile or humiliating working environment for the recipient."

Following such definition, Italian courts have reproved sexual harassment on several occasions.

In certain cases, courts have applied legal rules regulating matters of discrimination and equal opportunities in order to punish the employer's conduct. For example, through application of the obligation to preserve the physical and moral integrity of employees as provided for by Article 2087 of the Italian Civil Code, an employer who sexually harassed certain employees was found liable in contract. On another occasion, a court declared the dismissal of an employee who attempted to harass a female colleague as being based on just grounds.

Finally, the resignations of female employees who were the victims of sexual harassment were declared to be based on a just cause and the employer was ordered to pay them compensation for the "biological" damage they had suffered as a consequence of harassing behavior.

Other Grounds of Discrimination

The so-called Workers' Statute[13] also makes discrimination unlawful. In particular, Article 15 makes it illegal for an employer to discriminate against employees for joining (or not joining) a trade union or for participating in a strike. In particular, the employer may not refuse to hire, offer less favorable terms to, or dismiss an employee on account of his or her trade union activity.

Discrimination against the employee because of color, race, language, religion, or political beliefs is also illegal. Further, Article 16 provides that more-favorable economic treatments are forbidden where they are offered only to a certain group of workers on discriminatory grounds. Any act or agreement violating these provisions is deemed null and void.

A court may order reinstatement of any employee dismissed on discriminatory grounds. Furthermore, the labor courts may award compensation for damages to an employee who has been subject to discrimination. As Italian law does not provide for punitive damages, the amount of such compensation is quite limited (generally not exceeding €100,000).

With respect to discrimination on the grounds of racial/ethnic origin, race, etc., the Italian law has recently implemented[14] European Directive No. 43 of 2000 (concerning equality of treatment between persons irrespective of racial or ethnic origin) and European Directive No. 78 of 2000 (concerning equality of treatment irrespective of religion, personal opinions, disability, age, and sexual orientation).

As defined by these directives, direct discrimination occurs when one person is treated less favorably than another on grounds of racial/ethnic origin (race), religion, personal opinions, disability, age, or sexual orientation. Indirect discrimination occurs when an apparently neutral practice, rule, or condition is imposed on all employees, but produces a particular disadvantage to persons of one particular racial/ethnic origin, religion, etc. Thus indirect discrimination occurs not only when a particular disadvantage has an adverse impact on certain categories of employees, but also when a disadvantage simply occurs, as provided for by the above-mentioned law of 1991.

The prohibition against sexual harassment also applies to all aspects of employment relationships: recruitment, promotion, vocational training, conditions of dismissal, working conditions, etc.

SECTION VI

On the Horizon: What key labor and employment law developments should an employer doing business in Italy anticipate occurring in the coming years?

At the end of 2003, a major reform of labor legislation was implemented in Italy, the most significant aspects of which (introduction of new types of flexible contracts, reform of the rules on transfer of business) have been mentioned above.

The process leading up to the enactment of this reform involved exhausting negotiations with social parties and within the government. In order to reach a compromise, it became necessary to eliminate from the final draft the most important part of the reform: the amendment to the rules governing dismissals. This proposed amendment would have limited the right of automatic reinstatement, which is at the moment mandatory in every case of unjustified dismissal occurring in companies with more than 15 employees.

The proposed reform concerning dismissals has been transferred into a separate government bill, but it seems unlikely that the necessary parliamentary and social consensus will be achieved any time soon.

On the other hand, pension laws are undergoing important reforms. A pension law was enacted in 2004[15] providing for an increase of the minimum retirement age, in order to reduce the INPS expenses and therefore its deficit in the balance sheet. This law also provides for a series of measures aimed at enhancing the stability of private pension schemes. However, such measures will not have an immediate impact on the burden of Social Security charges, which will remain at the present level in order to finance the pension expense.

NOTES

1. Legislative Decree No. 152 of May 26, 1997 (which implements European Directive No. 91/533/EC).
2. Law No. 196 of June 24, 1997.
3. Legislative Decree No. 66 of February 3, 2003.
4. Legislative Decree No. 66 of February 3, 2003.
5. Such duty to notify the contracts is additional to the obligation to communicate the hiring mentioned under Form and Notice Obligations in Section I above.
6. *See* Legislative Decree No. 276 of September 10, 2003.
7. National Collective Agreement of 27 April, 1995.
8. Provided that they are staffed with more than 15 employees. The CIGS programs apply to all workers who were employed for at least 90 days, with the exception of *dirigenti* and apprentices.
9. European Directive No. 187 of 1977, now in the consolidated text introduced by European Directive No. 23 of 2001.
10. *See* Section 47 of Law No. 428 of December 29, 1990 (which also implemented the EC Acquired Rights Directive in Italy).
11. Law No. 903 of December 9, 1977.
12. Law No. 125 of April 10, 1991.
13. Law No. 300 of May 20, 1970.
14. Legislative Decree No. 215 of July 9, 2003, and Legislative Decree No. 216 of July 9, 2003.
15. Law No. 243 of August 23, 2004.

CHAPTER 8

Labor and Employment Law in Japan

Hideki Thurgood Kano
James M. Minamoto

Section I

My client wishes to establish a manufacturing facility in Japan and will need to hire a workforce. What are the key legal issues involved?

Legal Framework Governing Employment in Japan

The primary law governing employment conditions in Japan is the Labor Standards Law (*Roudou-Kijun-Hou*).

The Labor Standards Law (LSL) sets forth minimum standards for working conditions. For example, any provision in a company's Rules of Employment (*Syuugyou-Kisoku*), wage regulations (part of the Rules of Employment), collective bargaining agreements (*Roudou-Kyouyaku*), or individual employment contracts providing less protection to an employee than that offered under the LSL is null and void.

No "At Will" Employment in Japan

Generally, there is no "at will" employment in Japan by which an employer can terminate regular employees without cause. A unilateral termination by an employer is deemed to be an abuse of right and therefore null and void, unless such termination is based upon a strong and justifiable cause (see Statutory Restrictions on Dismissal without Cause under Section IV for further discussion).

Employees are categorized as "regular" or "contract" employees. A regular employee is one retained under an offer of employment for an unspecified or indefinite period.

Under a recent amendment to the LSL, the maximum employment period for contract employees is three years, with limited exceptions such as contracts tied to a specific project or involving certain types of professionals. If an employment contract provides for an employment period of three years but the employee continues to work without both parties' explicit extension or renewal of the contract after the three-year period expires, the contract is deemed to be extended for an indefinite period.

Further, Japanese courts often give contract employees whose contracts are explicitly and regularly renewed protection similar to that of regular employees with respect to the discontinuance of the extension/renewal of the definite-term employment contract. In other words, it becomes very difficult for an employer not to extend/renew the definite-term employment contract of those employees to whom the employer has, by way of statements or documents to them or treatment of other employees, given a reasonable expectation of continued employment until the mandatory retirement age.

Employment Contracts: Who Receives Them and What They Must Include

Employers generally must enter into written employment contracts with all persons performing work at the company or its workplace, regardless of the type of work they engage in.

Employment contracts must, by law, state the nature of the position, the period of employment (starting date and retirement date), the place of employment, and the working hours. Employment contracts in Japan are generally short and simple, as details of employment terms and conditions are usually set forth in the company's Rules of Employment and wage regulations.

Rules of Employment and wage regulations are legally required for any employer that continuously employs ten or more workers. The employer may refer to the Rules of Employment and wage regulations with regard to the above matters, as long as they are delivered to the employee when the employment contract is entered into.

Employment contracts do not have to be written in Japanese. Provided that the employee can read and understand English fluently, the agreement can be prepared in English without a Japanese translation.

Hiring Managerial Employees

Members of the board of directors are not generally considered "employees" and are not entitled to many of the protections that the LSL provides to employees. Directors are, therefore, excluded from the written employment contract requirement. However, directors of Japanese companies can hold dual positions as directors and employees. In such cases, an employment contract is required.

It is often advisable for employment contracts of foreign nationals transferred to Japan as executives to be governed by the law of the home country, because if it becomes necessary to dismiss an employee, it is often easier to recall the employee to the home jurisdiction and then terminate employment under the home country's law. If the only nexus with Japan is that the employee came because of his job, and if litigating the employment contract in the home jurisdiction would not impose any undue hardship on the complainant employee, there is a good chance that Japanese courts will uphold the application of the foreign jurisdiction's law. However, if the employee continues to stay in Japan after the dispute and a claim is filed at any court in Japan, the Japanese court may apply the Japanese labor laws to protect the status of the employee on the grounds that the laws protecting the employee constitute a matter of Japanese public order and cannot be waived by private agreement.

Wages and Benefits

Wages

Employees are generally paid a salary in Japan on a monthly basis, usually on a designated date between the 21st and 28th day of the month, by wire transfer to the employee's designated account, and not by check or cash. However, under the LSL the employer must have the employee's consent to this wire-transfer arrangement.

Bonuses

There is no legal requirement to give bonuses in addition to the monthly wages. However, Japanese companies commonly give a winter and summer bonus, which is typically a form of deferred salary and usually equivalent to two or three months' salary. The typical annual wage is thus the monthly salary multiplied by 16 or 18 months.

Once a bonus system is established in the Rules of Employment (including wage regulations) or through established practice, employees have the right to the bonus as part of their wages unless the Rules of Employment establish that the bonus is discretionary and subject to the performance of the company and the employee and that the payment amount has actually been discretionarily decided, as opposed to a consistent amount being regularly distributed.

Some companies have discretionary bonus systems, or performance-based bonus systems. Transforming a straight deferred salary bonus to a discretionary or performance-based bonus is more difficult than beginning with this system.

Vacation/Paid Leave

The LSL stipulates minimum amounts of paid annual leave, starting at 10 days and gradually increasing to 20 days based on years of service. For the period:

- 6–18 months after the starting date: 10 days
- 18–30 months after the starting date: 11 days
- 30–42 months after the starting date: 12 days
- 42–54 months after the starting date: 14 days
- 54–66 months after the starting date: 16 days
- 66–78 months after the starting date: 18 days
- More than 78 months after the starting date: 20 days

Overtime

The LSL specifies the following minimum additional compensation for overtime:

- 125 percent of hourly wages for overtime work on a normal work day;
- 135 percent for work on a holiday;
- 150 percent for late-night work (between 10 PM and 5 AM) on a normal work day; and
- 160 percent for late-night work on a holiday.

Managerial employees are entitled only to late-night work compensation, at a rate of 125 percent for work done between 10 PM and 5 AM (both regular working days and holidays).

Mandatory Social Security Programs

Employees generally receive four basic types of insurance: health insurance, welfare pension insurance, workers' compensation, and unemployment insurance. Health insurance and welfare pension insurance are "social insurance," to which directors are also entitled. Premiums are borne 50 percent by the company and 50 percent by the employee. This generally amounts to more than 20 percent of an employee's salary. Workers' compensation and unemployment insurance are "labor insurance," to which directors are not entitled. The company is responsible for 100 percent of workers' compensation premiums and more than 50 percent of unemployment insurance premiums. Foreign nationals who are directly paid by the company within the territory of Japan are required to be covered by all four types of insurance.

Retirement Benefit Programs

Although not required by law, many companies have retirement benefit plans, commonly in the form of lump-sum retirement payments with payment amounts varying based upon years of service and whether the employee leaves the company on a voluntary or involuntary basis.

It is advised that a deferred-bonus plan *not* be adopted. Quite a few companies have introduced some kind of deferred-bonus plan under which a portion of the incentive bonus is set aside and later paid as a part of the retirement allowance. That is, these companies defer some portion of the bonus amount payable to the employees until the employees leave the company. The purpose of this deferred-bonus plan is to reduce the tax burden on the employees and maximize the after-tax receipt by taking advantage of the beneficial tax treatment applicable to retirement allowances. Recently, the National Tax Authority (*Kokuzeityou*) started to question the legality of this scheme and has investigated several companies. As a result, the National Tax Authority has required some employees to pay additional withholding tax and penalties.

Leave

Maternity leave consists of voluntary leave from six weeks (or 14 weeks in case of multiple pregnancy) before the scheduled date of birth and mandatory leave for eight weeks (or six weeks where the employee desires to work and a doctor confirms it is safe to do so) after giving birth. In addition, the employer must grant, when requested, unpaid child-care leave until the child is one year old.

An employer is required to grant family-care leave for a minimum period of three months when an employee having a disabled family member applies for such leave.

Stock Option Plans

Before offering stock options to employees, employers should check whether such plans trigger the Securities and Exchange Law's reporting and registration requirements in Japan.

Tax

Income tax, which is part of the national tax, is imposed upon the salary and bonuses of employees. Companies are obligated to make withholdings from the salary or bonuses of each employee and pay it to the national government. The salary and bonuses of employees are also subject to inhabitant tax, which is part of the municipal government tax.

Labor Unions

The Labor Union Law bars employers from restricting employees from joining a union. Two or more employees can form a union and a single employee can join an existing union at any time and for any reason, including when they are dismissed due to redundancy, when their overtime compensation is not sufficiently paid, when they are unreasonably internally transferred, and when they feel they are not promoted because of discrimination. If a labor union is established within the workplace or an employee becomes a member of an outside labor union, the labor union will request that the company hold collective bargaining sessions (*Dantai-Kousyou*) in order to discuss the employee's complaint against the company. The Labor Union Law bars an employer from unreasonably refusing to hold collective bargaining sessions. In general, approximately ten collective bargaining sessions are held within a period of roughly three months for the purpose of reaching an amicable settlement concerning the matters involved.

SECTION II

My client is merging with an existing company in Japan. How do I assess the existing workforce and consider changes?

In Japan, "mergers" can refer generally to business transfers, stock acquisitions, and corporate splits, in addition to the case where one company is amalgamated into another surviving company.

Business Transfers/Stock Acquisitions

In general, employee contracts are not automatically transferred by law in the case of a business transfer; rather, they remain with the transferor. In a stock acquisition, the same principle applies; i.e., despite the stock acquisition, employee contracts will remain in place and will not be legally affected by the stock transfer.

Amalgamation Mergers and Corporate Splits

By contrast, where one company amalgamates with another, all obligations, including employee contracts, will, by operation of law, be transferred to the surviving company. Similarly, in the case of a corporate split or spinoff, employment agreements of those employees who are employees of, or whose duties are owed mainly to, the transferred business will also in principle be transferred.

Making Changes to Key Managerial Positions

Members of the board of directors can generally be changed at will by majority vote of the shareholders, but if a director is removed prior to the expiration of his or her statutory term the company may be required to pay the director's compensation through the end of the term.

The board of directors normally appoints top executive positions with a Japanese company, such as president, vice president, CEO, etc. Thus, top executive positions can also be changed at will by the board. But again, if the executive has an engagement or employment contract with the company, the company may be required to pay the executive's compensation through the end of the term.

Carrying Out a Workforce Reduction

Redundancy termination requires an employer to show that (1) there is a necessity to reduce the workforce; (2) there is a necessity to utilize unilateral termination as the method of workforce reduction (i.e., the company has exhausted other cost-reduction methods); (3) the selection of personnel to be terminated is fair and based upon a rational procedure; *and* (4) termination procedures are appropriate (including making full explanation to the employees or labor unions). If *all* elements are satisfied, an employer can terminate employees for redundancy on the basis of "just cause."

Courts have set high standards for each element. Generally, it is very difficult for a company to successfully establish the above-mentioned grounds for unilateral termination of employees for redundancy. Thus, as a practical matter, when redundancy terminations are desired, employers typically offer voluntary resignation packages to induce employees to resign.

The cost of such inducement varies with the employee's years of service, position, ability to find other work, and specific situation, but typically requires an offer of three months to as much as one year of salary.

An employee cannot be terminated for failing to accept a voluntary resignation package, even if the package is extremely generous.

Companies that are buying another company or business should require as a condition precedent to closing that the seller/transferor take responsibility for reducing the workforce to an appropriate level and also request that the seller/transferor make a payment of all of the retirement benefit amounts stipulated in its retirement benefit plans. Some employees may not wish to transfer to a new company and thus may leave of their own volition. Others may be offered a voluntary resignation package, at the seller/transferor's expense.

Reorganizing the Workforce

Japanese companies generally have wide discretion to change the position or title of nonexecutive managers and other staff, subject to the qualification that their employment contract does not contain a guarantee that they would hold a certain position or title for the entirety of their employment at the company.

Changing the Wage and Benefits Structure

It is generally not possible for an employer to unilaterally decrease the wages of any employee without just cause. The mere fact of a merger or similar business transaction does not constitute just cause.

The employer can change the Rules of Employment and other work conditions without consent from the employees if the change is *beneficial* to the employees.

The employer can change the Rules of Employment and other work conditions in a manner that may be detrimental to the employees only if the changes are deemed *"reasonable" in light of circumstances.* Note that changes are, according to the Supreme Court of Japan's precedent, deemed reasonable in light of factors such as

- The content of the unfavorable change;
- Any favorable treatment that is given in exchange for acceptance of the unfavorable change;
- The necessity for the company to implement the unfavorable change;
- Setting up of a grace period or a buffer system that alleviates a sudden drastic change;
- Discussions with a labor union or employees regarding the unfavorably changed content; and
- Whether other companies have implemented the same or a similar unfavorable change.

If the change is not deemed reasonable, a Japanese court could find such a change to be invalid and continue to apply past working conditions.

The LSL requires that if amended the revised version of the Rules of Employment must be submitted to the Employment Standards Inspection Office (*Roudou-Kijun-Kantokusyo*), together with the employee representative's written opinion about the revisions.

Even if a company generally wishes to retain the current Rules of Employment, it is advisable to review and update them before the employees are transferred to the company, in order to identify potential areas where change might be desirable or to conform to recent changes in the law. For example, amendments were recently made to the LSL, the Child-Care and Family-Care Leave Law, and the Equal Employment Opportunity Law (concerning sexual harassment); current Rules of Employment may not reflect such amendments.

Consulting with Labor Unions or Works Councils

An employer generally cannot change the terms of individual employment contracts with its employees or collective bargaining agreements with labor unions without consent, particularly if the changes are detrimental to the employees or labor union members.

Further, in the case of a corporate split, the splitting company must give prior notice to any union with which a collective bargaining agreement has been entered into, and allow for an objection period for employees who would or would not like for their employment agreement to be succeeded by the separated company. The splitting company should make genuine efforts to obtain the understanding and cooperation of its employees.

SECTION III

My client wishes to sell its existing facility. What restrictions do we need to consider?

Assessing Employment Contracts

If the facility sale is made through a corporate split or stock transfer, related employment contracts will generally transfer automatically to the purchaser.

If the facility sale is made through an asset sale, employment contracts will generally not transfer; i.e., the client will remain obligated under related employment contracts even though the affected employees will, as a practical matter, have no work to do after the facility is sold and will become redundant. Thus, the client should generally try to negotiate with the buyer with the goal of persuading the buyer to offer new employment to as many of the facility workers as possible.

Consulting with the Government

There is generally no need to consult with any Japanese governmental authorities concerning labor issues in connection with a facility sale. However, if a company is releasing 30 or more employees against their will, the company is under an obligation to notify the Public Job Stability Office (*Koukyou-Syokugyou-Anteisyo*) at least one month prior to the date of release.

Consulting with Labor Unions or Works Councils

As stated above, in case of a corporate split, labor union consultation is required.

Further, as a practical matter, the client should reserve sufficient time to explain the facility sale and the possible impact on employees. Without the cooperation and understanding of the labor union, employees may not agree to work at the facility under the new owners.

Negotiating with a Buyer: Special Labor Issues

If possible, in the case of an asset sale, the client should seek to transfer all pension reserves and obligations to the buyer and obtain a release from the employees and/or an indemnification from the buyer. The alternative is that the client will have to pay out pension distributions to all employees who resign and then commence work with the new owner, which can require a substantial cash outlay.

Some buyers naturally want to "cherry pick" only the best workers, leaving unproductive, undesirable workers with the seller. However, there is no guarantee that the best workers will agree to accept employment with the buyer, especially if the buyer seeks to phase in over time a stricter, more merit-based compensation system. To reduce the risk of getting stuck with unproductive workers, the seller may seek to persuade the buyer to accept as a closing condition that a certain percentage of workers will join the buyer, but without reference to the names of any particular workers since workers cannot be forced to work for the buyer in any case (even if their contracts are automatically transferred, they may simply resign and not show up for work).

SECTION IV

My client wishes to replace its senior manager(s). What restrictions do we need to consider?

Employment Contracts

The threshold question is whether the senior managers are members of the board of directors or not. Directors can be removed by majority vote of the shareholders, as explained in Making Changes to Key Managerial Positions under Section II above. Nondirector managers have the same rights as any other employee. See Carrying Out a Workforce Reduction and Reorganizing the Workforce under Section II above.

Discrimination Issues

Termination based on age alone is generally not permitted. However, a mandatory retirement age may be stipulated in the Rules of Employment. Amendments were made by the Japanese Diet to the Senior People Employment Stability Law in June 2004, and the statutorily permitted minimum mandatory retirement age, which is presently 60 years old, will be

- 62 years old, from April 1, 2006, to March 31, 2007;
- 63 years old, from April 1, 2007, to March 31, 2010;

- 64 years old, from April 1, 2010, to March 31, 2013; and
- 65 years old, from April 1, 2013.

Statutory Severance Pay Requirements

There is no statutory severance pay requirement under Japanese law, except the Unilateral Termination Notification Allowance amounting to the 30-day salary of the targeted employee. Employment can be unilaterally terminated only if just cause exists (see Carrying Out a Workforce Reduction under Section II above); otherwise, employment can be terminated only by mutual agreement (by, for example, entering into a voluntary resignation agreement).

Statutory Restrictions on Dismissal without Cause

As stated above in No "At Will" Employment in Japan under Section I, there is generally no "at will" employment in Japan. Notwithstanding express terms of an employment contract or the Rules of Employment to the contrary, unilateral termination of employment by an employer may be deemed an "abuse of right" and therefore null and void, unless such termination is for a strong and justifiable reason or cause, or "just cause," according to the LSL.

An employee who believes that his or her employment was improperly terminated can institute litigation seeking reinstatement with back pay, as well as a provisional injunction requiring the employer to pay salary during the pendency of the litigation. If the employee is successful in obtaining the provisional injunction, the employer will generally have to pay out the employee's salary for one to two years, but without receiving the benefit of services in exchange.

This is an extremely burdensome result for employers. Thus, even where an employer believes it has strong grounds to unilaterally terminate an employee, in order to avoid the legal risks attendant to an improper termination, employers will frequently seek to obtain the voluntary resignation of an undesired employee.

SECTION V

What prohibitions exist against discrimination on a basis of age, race, gender, disability, pregnancy, and other factors? What are the rights of employees, applicants, or former employees who believe that they have been discriminated against?

Gender, Nationality, Creed, Social Status, Pregnancy, Childbirth Leave, Etc.

An employee's termination is null and void if made on a discriminatory basis, e.g., reasons of nationality, creed, social status, or gender, or because the employee took child-care leave.

Also, it is prohibited to terminate the employment of women because of marriage, pregnancy, or during childbirth leave or for 30 days thereafter. Further, no company is permitted to treat female employees differently from male employees with respect to termination.

Termination based on age only does *not* satisfy the "just cause" requirement. However, if a mandatory retirement age is stipulated in the Rules of Employment, an employee can be required to leave a company for this reason only.

Physical or Mental Disability

If the disability was caused by work, the LSL restricts an employer from terminating employment.

If an employee has a physical or mental disability not caused by work, the employee can be dismissed if the disability prevents the employee from working, unless dismissal violates the employer's sick leave policy.

Union Membership

No company is allowed to terminate employees on the grounds that they are labor union members.

Rights

If an employee believes that his/her employment was improperly terminated, he/she can institute litigation seeking reinstatement with back pay, as well as a provisional injunction requiring the employer to pay salary during the pendency of the litigation so that the employee can maintain his/her standard of living. See Statutory Restrictions on Dismissal without Cause under Section IV above.

An employee has the right to form a labor union or join an existing labor union. See Labor Unions under Section I above.

SECTION VI

On the Horizon: What key labor and employment law developments should an employer doing business in Japan anticipate occurring in the coming years?

Pension Deficits of Japanese Companies

Before an amendment in June 2000 brought Japanese generally accepted accounting principles up to international GAAP standards, Japanese companies (including those listed on the Tokyo Stock Exchange) had wide discretion about how to reflect pension liabilities on their books, and it was hard to accurately determine a company's true liability. Post amendment, there is still inconsistency in reporting among companies not listed on the TSE as they are not required to follow the Japanese GAAP standards. Furthermore, even if a company lists its pension liability, it is not always the case that funds have actually been set aside. In fact, the underfunding of pension systems among Japanese companies has recently come to light as an important social issue in Japan, having an adverse effect on the financial stability of Japanese companies. Accordingly, there are hidden risks for companies wishing to acquire

Japanese companies, who might find themselves with obligations to the employees of the target company that do not come to light until quite late in the deal. Recently, in response to the problematic deficits, Japan's lower House of Parliament approved a bill aimed at overhauling the current pension scheme in Japan by gradually raising premiums and lowering minimum benefits paid to employees.

Additional Compensation

When Japan's economic bubble collapsed in the early 1990s, ailing companies tried to reduce the impact of decreased profits by lowering their overhead expenses. Employers first tended to reduce their workforces, but the effect of these cutbacks in manpower was an increase in the work volume for the remaining employees, which translated into longer working hours. Their health deteriorated, and death by overwork and suicide resulting from overwork increased. Nevertheless, employers continued not to pay overtime compensation to their employees, and employees found themselves in a position where they could not demand the compensation, because the company could claim that it might become bankrupt if it had to pay the claims. In response to this situation, the Ministry of Health, Labor, and Welfare (*Kousei-Roudou-Syou*) declared that the nonpayment of overtime compensation was unacceptable, and began a crackdown in 2002. Since then, many companies were investigated and ordered to make a payment of the unpaid compensation by the Employment Standards Inspection Office, which is under the umbrella of the Ministry of Health, Labor, and Welfare.

Control of Working Hours

There are many employees throughout Japan who suffer emotional illness or die due to overwork. If an employee becomes sick and files a motion (or if an employee dies and his or her family files a motion) seeking workers' compensation, inspectors of the Employment Standards Inspection Office will come to the workplace and investigate the company. This situation would defame the company's reputation and damage the morale of other employees of the company. To avoid this, it is recommended that a company control the working hours of each employee. This is an obligation recently imposed by the Ministry of Health, Labor, and Welfare upon companies. A company should know the working hours of each employee so it can stop a particular employee from working too much, to circumvent the risk of emotional damage or death due to overwork.

Individual Employment Disputes Hearing/Order

The Japanese Diet enacted a statute on April 28, 2004, that concerns special proceedings at courts with respect to employment law cases. The statute, the Labor Tribunal Dispute Resolution Law (*Roudou-Sinpan-Hou*), adopts simplified proceedings that aim at swift resolution of disputes between individual employees (not labor unions) and their companies. It will take effect on April 1, 2006. District courts have jurisdiction over the Labor Tribunal. A district court has one or more panels, each of which comprises one judge and two experts (one being chosen from among management people throughout Japan and the other chosen from among labor union members throughout Japan). The panel is expected to put an end to any individual employment disputes by way of discussion and rendering an official order after holding up to three closed hearing sessions (possibly occurring within a three-month period). As a rule, the official order is binding on both parties. We can reasonably project that there will be a remarkable increase in employment law cases in the coming two years.

CHAPTER 9

Labor and Employment Law in Mexico

Jorge G. De Presno

SECTION I

My client wishes to establish a manufacturing facility in Mexico and will need to hire a workforce. What are the key legal issues involved?

The Labor Relationship and the Individual Employment Agreement

However it arises, a labor relationship is understood to be the rendering of personal services subject to the authority of another person, with payment of a salary.

An individual labor agreement must contain the employment conditions, which are

- The name, nationality, sex, age, marital status, and domicile of the employee and the employer;
- Whether the labor relationship is for a specific task or period of time, or for an indefinite term;
- The service or services to be rendered, which are to be stated as precisely as possible;
- The place or places where the work is to be performed;
- The length of the workday;
- The form and amount of salary;
- The day and place for payment of salary;
- The statement that training for the work will be given in the manner provided in the plans and programs established or to be established within the company, as provided in the Federal Labor Law;
- Other work conditions such as days off, vacations, and other matters agreed upon by the employee and the employer.

Written employment agreements and employment relationships produce the same legal consequences. The absence of a written individual employment agreement does not deprive the employee of the rights arising from the employment relationship and the services rendered, because the absence of the formality is imputed to the employer.

Positions of Trust

Upper-level employees and officers are individuals who work for and are subject to the authority of other individuals or companies in general management and administration positions that bind the employer in its relationships with its employees. Thus we have officers, directors, and managers, who in addition to being employees hold positions of trust.

Employees holding positions of trust are the employees who engage in inspection, oversight, and investigation. They are not necessarily representatives of the employer, but in some cases they may represent the employer.

Salaries and Benefits

Salary

Salary may be freely fixed by the parties (employer and employee), or may be subject to minimums set by the government. In Mexican legislation there is no upper limit on salaries. Salary caps are mentioned only in the context of indemnification for professional risks and seniority payments.

There are various ways of fixing salary: by unit of time, by unit of work, by commission, or as a fixed price. In the first case, the employee is required to work during the agreed workday, which must appear in the respective agreement, and receives the agreed salary. In the second case the agreement is to pay an amount of money for each piece or unit made by the employee. The sum of the units made during the workday is the basis for calculating the salary. In salary by way of commission, a percentage of the sales made constitutes the salary that is to be paid. Finally, in the case of salary at a fixed price all the work is contracted for a specified amount. The only thing that must be taken into account is that, in the normal case of performance of the work, the provisions regarding minimum salary are not violated.

In addition to the fixed payment or base salary, a sum certain of money, salary includes services or goods that can be valued in money, such as periodic bonuses at Christmas, the end of the year, and the like; overtime payments; travel expenses and per diems; housing and fuel allowances; etc. Article 84 of the Federal Labor Law provides that "salary is integrated of payments made in cash on a daily basis, bonuses, compensation, housing, fees, commissions, benefits in kind and any other amount or benefit delivered to the employee for his work."

Salary is integrated, nonetheless, only for purposes of payment of indemnifications.

Regarding payment of salary, the following must be taken into account:

- Salary must be paid directly to the employee. In cases in which the employee cannot personally collect the salary, the payment will be made to the person appointed as attorney in fact by means of a power of attorney signed by two witnesses.
- Cash salary must be paid in currency of legal tender. It is not permitted in merchandise, vouchers, tokens, or any other representative item intended to replace money.

- Employee salaries cannot be subject to any setoff whatsoever.
- Salary must be paid at the place the employees render their services.
- Payment must be made on a workday, fixed by agreement between the employee and the employer, during or at the immediate end of work hours.

Benefits

The Federal Labor Law provides that every employee has a right to vacation days and bonuses.

Vacations

- Employees who have worked for more than a year enjoy annual paid vacations of no less than six working days. The number is increased by two working days for each following year of services, until reaching 12 days. After the fourth year, the vacation period is increased by two days for every five years of services.
- Employees who render services on an irregular basis and seasonal workers have a right to an annual vacation period in proportion to the number of days worked during the year.
- Employees must take at least six days of uninterrupted vacation.
- Vacation entitlements may not be replaced by remuneration.
- If the employment relationship ends before one year of services has been completed, the employee has a right to remuneration for vacation days in proportion to the period worked.
- Vacations must be granted to workers within the six months following completion of the year of services. Employers annually must deliver to their employees a statement of their seniority and, based thereon, the vacation period owed to them and the date they are to take it.

Vacation Bonus

Employees have the right to receive a vacation bonus of not less than 25 percent of their salary during the vacation period.

Year-End (Christmas) Bonus

Employees have a right to a year-end (Christmas) bonus consisting of 15 days of salary, to be paid before December 20. Those that have not completed a year of services, regardless of whether they are working on the date of payment of the year-end bonus, have the right to payment of the proportional part thereof.

Seniority Bonus

Permanent employees who have been employed for at least 15 years have a right to a seniority bonus, which consists of 12 days of salary for each year of service. In those cases in which the employee's salary exceeds two times the minimum salary in the economic area where he or she renders services, that amount is taken as the maximum for payment of the seniority bonus.

Unions

A union is an association of employees or employers formed for the study, improvement, and defense of their respective interests.

Classifications of Unions

Employee unions are classified as

- Guilds, being those formed by workers of the same profession, occupation, or specialty;
- Company unions, being those formed by employees who provide their services within the same company;
- Industrial unions, being those formed by employees who render services in two or more companies in the same branch of industry;
- National industrial unions, being those formed by employees who render their services in one or more companies of the same branch of industry, established in two or more states within the country; and
- Multi-occupation unions, being those formed by employees in various professions. These unions may be formed only when, in the municipality in question, the number of employees within a given profession is less than 20.

Employer unions are classified as

- Those formed by employers from one or more branches of activity; and
- National, being those formed by employers from one or more branches of activity in various states within the country.

Formation of a union must satisfy certain requirements, such as

- The members must be more than 14 years old.
- Employees holding positions of trust may not be members of unions of other employees. Under Article 123, Subsection XVI, paragraph A of the Federal Constitution, this prohibition does not prevent them from forming their own unions.
- The union must be comprised of at least 20 active employees or three employers.
- No one can be forced to be a member or not be a member of a union. Any provision establishing a fine or similar penalty in the event of leaving the union is void.
- Unions must be registered with the Ministry of Labor and Social Welfare in cases of federal jurisdiction and with the Conciliation and Arbitration Boards in cases of state jurisdiction.
- Unions represent their members in the defense of their individual rights, without prejudice to the right of the employees to act and participate directly, the participation of the union then ceasing on the request of the employee.
- Representation of the union is exercised by its secretary general or the person appointed by its direction committee, absent a special provision in

the bylaws. Members of the direction committee who are fired by the employer or leave their jobs for reasons imputable to the employer will continue in their union positions absent a contrary provision in the bylaws.

Collective Employment Agreements

A collective employment agreement is entered into between one or more employee unions and one or more employers or one or more employer unions, with the purpose of establishing the conditions pursuant to which work is to be performed in one or more companies or business units. For the employer it is mandatory to enter into a collective agreement when so required by the union representing the majority of its employees. It may be, however, that employees belonging to different unions work for a company, because their professions or specialties are different. In this case, the law sets the rules to be followed when entering into the collective employment agreement or agreements.

Regarding the term and form, the collective agreement may be entered into for an indefinite term, for a fixed term, or for a specific task. It also must be entered into in writing, or it will be null. Three copies must be signed, one to be retained by each of the parties and the third to be deposited for registration with the Conciliation and Arbitration Board having jurisdiction, whether federal or state. Regardless of the term of duration of the collective employment agreement (which can be no more than two years, per Article 399 of the Labor Law), it will be subject to revision, in whole or in part, 60 days prior to maturity.

The collective employment agreement must include the following content:

- Name and domicile of the contracting parties;
- Companies and business units covered;
- The term or a statement that it is for an indefinite term or specific task;
- The workdays;
- Days off and vacations;
- Salary amounts;
- Clauses regarding training of employees in the company or business unit in question;
- Provisions regarding initial training to be given to those who will begin working for the company or business unit;
- The bases for formation and operation of the committees that must be formed pursuant to law; and
- The other provisions agreed upon by the parties.

An agreement that lacks the wage scale determining salaries will not have the effect of a collective employment agreement. If there are no provisions regarding workday, days off, and vacations, the legal provisions will apply, and conditions less favorable to the employees than those contained in agreements in effect in the company or business unit may not be agreed upon.

Within the collective employment agreement a so-called exclusion clause generally is included. This is a provision by virtue of which the parties may agree that, within a company, only those employees who are members of the union that is a party to the collective agreement in effect within the company or business unit may render their services. This includes two possibilities:

1. Exclusion Clause upon Admission: The employer will hire only employees who are members of the contracting union.
2. Exclusion Clause upon Separation: The employer must terminate the individual employment relationship of an employee who quits or is expelled from the contracting union upon request from the union and without responsibility on its part. In order for a union to be able to apply this clause it must meet the statutory (bylaws) requirements set forth in Subsection VII of Article 371 of the Labor Law.

Union Leading Collective Agreement

The union representing the greatest professional interest within the company may demand that the labor authorities recognize it as the leading union in the collective agreement, not by way of strike but rather through special proceedings set forth in Article 782 of the Labor Law, which include a majority vote.

If within the same company there are several unions, the following rules will be observed:

- If there is more than one company or industrial union, the collective agreement will be entered into with the one having the greatest number of employees within the company.
- If there is more than one guild, the collective agreement will be entered into with the group of majority unions that represent the professions, provided that they reach agreement. If not, each union will enter into a collective agreement for its profession.
- If there are both guilds and company or industrial unions, the guilds may enter into collective agreements for their professions, provided that the number of their members is greater than that of the workers in the same profession that are members of the company or industrial union.

Termination of Collective Agreement

A collective agreement terminates

1. By mutual consent;
2. By completion of the task; or
3. In cases of collective termination of employment relationships referred to in Article 434 of the Law, which result in the closing of the companies or business units or the permanent reduction of their work, provided that they are caused by:
   a. Force majeure or acts of God not imputable to the employer, or the employer's physical or mental disability or death, which as a necessary, immediate, and direct consequence results in termination of work;
   b. Notorious and obvious lack of profitability in the business;
   c. Exhaustion of the material that is the subject matter of an extractive industry;
   d. Legally declared insolvency or bankruptcy if the permanent closing of the company is ordered.

In the case of dissolution of the workers union that leads the collective agreement or termination thereof, the employment conditions will continue in effect within the company or business unit.

Industry-Wide Labor Agreement

The industry-wide labor agreement is entered into between one or more employee unions and several employers, or one or more employer unions, for the purpose of establishing the conditions pursuant to which work is to be performed within a specific branch of the industry. Such an agreement is declared to be obligatory in one or more states in the country, in one or more economic areas that cover one or more of those states, or in the entire country.

An industry-wide labor agreement must contain

- The names and domiciles of the employees unions and employers attending the convention for its execution;
- The state or states, the area covered, or the statement that it applies throughout the country;
- Its term, which may not exceed two years;
- The employment conditions indicated in Article 391, Subsections IV, V, VI, and IX (workdays, days off and vacations, salaries, and commissions);
- The rules in accordance with which plans and programs will be prepared for training in the branch of the industry in question; and
- The other provisions agreed upon by the parties.

Clauses of exclusion upon admission and exclusion upon separation also may be established. They are applied by the union managing the industry-wide labor agreement within each company.

Strike

A strike is a temporary suspension of work carried out by a "coalition of workers," that is, a registered union.

The principal purposes of strikes include

- Achieving equilibrium between various factors of production and harmonizing the rights of workers with those of investors;
- Causing an employer or employers to enter into a collective labor agreement or industry-wide labor agreement, and requiring its revision at the end of its term;
- Requiring performance of the legal provisions regarding profit sharing; and
- Requiring revision of contractual salaries.

It is a necessary requirement that the majority of the workers in the company or business unit vote to strike. The votes of employees in positions of trust and general employees who have been hired after the date of presentation of the written strike notice are not counted. On the other hand, those dismissed from work after the date of presentation of the strike notice are considered to be employees of the company.

Once the strike has been voted by the workers, as the next step, under Article 922 of the labor law, a written list of demands must be prepared and addressed to the employer. It must state that if the demands are not accepted, the employees will go on strike within a term of not less than ten days in the case of companies providing public services, or not less than six days in other cases.

The list reaches the employer through the corresponding Conciliation and Arbitration Board, the president of which has the strict responsibility of delivering it to the employer within 48 hours of receipt. The custom in fact is to address a document to the labor authorities together with the original list of demands, so that the employer receives both a copy of the writing addressed to the board and the referenced list that gives notice of the intention to go on strike.

In the case of entering into or revising a collective agreement, it is necessary for the employees to attach a copy of the respective draft agreement, so that the employer may decide whether or not to accept it. The means by which the president of the Conciliation and Arbitration Board delivers it to the employer is through a clerk of that body. If the board is not present in the locality where the company or business unit is located, the document may be presented to the nearest labor authority or the highest-level political authority of the place where the company or business unit is located. These authorities give the notice and, within the following 48 hours, return the file to the Conciliation and Arbitration Board.

The term after which the strike may commence begins to run from the time of the notice. The effect of the notice is to make the employer, for the entire term of the notice, a depository of the company or business unit affected by the strike, with the rights and obligations inherent in that position.

It is necessary to highlight that the labor law provides: "Upon notice of the list of demands and intention to strike, the enforcement of all judgments must be suspended and there may be no embargo, assurance, proceedings, or eviction against the company or business unit, nor any seizure of the assets of the premises where it operates, except when prior to commencing the strike it involves: (I) Assuring employee rights, particularly indemnifications, salaries, pensions and other accrued benefits, up to the amount of two years of salary; (II) Credits derived from failure to pay contributions to the Mexican Social Security Institute; (III) Assuring the collection of contributions the employer is obligated to make to the National Workers Housing Fund; and (IV) Other tax credits. . . ."

If the day and hour indicated for the strike arrives and there is no agreement between the employees and employers, the strike must be carried out and the employees must abandon the workplace. The employees normally post guards to prevent entry to other employees who might break the strike, known as *esquiroles* ("scabs"). Nevertheless, it is necessary for the employer and some of its representatives and employees in positions of trust to be present at the work center, where the files and documents they need during the conflict are located. It also is essential for the treasurer or cashier and payment personnel to be present on the premises, to pay the salaries of emergency personnel.

In the case of a strike to obtain the execution or revision of an industry-wide labor agreement, the term required between the date of presentation of the strike notice to the Conciliation and Arbitration Board and the day and hour for suspension of work must be 90 days.

SECTION II

My client is acquiring an existing business in Mexico. How do I assess the existing workforce and consider changes?

A due diligence process must be performed whenever a merger or acquisition will take place in order for the purchaser to detect any issues related to labor and employment that may be relevant to the operation, as well as for the company to be acquired to disclose any relevant matters related thereto. Under a legal as well as a business perspective, the most important aspect to be considered when acquiring an existing company is that as a matter of law, the purchaser will become the substitute employer of the employees of the previous employer. This means that all terms and conditions of employment previously agreed upon between the employees and the acquired employer must be fully honored by the new employer, such as hiring date, salary and benefits, and work hours. During a period of six months following the sale and purchase agreement, and once written notice of the substitution is given to each and every employee and/or the union, a joint responsibility among the two employers (substitute and substituted) will be in effect. Once this term elapses, only the new employer will be responsible for any issue related to the workforce.

In order for there to be a substitution of employer, it is essential that ownership of the entity, taken as an economic and legal unit, whether called an enterprise, factory, company, shop, business, etc., be transferred to another person. That is, the assets, rights, and obligations inherent therein that are dedicated to the conduct of the business must leave the patrimony of one person and enter that of another.

This in principle should not affect existing employment agreements. Nevertheless, for a term of six months counted after the date the former employer gives written notice of the substitution of employer to the union or to the employees, the former employer and new employer are jointly and severally liable to the employees. When this term concludes, only the liability of the new employer remains. It should be noted that the former employer has joint and several liability only with respect to those obligations that existed at the time of the substitution. Acts performed thereafter by the new employer in no way may prejudice or compromise the prior employer. Likewise the labor legislation does not contain any authorization for the new and former employers to stipulate that only one of them will be responsible for the obligations arising before the date of substitution, with the other being relieved of any liability. For this reason, any agreement they reach in this regard is illegal and has no effect against the employees of the company or business unit.

Under Article 41 of the Federal Labor Law, if employees in labor litigation sue a person and thereafter amend the suit to apply to another, but fail to assert the liability of the latter arising from the substitution of the employer, the omission does not prevent the Conciliation and Arbitration Board from deciding regarding that legal status. This is because it is based on the transfer of the source of work, and what the law intends is the protection of the rights of the workers. Therefore it is not necessary to claim the liability deriving from the substitution of employers in labor litigation, when from the complaint or the answer the facts appear that give rise to the substitution of employer and, further, both the replaced and new employers have been properly served.[1]

To conclude this point in accordance with the criterion of the highest courts, there is substitution of employers with respect to an economic production unit provided that there is an intimate relationship between that source of work and the employer, without interruption of the employment activities or production or services; that is, when the new employer continues to conduct the activities of the prior employer, within the work center, using the same machinery and tools, occupying those premises, maintaining the same business cycle, and maintaining the same productivity, provided there is no stoppage of work. In other words, it must be understood that there is a substitution of employers not just because the former employer directly or indirectly, over time or immediately, transfers its business to a third person. In addition, as an essential element, it is required that the business continue without stoppage of work, with the purpose of maintaining the same productivity and cycle. Otherwise, if there is stoppage of work based on a declaration of cessation of labor relationships, as may occur after a strike in which the assets of the company that is said to have undergone a substitution are transferred by means of auction to another enterprise, it is clear that the substitution of employers contemplated by law is not present.

When only a purchase of shares or stock of a business takes place, as happens every day in the world's markets, no implication pertaining to labor or to the terms and conditions of employment exists. Even if the shares of a nonpublic company are acquired in a private operation by which no asset transmission agreement is in place, the terms and conditions of employment prevail without the obligation to issue to the employees the notice of substitution referred to above. In this case, the company subsists as is with only a change in the stock ownership, which may not even be known to the employees.

SECTION III

My client wishes to sell its existing facility. What restrictions do we need to consider?

As mentioned above, when a company is being acquired, the relevant labor issues are those related to the purchaser and not to the seller. If the client is willing to sell the company's assets, the liabilities as to the workforce will lie principally with the new employer (the purchaser); as long as the legal documentation referred to in Section I above is in order, the new employer must honor those terms and conditions of employment and the client, the seller, should concentrate on the negotiations for the final sale of the company. It is common that notwithstanding the above, both the seller and the purchaser will cooperate to make the operation a successful one and not let the labor issues obstruct the main objective, the merger or the acquisition.

If the sale is solely of stock or shares, no relevant labor issues to the seller are to be considered, as described above.

SECTION IV

My client wishes to replace an officer. What restrictions do we need to consider?

The services of an officer or in general an employee in a position of trust in a company are contracted so that, in accordance with the instructions of the employer, it may represent and direct the work of the business, there being a clear legal subordination.

In the case of tacit labor powers of representation, which exist in the case of labor representatives, and even in the case of general attorneys in fact, appointed in accordance with the civil law, neither one nor the other may exceed the terms of the instructions received from the grantor of the power of attorney or the employer.

High-level employees have workdays, compensation and salaries, and general situations that are in no way different from a labor relationship point of view than those of the rest of the employees of a company. It is just that there are several steps regarding legal subordination. High-level employees are subordinate only to the employer. Other employees are subordinate both to the employer and to the high-level employees, in their capacities as representatives of the employer.

On the other hand, agreements with high-level employees cannot be likened to agreements for the rendering of professional services (contemplated in civil legislation). This is because in the latter the characteristic feature of legal subordination is not present. In reality, high-level employees do not cease to be employees of the employer, to which they must account fully for very high levels of responsibility. But in the end, it is a part of the work that is conducted within a company.

The greater knowledge of officers, managers, and other executives of a company, in excess of that of the employer itself, does not prevent their being employees, regardless of their technical specialty, with respect to which the employer might have difficulty correcting them. In their administrative behavior they are subject to the discipline inherent in the relationship, pursuant to which the responsibility of such functionaries may be required in accordance with the policies set by the owners of each company. If they violate those policies, they will be subject to the sanctions to be imposed on them, including dismissal.

To the foregoing it should be added that managers, officers, executives, and in general high-level employees of a company must be considered to be employees only when they are an integral part of the company, and are not tied to the economic results of its activities. In the latter case, without doubt, they have the character of employers. In the first case, such categories are subject to the benefits, rights, and obligations established by law as for any other employee.

SECTION V

What prohibitions exist against discrimination on a basis of age, race, gender, disability, pregnancy, and other factors? What are the rights of employees, applicants, or former employees who believe that they have been discriminated against?

The minimum rights fixed by law for employees, such as the employment conditions under Articles 56 and 133 of the Federal Labor Law, based on the precepts of Articles 1 and 123 of the Constitution, in no case may be less than those fixed by law, and they must be proportional to the importance of the services and equal for equal work. Differences may not be established by reason of race, nationality, age, sex, or religious or political belief, except in cases that are expressly contemplated by law for special work, which merits special treatment. Such work is performed by workers in positions of trust, sailors, aircraft crews, railroad men, vehicle drivers, public service providers in areas under federal jurisdiction, field workers, commercial agents and the like, professional athletes, actors, musicians, home workers, servants, workers in family industry, and workers in hotels, restaurants, bars, and similar establishments.

Even when these conditions and rights of employees are at the minimums fixed in the Constitution and regulated in the law, under Article 57 the employee may request the Conciliation and Arbitration Board to modify the conditions of work when the salary is not remunerative, or the workday is excessive, or there are economic circumstances justifying it. The same right is given to the employer.[2]

Thus employees that have been, are, or believe that they are victims of discrimination may apply to the Federal Workers' Protection Agency, which is the authority that advises, guides, or represents them without charge in such cases of conflict with their employers.

SECTION VI

On the Horizon: What key labor and employment law developments should an employer doing buisness in Mexico anticipate occurring in the coming years?

Over many years of discussion regarding reform of the Federal Labor Law, the parties and groups representing businesses and unions (the CTM and the UNT) have prepared proposals in accordance with their particular interests. Each proposal at first included demagogically large benefits for employees. But as the negotiations advanced they were thrown aside to concentrate on the central issues in the disputes, with no truces among the various sectors involved.

In 2002 it was the turn of the Employment and Social Welfare Committee of the Chamber of Deputies of the Federal Congress to prepare a proposal, after a year or two of adjournment around the change of six-year programs. The controversy regarding proposals reappeared as the Abascal Proposal (named for the current Secretary of Labor) and that of the UNT (National Workers' Union). The National Action Party, currently in power, sent its employment proposals in response to the official proposal, the demagogic wrapping disappearing in the process, since the PRD and the UNT supposedly agreed on a proposal adopting the proposals of that party to democratize the unions, and limited itself to supporting the interests of the UNT.

To summarize the content of the draft, highlighted here are the principal proposals:

- Concepts of discrimination based on ethnic origin, opinions, political belief, marital status, or any other basis contrary to human dignity are included. It is stated that distinctions, exclusions, or preferences supported by the particular qualifications required by specific work are not considered to be discriminatory.

- It is established that it is in the social interest to promote and monitor training, productivity, and quality of work, as well as the benefits they must generate for both employees and employers.
- It is stated that officers of companies bind the employer only within their areas of responsibility.
- The employees in a company's business unit are a part of that company for purposes of employee profit participation.

Proposals regarding individual labor relationships include the following:

- The hiring of employees between 14 and 16 years of age who have not finished primary education would be prohibited.
- Temporary relationships would extend over all of the period that circumstances of the same nature persist.
- A trial period of no more than 30 days would be created in employment relationships of an indefinite term, or when the relationship exceeds 180 days. The purpose is to verify that the employee meets the requirements and has the knowledge necessary to perform the work requested. The trial period may be extended for up to 180 days when the positions are for officers, managers, and others performing functions of officers or managers in the company or business unit. The employment relationship can be terminated without employer liability if abilities are not shown.
- An employment relationship or agreement for a period of initial training would be established. The purpose is for the employee to acquire the knowledge or skills necessary for the activity for which he is to be hired. The term would be up to three months or up to six months when the positions are for employees who are officers, managers, and other persons exercising functions of officers or managers in the company or business unit, or when the positions are for those who will perform technical work or exercise specialized professions. At the end of the initial training agreement the employment relationship may be terminated without employer liability if competence is not shown.
- Absence of notice of dismissal would be cause to consider the dismissal to be unjustified, absent proof to the contrary, and notice of dismissal would not be required in the case of domestic workers.
- A worker could terminate the agreement for causes imputable to the employer in the event of sexual harassment.
- Voluntary resignation of an employee would be included as a cause of termination of a labor relationship.

Proposals regarding conditions of employment include the following:

- The employee and the employer could fix the length of the workday, without exceeding the legal maximums, and with that limitation and based on the total working hours in the week, the employees and the employer could agree to increase the workday, in order to allow the employees cumulative days off during the week. A program for monthly accumulation could also be established provided that it is by agreement of the parties, that no inhumane workday is required, and that time off is proportionate to that established in this law.

- Salary would continue to be paid directly to the employee, but "directly" would be extended to include payment made by deposit in bank accounts, debit or credit cards, by wire transfer, or using any other electronic means to which the employee agrees. These alternative forms of payment must not have any cost to the employee.
- Employers would be prohibited from engaging in any sexual harassment of any person in the workplace. Sexual harassment is understood to be any conduct constituting unwanted behavior that, based on sexuality, offends the dignity of any person in the workplace.
- Dismissal or direct or indirect inducement of the resignation of an employee because she is pregnant, has changed marital status, or has minor children in her care would be prohibited.
- Blind promotion (based solely on seniority) would be ended. Employers would be required, under equal circumstances, to prefer Mexican over non-Mexican employees, those who have completed their primary education, those trained over those who are not, those who have greater aptitude and knowledge to perform the work, and unionized employees over those who are not.
- The direction committees of unions, every six months and within a maximum period of 30 days, would be required to render complete and detailed account to the membership regarding the patrimony of the union.
- A strike notice to an employer receiving the services of employees who are members of a union, and having the obligation to enter into a collective agreement when the union so requests, would be required to be in writing and to contain the signatures of the representatives of the union as well as the signatures of the employee members of such union. The current certificates issued by the registering authority are to be attached: the list of directors; the bylaws, to the extent related to the purpose and radius of action within the branch of the industry or activity of the company or business unit; and the employer of the unionized members working in the company or business unit.

The Abascal Law contains two large categories of reforms.

1. Employers' proposals for making employment more flexible:

   Workdays, days of work, tasks and work "to be agreed upon," training and trial agreements, promotion based on aptitude and seniority, and elimination of some other obstacles to dismissal of employees. All of this is subject to agreement between the employer and the union. This eliminates the protectionist nature of the labor law regarding these matters. In this regard it must be said that the UNT proposal covers a good part of this flexibility and a bit more. It increases the possibilities of agreement between the employer and the union or employee.

2. The aspects of the supposed agreement that would be favorable to the UNT:

The acceptance of the Public Registry of Unions and Collective Agreements with some characteristics promoted by the UNT; universal, direct, and secret voting for the appointment of union boards; the signature of a collective agreement must be with the elected union, and a strike may be brought only by the elected union in cases of intra-union disputes; the productivity chapter with payment of benefits is included in the agreement. In the area of free unionization, in place at the current radius of action, there also is the right of employees to know the bylaws, the agreement, etc., and the obligation of boards to render accounts with an applicable penalty.

In conclusion, after more than ten years of production of proposals, declarations, or complete initiatives regarding reforms of the Federal Labor Law and Article 123 of the Federal Constitution, unfortunately they have not managed to enter into a true debate, generating dialogue and, above all, consensus for reform. Under the current conditions of recession and crisis in the Mexican economy it is likely that labor reform will be even further delayed before approval. Regarding the principal disputes that exist regarding the referenced reform, in the eyes of some conservative sectors the protection and achievements obtained by the working class over many years will be abandoned. Nevertheless the need to make decisions regarding changes supporting growth of the country in a world of constant change and globalization is urgent and imperative. The Mexican working class must acquire a new work ethic and be highly competitive, including at the international level.

A most appropriate approach is to achieve a point of equilibrium among the employee, employer, union, government, and other sectors, setting personal interests aside, working with an objective, clear view, with benefits for all levels participating in or intimately connected to the labor reform. What is very true and should always be considered is that labor laws in Mexico have never been nor will ever be an obstacle for foreign or domestic investment and job creation in the country.

NOTES

1. Substitution of employer. The board may resolve regarding liability derived from it when the facts giving rise to it appear in the file and both the replaced and the new employers have been served. Op. I.6o.T.138 L, 16 S.J.F. 1195 (Tribunales Colegiados de Circuito [Collegiate Circuit Courts] Nov. 2002).

2. Dionisio J. Kaye, Relaciones Individuales y Colectivas del Trabajo [Individual and Collective Labor Relationships] (Ed. Themis, Colección Ensayos Jurídicos [Legal Works Collection]. México 1995).

CHAPTER 10

Labor and Employment Law in the Netherlands

Maartje M. Govaert
Liesbeth (E). Th.M. Sneek

Section I

My client wishes to establish a manufacturing facility in the Netherlands and will need to hire a workforce. What are the key legal issues involved?

Employment Contracts

General

An employment contract may be concluded orally or in writing (not necessarily in Dutch; any language that the employer and employee can be deemed to understand would be valid). However, certain provisions, such as a noncompetition clause, are valid only if in writing. Moreover, the employer is obliged to provide all employees (regular, full time, and temporary) the conditions of employment in writing[1] within one month of the commencement of the employment, or sooner if the employment is for less than a month. The document containing this information must be signed by the employer.

Types of Contracts

Several types of employment contracts are possible under Dutch law. An employment contract may be concluded for an indefinite period of time or for a definite period. A contract for a definite period may be for a specific time frame or for a period that can be determined on the basis of objective standards (e.g., as long as a specific project is handled by the employer). Under either type of contract, an employee may work full time or part time.

Several forms of atypical work arrangements also traditionally exist in the Netherlands. These vary from on-call types of arrangements to zero-hours contracts (those without any guarantee with respect to the number of hours of work). Many employers also use temporary agency workers. If the requirements for temporary contracts under Dutch law (Article 7:690 Dutch Civil Code, hereinafter DCC) are met, the employee has an employment contract with the employment agency and not with the employer (where the employee will actually perform work). The employer and the employment agency should have concluded an agreement for professional services (*overeenkomst van opdracht*).

Pursuant to Article 7:668a DCC (referring to a "chain" of contracts), a contract for a definite period of time may, if extended, and once certain criteria are met, be automatically converted into a contract for an indefinite period of time. This article also applies in the event an employee continues his or her employment contract with another employer that—depending on the nature of the work—can be considered to be the successor of the former employer. An employment agency and the employer will usually be considered each other's successor. So will different group companies.

Hiring Managerial Employees

The first managing directors of a business that is carried out through a legal entity are appointed in the deed of incorporation of the legal entity. After incorporation, the managing directors are appointed by the corporate body that is authorized by the articles of association (e.g., the general meeting of shareholders or the supervisory board). In most cases, members of the management board will not only have been appointed as managing directors under the articles of association, but will also have an employment contract with the legal entity. According to the Works Council Act (*Wet op de Ondernemingsraden;* hereinafter WCA), the prior advice of the works council (if any) on a proposed decision to appoint or dismiss a managing director is required, provided the managing director in question qualifies as the manager of the business as defined in the WCA. (See Works Council below.) Appointment, dismissal, and suspension of managing directors must be registered with the trade register.

Employment Contracts

Wages and Benefits

In principle, the parties to an employment contract are free to agree to the wages to which an employee shall be entitled. However, the Act on Minimum Wages and Minimum Holiday Allowances contains certain minimum wages and minimum holiday allowances, which are normally adjusted each year. Furthermore, the freedom of contract of the parties is limited by Article 7:646 DCC and the Act on Equal Treatment of Men and Women (*Wet gelijke behandeling van mannen en vrouwen*). A collective bargaining agreement (*Collectieve Arbeidsovereenkomst;* hereinafter CBA) may also contain salary scales that are binding on individual employers.

The parties may agree to certain fringe benefits, such as a so-called 13th month, a contribution to health insurance premiums, and a bonus. See Pension below for pension-plan provisions.

Wages are not due over a period during which the employee has not performed work. However, this is not the case if the employee could not perform the agreed-upon labor due to (1) sickness, pregnancy, or delivery or (2) circumstances that are reasonably deemed to be for the employer's account.

Trial Period

An employment contract may contain a trial period during which either party may terminate the contract with immediate effect. The employer is obliged only to provide the reason for termination (in writing) on request thereto by the employee. The trial period has to be concluded in writing and has a maximum length of (1) one month for employment contracts of less than two years and (2) two months for employment contracts of two years or more or for indefinite-term contracts.

Restrictive Conditions

Confidentiality

It is a criminal offense for an employee to disclose any confidential information about the employer's business during or after employment. Employment contracts often provide what kind of information is to be kept confidential and to whom it may not be disclosed.

Noncompetition

An employment contract may contain a noncompetition clause restricting the employee from competing with his or her formal employer during a certain period after termination of the employment contract.

The employee may petition the court with the request to mitigate or annul the noncompetition clause. The court will assess whether the noncompetition clause is too burdensome for the employee in relation to the interest of the employer in (fully) maintaining it. The court may also order the employer to compensate the employee during the period in which the noncompetition clause is maintained.

Protection of Intellectual Property Rights

According to the Patent Act (*Rijksoctrooiwet*), the employer is entitled to patents concerning inventions made by an employee if such inventions fall within the scope of the work for which the employee was hired. If the salary of the employee cannot be considered to include compensation for such inventions, he is entitled to a reasonable reward. If a work of literature, science, or art is created by an employee, the employer is entitled to the copyright with respect to the work, but only if the job entails making such works (the Copyright Act (*Auteurswet*)). According to the Uniform Benelux Design Act (*Eenvormige Beneluxwet inzake Tekeningen of Modellen*), designs made by employees in the performance of their job will normally belong to the employer.

Working Hours

The legislation on working hours and working conditions based on the Working Hours Act (*Arbeidstijdenwet*) is extensive and complicated. The number of working hours depends upon the sector of industry and kind of labor performed. In general, an employee is allowed to work a maximum of nine hours per day, for a maximum of 45 hours per week. Over a period of 13 weeks the maximum number of working hours is 40 hours per week. CBAs often contain provisions with regard to this subject. Arrangements on working hours included in an individual employment contract that are not in conformity with the Working Hours Act can be declared null and void.

Part-Time Work

The Working Hours Amendment Act 2000 (*Wet aanpassing arbeidsduur*) allows an employee to request a reduction (or an increase) of working hours. In general, the employer must grant such a request, provided that (1) the employee has worked for more than one year with the said employer, and (2) granting the employee's request does not conflict with considerable business interests (e.g., restaffing, safety).

Holidays[2]

The statutory minimum number of holidays per year to which an employee is entitled is four times the number of full working days per week. The parties may agree on a more generous holiday entitlement and in practice this regularly happens (an entitlement of five to six weeks is quite common in the Netherlands). CBAs often also provide for more days than the statutory minimum number. An agreement on a smaller number of days than the statutory minimum is invalid. Apart from the statutory number of vacation days, the employee is entitled to have paid leave on customary public holidays and for special events (such as the birth of a child or the death of a close relative).

Vacation days cannot be replaced by monetary payment. However, days in excess of the statutory minimum may be bought off if this has been agreed upon by the parties. Upon the termination of the employment contract the employee is entitled to payment for outstanding vacation days. Unused vacation days lapse after five years.

Special Leave

Most special leaves are provided for in the Work and Care Act (*Wet arbeid en zorg*). Sickness, maternity and adoption, parental, and political leaves are described next. Other special leaves include leave for domestic emergencies, short-term-care leave, and birth leave for a husband/partner.

Sickness

The employer is obliged to pay the employee during the first two years of sickness (1) at least 70 percent of the employee's last wages (but not below the minimum wage) during the first year and (2) no more than 70 percent of the last wages over the second year. The statutory minimum wage guarantee does not apply to the second year of sickness. Most employers in the Netherlands are obliged to pay 100 percent of the wages over the first year, either by arrangement in the individual employment contract or through CBAs. There is also a prohibition against terminating the employment contract by giving notice during the first two years of sickness, as further described below.

On the other hand, the employee also has certain obligations. Among other things, the employee may be required to fulfill alternative positions for the employer or a third party. The employee is also obliged to undergo reasonable medical exams as requested by the employer.

Maternity and Adoption

Employees have the right to 16 weeks of maternity leave. Adoption gives a right to an unpaid leave of four consecutive weeks in an 18-week period commencing two weeks before the day the child is adopted. During the maternity leave the employee will receive certain minimal benefits from the Social Security Authority (*UWV*). A CBA or individual employment contract may call for an additional payment by the employer.

Parental

Parents or guardians whose children are not more than eight years of age and who have worked for the employer for at least one year have the right to unpaid parental leave. The duration of the leave depends on how many hours the employee works in a week.

Political

Employees may request permission from the employer to attend meetings of certain representative bodies. There is no statutory right to salary during this leave.

Safety and Health

The Working Conditions Act (*Arbeidsomstandighedenwet*) and related laws impose significant obligations on the employer relating to the health and safety of the employees. The employer must, among other things, prevent sickness and any danger to the health of employees and make an effort to reintegrate sick employees in the working process. The employer is required to use the services of a working-conditions service (*Arbo dienst*), an institution that assists the employer in the overview and evaluation of the risks, assists sick employees, advises the employer on reintegration of sick employees, and more.

Pension

In general, employers are not obligated to provide a pension plan. However, in most cases pension plans are based on CBAs and there are also employers who offer pension arrangements in the individual employment contract. Some industry sectors have an industry pension fund. Participation in an industry pension fund can be prescribed on a mandatory basis for all employees in a certain industry by the Minister of Social Affairs and Employment Matters, if requested by a sufficiently representative sample of businesses in the respective industry sector. In the event the employer has a pension plan, the provisions of the Pensions and Savings

Funds Act (*Pensioen en Spaarfondsenwet*) will apply. One of the most important obligations under this Act is the requirement to engage a third party for the administration and execution of the plan.

Reintegration of Disabled Employees

In the event an employee becomes disabled, the employer is obligated to provide suitable employment to the employee by either amending the working conditions and working circumstances such that the disabled employee can once again perform his or her own work or by providing a suitable alternative. Obligations of the employer in this respect have been incorporated in the Reintegration of Disabled Employees Act (*Wet Reïntegratie Arbeidsgehandicapten*) and the Gatekeeper Act (*Wet Poortwachter*).

The employer is obliged to prepare an "action plan," in joint cooperation with the working-conditions service and the disabled employee, to actively reintegrate the disabled employee. The employee is obliged to actively cooperate with the preparation and the evaluation of the action plan, to accept suitable work, and to accept, if necessary, a change in employment conditions resulting therefrom. If the employee does not cooperate or is not willing to accept suitable work, the employer is not obliged to pay wages. On the other hand, if the employer does not comply, the Social Security Authority (*UWV*) can order the employer to pay wages for a longer period than two years.

Liability for Damages

The employer is liable for damages of third parties if one of its employees has caused damage while performing his or her employment. For damages suffered by the employee during employment, the employer may be liable.

Trade Unions and Employers Associations

Trade Unions

The most important trade unions are the Federation of Dutch Trade Unions (FNV) and the National Federation of Christian Democratic Workers (CNV). In case of a closure or a reorganization resulting in a collective dismissal, it is common practice in the Netherlands to agree with the unions and/or the works council and/or the employee representative body on a so-called social plan.

Employers Associations

The most important employers association is the Confederation of Netherlands Industries and Employers (VNO-NCW), which consists of various employers' organizations in trade, industry, transport, banking, insurance, and wholesale and large retail stores.

Collective Bargaining Agreements

General

Trade unions and employers associations often conclude CBAs (which then apply to all the employees that are members of the specific employer's association). CBAs are sometimes also concluded by trade unions and large individual businesses. Such a CBA then applies only to the individual business.

Applicability

Pursuant to the Act concerning the Declaration of General Applicability of Provisions of Collective Bargaining Agreements, the Minister of Social Affairs and Employment may, at the request of the parties to such agreement, under certain circumstances declare certain provisions of a CBA generally applicable to all labor relations in a specific sector of industry. In such cases, employers who are not members of an employers association will nevertheless be bound by those provisions in the CBA. In practice, an "organized" employer will treat its employees equally irrespective of whether they are members of the relevant trade union(s). The employer and the employee may in principle not deviate from the applicable CBA provisions.

Works Council

Obligation to Establish a Works Council

Works Council

According to the Works Council Act (WCA), a business in which, as a rule, at least 50 persons are employed is obligated to establish a works council for the purposes of consultation with and representation of the employees of the business. The obligation to establish a works council may also result from a provision to this effect in a CBA. In that case the WCA will also be applicable.

Central Works Council

A company that maintains more than one business may establish a central works council for all the businesses, which then exists next to the works councils of the individual businesses. A company is obliged to establish a central works council if this is demanded by the majority of the works councils in the businesses involved. The central works council deals only with those matters that are "of common interest" to all or the majority of the businesses for which they have been established. The individual works councils can then no longer exercise their rights over that specific issue.

Group Works Council

A company may also establish one or more group works councils for some but not all of the businesses it maintains.

Representation of Employees (Small Business)
The WCA contains special provisions regarding a mandatory representation of employees (*personeelsvertegenwoordiging*) in small businesses employing at least 10 but less than 50 employees. The authority of the small works council to render advice is limited to proposed decisions that may result in a loss of jobs or in an important change in the nature of the work, the employment conditions, or the circumstances under which the work is being performed, for at least one quarter of the employees in the business.

Protection of Members of the Works Council

In order to protect the position of members of the works council (including the members of its committees), the WCA provides that the employer shall ensure that the candidates as well as members and former members of the works council do not suffer any disadvantage in their position in the business because of their candidacy for or membership of the works council. Furthermore, it is prohibited to terminate the employment contract with a member of the works council, unless (1) the employee has agreed in writing to the termination, or (2) the employee is dismissed for cause. In addition, an employee can be dismissed for important reasons not related to membership in the works council (e.g., disfunctioning, closing down the business; see Section IV), but only with the permission of the District Court, Cantonal Division.

Rights of the Works Council

Right to Receive Information
The works council is entitled to receive all information (if it so requests in writing) that it reasonably needs to properly perform its duties.

Right to Consultation
The employer and the works council shall meet in a so-called consultation meeting within two weeks after a request, setting out the reasons for such meeting, by either the employer or the works council. At least six consultation meetings per year must be held in order to discuss matters on which consultation is mandatory by virtue of the WCA. The works council is entitled to submit proposals on these matters and to present its views.

Right to Render Advice
According to Article 25 WCA, a company must request the prior advice of the works council in respect of specific proposed decisions (and the implementation thereof) on such "business" matters as, for example, the transfer of control over the business or any part thereof; the establishment, takeover, or relinquishment of control over another business; the termination of the activities of a business or a substantial part thereof; a substantial reduction, expansion, or other change in the activities of the business; a substantial change in the organization of the business or in the allocation of the authority within the business; and the appointment of

an outside expert to provide advice on one of these matters. The advice must be requested at such a time that it can still substantially influence the decision to be made.

After advice has been rendered, the company is free to make a decision, either following the advice or not. The company should, as soon as possible after the decision has been made, give written notice of its decision to the works council. If the decision is not (completely) in conformity with the works council's advice, the entrepreneur must explain to the works council in writing why he or she has deviated from the advice. If the decision differs from the advice, the entrepreneur may not take any actions to implement the decision during a waiting period of one month.

The works council may file an appeal with the Enterprise Chamber (*Ondernemingskamer*) of the Amsterdam Court of Appeal if the decision deviates from its advice or if facts or circumstances have become known that, had they been known to the works council at the time of rendering its advice, might have led to different advice. A full description of this process is beyond the scope of this chapter.

Right of Approval

According to Article 27 WCA, an employer should request the prior approval of the works council in respect to specific proposed decisions concerning the introduction, modification, or repeal of "social" regulations within the business, such as regulations on pension plans, on profit sharing or saving plans, on working hours or holidays, and on salary or job classification systems.

If the employer does not obtain the approval of the works council, it can—after having fulfilled and not succeeded in a mediation by a special committee (*bedrijfscommissie*)—request permission from the District Court, Cantonal Division to nonetheless make the proposed decision.

Any decision made by the employer without the prior approval of the works council or without the permission of the District Court, Cantonal Division is null and void.

SECTION II

My client is acquiring an existing business in the Netherlands. How do I assess the existing workforce and consider changes?

Implications of Employee Legislation

Acquiring an established business in the Netherlands can take place by (1) a share purchase, (2) an asset purchase of a business (or part thereof),[3] or (3) a legal merger. This section focuses on the implications of employment legislation with respect to an acquisition.

Two regimes aimed at the protection of employees in the case of the acquisition of control (meaning, in this context, an interest of 50 percent or more) in another business are the Merger Code (*SER Fusiegedragsregels*) and the Works Council Act (WCA). Furthermore, the Netherlands implemented European Directive No. 77/187[4] of 14 February 1977 on employees' acquired rights in a transfer of a business in Articles 7:662–666 DCC. CBAs may contain certain protective provisions. Generally speaking, except for articles 7:662–666 DCC, these regimes apply irrespectively of the manner in which an acquisition takes place. Articles 7:662–666 DCC generally apply only in the event the acquisition takes place through an asset purchase of a business.

Merger Code

Applicability

The Merger Code is applicable if (1) the merger involves at least one business that is established in the Netherlands and normally employs at least 100 employees or (2) a business that is involved in the merger belongs to a group of businesses where the businesses established in the Netherlands together normally employ at least 100 employees. A CBA may render the Merger Code applicable irrespective of whether or not these criteria have been met.

The Merger Code does not apply (1) when all parties to the merger form part of one group or (2) in the case of mergers outside the jurisdiction of Dutch law. The Merger Code has territorial application.

Rules for the Protection of the Employees

The trade unions must be given the opportunity to express their opinion with regard to the employees' interests involved in the intended merger. The involvement of the trade unions should be sought at such time that the judgment of the unions can still significantly influence (1) the decision of whether the merger will be realized and, if so, (2) the conditions of the merger. Approval of the merger by the trade unions is not required.

Simultaneously with the notification of the trade unions, the Social and Economic Council should be informed in writing of the intended merger.

Penalties

The Code does not have statutory effect. It is a code of conduct. Failure to comply with its rules may lead the Committee of Merger Affairs (*Commissie voor Fusieaangelegenheden*), instituted under the Merger Code, to impose limited sanctions on the businesses involved.

Works Council Act

As discussed in Section I under Rights of the Works Council, an employer must request the prior advice of the works council according to Article 25 WCA in respect to specific proposed decisions (and the implementation thereof) on several "business" matters, among which are (1) the transfer of control over the business or any part thereof and (2) the establishment, takeover, or relinquishment of control over another business. According to the Merger Code, this advice procedure may not be started until a first meeting with the trade unions has taken place.

Transfer of Employees

Purchase of a Business

Articles 7:662–666 DCC apply in case of the transfer of a business by means of an asset deal. Pursuant to Section 7:662b DCC, the term "transfer of a business" presumes a transfer as a result of an agreement. According to case law, in order for Articles 7:662–666 to apply, an agreement that leads to the transfer of the activities of the business is required. In general, this would be an "asset-liability purchase agreement."

If and when the criteria of Articles 7:662–666 DCC are met, upon the transfer of a business, the rights and obligations of the employer and that business under the existing employment contracts with the employees will be assumed by the acquirer of the business by operation of law. For one year after the transfer of the business, the seller and the acquirer are jointly and severally liable for the fulfillment of obligations under the employment contracts insofar as these obligations have accrued before the transfer.

Share Purchase and Legal Merger

A transfer of a business as a result of a share transaction, which causes no change in the identity of the person of the employer, is excluded from the applicability of Articles 7:662–666 DCC. The same applies if the employing business merges with another business by means of a legal merger.

Employment Conditions after the Acquisition

General

As indicated above, in case of a (1) share transaction, (2) purchase of a business through assets acquisition, or (3) legal merger, the employment conditions of the employees of the acquired business remain in force after the acquisition.

Article 7:663 DCC and CBA

Pursuant to Article 7:663 DCC, the employment conditions set out in a CBA will be transferred by operation of law to the acquirer, until such time as (1) the acquirer is bound by a new CBA (or the renewal of an existing CBA) concluded after the transfer, or (2) the acquirer is required by law[5] to comply with the provisions of another CBA, or (3) the CBA of the seller expires (even if the sellers' CBA is renewed).

Pension

Pension and savings plans arising from employment contracts or CBAs fall under the scope of Article 7:663 DCC. In case of a transfer of a business the rights and obligations of the seller arising from pension commitments will be assumed by the acquirer of the business by operation of law. Applicability of Article 7:663 DCC also means that the length of service of the transferred employee transfers with the employee. The acquirer is obligated to take into account the length of service of the transferred employee built up at the transferred business of the seller. This is important to consider when calculating the past service commitments (*backservice verplichtingen*) in the event the pension commitment is based on a final pay pension plan (*eindloonregeling*).

However, Article 7:663 DCC is not applicable on the rights and obligations arising from pension commitments, and will therefore not transfer to the acquirer by operation of law, in the event (1) the acquirer offers the transferred employee the same pension commitment as offered to his employees before the transfer, or (2) the acquirer is obligated to participate in an industry pension fund in which the employee shall participate as well, or (3) insofar as provisions of public law or provisions in a CBA deviate from the pension commitment.

The events described above under (1) and (2) concern new pension commitments. In that case, the acquirer is no longer obliged to take the seller's pension commitment (e.g., length of service and past service commitment) into consideration. The exceptions set forth above under (1), (2), and (3) do not apply in the event the employee is obliged to participate in a specific industry pension fund and this obligation is still in effect after the transfer of the business. In that case, the acquirer shall assume all rights and obligations arising from the industry pension fund by operation of law.

Reducing, Reorganizing, and Harmonizing Employment Conditions

Reducing and Reorganizing the Workforce

The employer is prohibited by law to terminate the employment contracts with employees solely as a result of a transfer of a business. This prohibition pertains to the seller and the acquirer of the transferred business. However, in the event certain economical, technical, or organizational reasons apply, termination of the employment contracts is normally allowed, provided strict rules on selection are applied (see Section IV).

Harmonizing Employment Conditions

Unilateral Adjustment by the Employer of the Employment Conditions

According to Article 7:613 DCC, the employer has the right to unilaterally adjust the terms and conditions of employment of an employee, in case (1) parties have agreed on this right in writing and (2) the employer can show a substantial interest (*zwaarwegend belang*) in adjusting the terms and conditions of employment in the way the employer desires.

In case parties have not agreed in writing on the right of the employer to unilaterally adjust the terms and conditions of employment, the employer cannot, in principle, unilaterally adjust these terms and conditions of employment. Despite the foregoing, there are a few options for an employer to nonetheless attempt to adjust the terms and conditions of employment of an employee.

Adjustment of the Employment Conditions by Means of an Agreement with the Employee

An employer can try to reach agreement with the employee on adjusting the terms and conditions of employment.

Adjustment of the Terms of Employment: Case Law

If the employee does not agree with the proposed adjustments of the terms and conditions of employment by the employer, the employer may bring the matter before the District Court, Cantonal Division. Based on a ruling by the Supreme Court of the Netherlands,[6] an employee should comply with reasonable propositions of the employer in connection with altered circumstances at work. An employee may reject these propositions only if acceptance of these propositions cannot reasonably be demanded from the employee.

Depending on the character of the employment conditions to be changed, the changes might fall under the definition of Article 27, Paragraph 1 of the Works Council Act. In that case, the prior consent of the works council is needed on the changes, along with the individual consent of the employee.

SECTION III

My client wishes to sell its existing facility. What restrictions do we need to consider?

Implications of Employee Legislation

General

Selling an established business in the Netherlands can take place by (1) a share sale, (2) an asset sale of a business, or (3) a legal merger. As indicated in Section II, the following employee legislation could have implications on the acquisition process: (1) the Merger Code, (2) the WCA, (3) Articles 7:662–666 DCC, and (4) a CBA. Generally speaking, except for Articles 7:662–666 DCC, these regimes apply irrespectively of the manner in which an acquisition takes place. Articles 7:662–666 DCC generally apply only in the event the acquisition takes place through an asset sale of a business.

Notification, Consultation, and Advice Procedure

If applicable, the Merger Code and the WCA prescribe certain procedures that have to be followed quite strictly before agreement can be reached. These procedures can take a considerable amount of time.

Assessing Employment Contracts

Due Diligence

In general, before starting the due diligence investigation, the acquirer will provide the seller with a request list. Among other issues (depending on the sort of business), the following labor issues should be reviewed by the acquirer:

Key Personnel

The acquirer shall probably want to assess the contents of the employment contracts of key personnel, including total annual salary, bonus and other profit-related plans, provisions regarding severance or layoffs (so-called golden parachute arrangements), job position and years of employment, share-based options and share incentives, and details on any noncompetition and confidentiality arrangements.

CBA, Works Council, and Other Employee Representative Bodies
The acquirer should review a list of members of works council and other employee representative bodies and the relation therewith; history of previous advice and consent procedures under the WCA and any court cases related thereto; and applicable CBA and other agreements between the business and trade unions, works councils, or other employee representative bodies.

Employees
The acquirer should assess the total number of employees, specified by number of sick employees, part-time employees, disabled employees, and definite-term period employees; details on employee benefits, including insurance, health care, and cars made available, and pension plans; and employment conditions. The acquirer should verify the possibility for the employer to unilaterally adjust the employment conditions inserted in the individual employment contracts.

Legal Proceedings, Dismissals, and Redundancies
The acquirer should review any legal proceedings or threatening legal proceedings due to a dismissal or redundancy or damages, and any previous labor incidents or strikes.

Protection of Privacy

The Act on Data Protection (ADP), an implementation of the European Data Protection Directive No. 95/46, is applicable to any fully or partially automatic processing of personal data as well as to non-automatic processing of personal data held in a database or designated to be held in a database.

The ADP requires that personal data administered in a database should be registered with the Registration Board before such data can be processed, unless the administration falls within the scope of the Exemption Decree. Under this decree, a salary administration and/or personnel register are, amongst other exceptions, exempt from the registration obligation; however, the type of data is limited to that required for salary administration. Personal data must be deleted from the registration no later than two years after the employment contract or the activities of the registered person on behalf of the employer have been terminated.

Pursuant to Article 76 of the ADP, the transmission of data to a country outside the European Union is allowed only if that country has statutory or other legal provisions that offer an adequate level of protection similar to the Data Protection Directive. However, a transfer of personal data to a third country that does not ensure such protection may nevertheless take place provided the data subject (i.e., the individual employee) has unambiguously given consent to the proposed transfer.

In case of an intended merger, it is not convenient to ask the consent of the employees. It is highly advisable that the seller seek legal advice with respect to the information it may provide and whether or not it is allowed to provide the acquirer with the requested information.

Negotiating with the Acquirer

Outcome of Due Diligence

All obligations and rights under the employment contracts and CBAs remain in force after the transfer of the business. After the outcome of the due diligence, negotiations between the acquirer and the seller with respect to the sale and purchase agreement will take place. Besides the general representations and warranties on labor issues, the acquirer might want to be indemnified by the seller for specific labor issues that have become apparent from the due diligence investigation.

Sick and Disabled Employees; Safety and Health

The Working Conditions Act and related laws impose substantial obligations on the employer relating to the health and safety of employees. With respect to sick employees, the employer has to pay wages during the first two years of sickness and the employer is obliged to (actively try to) reintegrate the sick employee. Furthermore, employers are prohibited from terminating the employment contract by giving notice during the first two years of sickness. In the event an employee becomes disabled, the employer is obliged to provide suitable alternative employment for the employee, even to rearrange the business if necessary. The employer is obliged to offer the employees a safe and healthy workplace.

Legal Proceedings

In the event that court proceedings are in progress at the time of transfer of the business, the proceedings will transfer along with the employees.

Employment Conditions

In the event the merger takes place by sale of shares or a legal merger, the employment conditions and the applicable CBA remain in force. In case of a sale of a business, the rights and obligations under the employment contracts and CBAs transfer by operation of law, and thus remain in force. The acquirer might desire to harmonize the employment conditions after the transfer. In this respect, the acquirer might want to estimate the possibilities to harmonize the employment conditions (e.g., unilateral adjustment clause in the employment contract).

Pension

The rights and obligations arising from pension commitments may transfer to the acquirer by operation of law in the event that certain conditions apply. Since pension claims can result in considerably large amounts, the acquirer shall want to be informed on the possible risks and liabilities with respect thereto. Furthermore, the acquirer shall want to investigate the possibility to harmonize the pension plans. The third parties involved for the administration and execution of the pension plans shall have to be consulted.

Key Personnel

Depending on the future plans of the acquirer with respect to the transferred business, the acquirer might want a guarantee that the key personnel of the business is willing to transfer along with the business for a period of time to be agreed upon and if not, that these employees will not compete with the business. On the other hand, if the acquirer is planning to replace key personnel with its own employees, the acquirer shall be more interested in the details of any "golden parachute" arrangements made between the seller and key personnel. The negotiations in this respect also depend on the line of business.

Works Council

As the works council may block the intended merger, and in light of the other rights of the works council (especially the right of approval), a good relationship with the works council is important to the acquirer. In light of a future reorganization and possible redundancies in that respect, a list of the members of the works council is usually relevant for the acquirer.

Representations, Warranties, and Indemnifications

In general, the representations and warranties that form part of the sale and purchase agreement are standardized. The indemnifications depend on the outcome of the due diligence investigation and the following negotiations between the acquirer and the seller.

SECTION IV

My client wishes to replace its senior manager(s). What restrictions do we need to consider?

Termination of an Employment Contract

General

Dutch statutory rules concerning the termination of an employment contract are designed to protect the interests of the employee to a larger extent than is the case in most other European jurisdictions. The most striking difference with other jurisdictions is that, basically, an employer needs prior approval—of the Center for Work and Income (CWI) or a District Court, Cantonal Division (hereinafter the Court)—before being able to terminate an employment contract. However, prior approval is not required in the event that (1) the term of an employment contract for a definite period of time lapses and no giving of notice is agreed upon in the contract; (2) the employment contract is terminated during the trial period; or (3) the employment contract is terminated on the spot for an urgent reason.

The information provided in this chapter is of a general nature only and hence cannot be relied upon as a basis for dismissal decisions in a particular case, as applicability of a CBA, deviations in the individual employment contract, or other specific circumstances may change the legal framework.

Termination of a Definite- or Indefinite-Term Contract

Definite-Term Contract

An employment contract entered into for a definite period of time ends by operation of law after the agreed period has lapsed. An employer that wishes to terminate the contract prematurely must apply for a dismissal permit, provided the employment contract allows for giving notice during its course, or should request the Court to dissolve the employment contract.

Indefinite-Term Contract

An employer may terminate an indefinite-term employment contract by (1) giving notice to the employee after having obtained a dismissal permit from the CWI; (2) obtaining a dissolution judgment from the Court; (3) dismissal on the spot for an urgent reason; or (4) mutual agreement.

Termination during Trial Period

During the trial period both the employer and the employee may give notice with immediate effect. Upon request the employer must provide the reasons for the notice to the employee in writing.

Termination for Urgent Reasons

An employment contract may be terminated with immediate effect if there is an urgent reason justifying such immediate dismissal. In general, only such events as theft of property of the employer or violent behavior are a sufficiently urgent reason to dismiss the employee on the spot. Strict procedural requirements apply with regard to how and when the employee should be informed of the dismissal.

Severance Payment

In the dissolution procedure before the Court, the Court may award compensation to one of the parties. In order to avoid too many differences between the Courts in amounts of compensation being awarded, the Courts have developed a formula by which the amount of compensation can be calculated more or less accurately. This formula has been made public as the "Cantonal Judges Formula."[7] Under the formula, three factors have to be taken into account to determine the amount of compensation:

(A) Length of employment, rounded off to a whole number of years. Years of employment served before the employee's 40th birthday count as one year; years of employment served between the employee's 40th and 50th birthday count as 1.5 years; years of employment served after the employee's 50th birthday count as two years.

(B) Gross monthly salary, including fixed monetary emoluments such as holiday allowance and a fixed (or average, if varying) bonus. Generally excluded are the employer's contributions to a pension plan, use of company car, expense allowances or royalties, the employer's contribution to medical insurance payments, and payments under nonstructural profit-sharing plans.

(C) A multiplier, to be set at 1 when the Court decides that neither of the parties can be held solely accountable for the reasons that have led to the dissolution. Depending on the circumstances of the case, the Court will set the adjustment factor between 0 and 1 (i.e., no compensation or a lower compensation) if it finds that awarding (full) compensation would be unfair because the termination is mostly or entirely the fault of the employee. On the other hand, if the employer is to be blamed to a large extent that there is such a change in the circumstances that the employment relationship has to be terminated, the Court may set the adjustment factor higher than 1 and even double the outcome of the formula. Officially there is no maximum to the C factor, but it is rarely set above 2.

The total amount to be awarded is (A) × (B) × (C).

The Court will usually not apply this formula in cases of relatively short employment periods (less than two years).

The formula is often also used in social plans or in cases of termination by mutual agreement.

Paying a severance compensation does not replace the obligation to terminate the employment contract validly, either by giving notice while observing the statutory or agreed-upon notice period, or by dissolution of the employment contract by the Court. An employee continues to be entitled to full wages and all benefits and to perform work for as long as the employment contract has not been validly terminated.

Termination by Giving Notice with a Dismissal Permit

Dismissal Permit

To terminate an employment contract by giving notice, a "dismissal permit" is required. The employer may obtain a dismissal permit by filing a written request for a dismissal permit with the appropriate office of the Center for Work and Income (CWI), which generally is the office in the district in which the employee works. The procedure before the CWI is primarily conducted in writing and may take several weeks to months, depending on whether or not the employee puts up a full-fledged defense. In order to safeguard any entitlement to unemployment benefits, the employee is required to oppose the dismissal. However, this can be different if the permission to dismiss was sought on "economic grounds" (and such grounds can be proven to exist). In that case the employee could sign a waiver to his or her right of defense (*verklaring van geen bezwaar*) without jeopardizing entitlements to unemployment benefits. These waivers are common practice in case a collective dismissal (and an appropriate accompanying social plan) has been agreed upon with the works council and the unions. If the waivers are signed, the procedure before the CWI, assuming all its criteria are met, will be considerably shorter (usually less than one month).

As of March 1, 2006, the rules that apply in case of dismissal for economic reasons are as follows: the CWI will grant permission only if the so-called age-reflecting principle (*afspiegelingsbeginsel*) is applied (unless all of the employees are dismissed). Following this principle employees with exchangeable positions have to be divided into five groups according to their age. Within each group the last-in, first-out (LIFO) principle has to be applied to determine both the number of employees within each group that may be dismissed and the choice of the specific employee within the group. If the employer has reached agreement with the unions on the necessity to make employees redundant and the number of employees to be dismissed, the CWI will generally grant a dismissal permit without carrying out too much of an individual check as to the reasons, provided the dismissal will not violate the age-reflecting principle, and the employer has sufficiently attempted to find alternative solutions, such as placing the employee in another job or at another location.

In case of a dismissal for nonperformance reasons, the CWI will investigate the nonperformance reasons. A clear file, showing that the employee has been warned that he or she is underperforming and has been given sufficient time and guidance to improve, is required. The age-reflecting principle does not apply in this situation. However, in individual labor conflicts, termination through dissolution by the Court is usually preferred.

Notice

Once a dismissal permit is granted, the employer can effectively give notice to the employee. The applicable (statutory or contractual) notice period will have to be observed. The statutory notice periods for the employer are (1) one month for an employee who has been employed for less than five years; (2) two months for an employee who has been employed between five and ten years; (3) three months for an employee who has been employed between ten and 15 years; and (4) four months for an employee who has been employed longer than 15 years.

If the employment contract is terminated without the required prior permission of the CWI, the termination is invalid. The employee may invoke the invalidity (nullity) of the termination within six months after receipt of the notice of termination. Terminating the employment contract, after obtaining the permission of the CWI, by giving an incorrect term of notice does not result in the invalidity of the termination as such, but it triggers the liability of the employer for (at least) an amount of damages consisting of the salary that would have been paid over the remainder of the correct notice period. Also, in that case any entitlements of the employer under a noncompetition clause are no longer valid.

If an employment contract is terminated by giving notice after having obtained a dismissal permit, there are no legal requirements regarding severance payments to an employee. Naturally, both parties may agree on such a payment and in practice this is often the case, taking into account what could have been the outcome of a dissolution procedure before the Court.

Termination through Dissolution by the Court

An employer may at all times attempt to terminate the employment contract with an employee by filing a request for dissolution of the employment contract before the Court. The Court will dissolve the employment contract if there are serious reasons (*gewichtige redenen*) for a termination. Dissolution judgments cannot be appealed against, unless a party can show a "mistake of law."

In the dissolution procedure, both parties will file a statement. Thereafter, an oral hearing will take place. Hearings at the Court tend to be informal. The entire procedure may take approximately six to eight weeks.

Termination by Mutual Agreement

An employment contract may be terminated by mutual agreement between the parties. However, under the relevant Social Security legislation (unemployment benefits), an employee is normally not entitled to unemployment benefits if termination of employment is due to the employee's own fault (imputable or voluntary unemployment). This may be the case if an employee has voluntarily agreed to the termination. To avoid risking the employee's entitlement to unemployment benefits, the employer and employee usually agree to file a pro forma petition for dissolution of the employment contract with the Court. However, the pro forma procedure is no guarantee that the employee will be granted an entitlement to unemployment benefits.

Collective Dismissals

General

In the event an employer intends to dismiss at least 20 employees within a period of three months in one CWI region, the Act on the Notification of Collective Dismissals (*Wet melding Collectief Ontslag*) is applicable. According to this act, the employer has to notify the CWI and the trade unions concerned of the intended dismissals and must first discuss the intended decision and its social consequences with these trade unions. Application for individual dismissal permits can only be filed starting one month after the notification of the intended collective dismissal. The employer can then once again only validly dismiss the individual employees concerned after the prior approval of the CWI has been obtained.

Social Plan

It is customary to agree with the trade unions and/or the works council (if any) and/or the employee representative body on a social plan in case of a closure or substantial number of dismissals. It is important to create a social plan that can stand the criticism of the CWI and/or the Court. In this respect, although there is no obligation to agree with the trade unions on a social plan (except as provided for in a CBA), it is preferable to do so.

There are no regulations with regard to the contents of a social plan, nor is there a set legal framework or timetable with respect to the negotiations regarding a social plan. The contents of a social plan and the elements to be included depend on the results of the negotiations between the employer and the unions (or works council). It is advisable to negotiate a social plan with the trade unions instead of with the works council, since the courts in general tend to accept the social plan agreed upon with the unions and be more critical toward social plans negotiated with the works council.

The budget for a social plan depends on the available funds. However, in practice the budget of a social plan is based on the Cantonal Judges Formula plus some additional benefits (like professional assistance in finding a job elsewhere).

Advice of the Works Council; Timetable

A "regular" restructuring/closing window of at least six to eight months, before the whole process is completed and the employment contracts have been terminated, should be taken into account. In a worst-case scenario, involving litigation by the works council, the whole process of a "regular" restructuring/closing may take up to one year.

In general, the negotiations with the trade unions coincide with the consultation of the works council under the WCA. As indicated above, there is no legal requirement to actually agree on a social plan with the trade unions; mere consultation is sufficient. The employer may—in principle—proceed once the consultation process has been followed. However, in general the employer will encounter difficulties in obtaining positive advice from the works council without a social plan having been agreed upon.

There is no set timetable for the process of a collective dismissal. The one-month waiting period mandated by the Act on the Notification of Collective Dismissals should be taken into account. In practice it can take up to three or four months before the works council has rendered its advice and a social plan has been concluded.

After the employer is entitled to implement its decision according to the WCA, the employer must apply for dismissal permits from the CWI. This process usually takes about two to three months. After the dismissal permits have been obtained, notice should be given to all the individual employees with due observance of the notice period. Instead of giving notice, dissolution proceedings may have to be followed for those employees for whom a statutory prohibition applies.

Dismissal of Managing Directors

General

When determining the manner in which dismissal of a managing director should be effected, it is necessary to make a distinction between the procedure in which the decision to dismiss the managing director from his corporate position must be taken (which process is governed by Dutch corporate law) and the termination of his employment agreement itself (which is ruled by Dutch employment law).

Dismissal Governed by Corporate Law

Book 2 of the DCC provides that managing directors of virtually all businesses can, at any time, be dismissed by the corporate body that was authorized to appoint them (e.g., the general meeting of shareholders or the supervisory board). The supervisory board must, on penalty of the decision to dismiss being voided, consult the general meeting of shareholders before the dismissal of the managing director is effected.

The decision to dismiss is void if the decision is in breach of Dutch law or the articles of association of the business, and it can be annulled if it is in breach of provisions that pertain to the procedure in which decisions must be made. The decision to dismiss is also annullable if it contradicts principles of reasonableness and fairness *(redelijkheid en billijkheid)* that must be taken into account in the behavior among the different corporate bodies of a business. The managing director must first be informed of the fact that the relevant corporate body intends to effect the dismissal and must then be given the opportunity to communicate an opinion to the authorized corporate body.

A former managing director cannot successfully have the decision to dismiss him or her annulled purely on the basis that the grounds for dismissal were unsound. In other words, only the manner in which the decision to dismiss the managing director has been brought about is subject to annulment in case of breach of the requirements of law, articles of association, or the principles of reasonableness and fairness. All other "defects" in the dismissal can be translated into claims for compensation.

The works council must be given the opportunity to render its advice in respect of the intended dismissal of a managing director (provided the managing director qualifies as the "manager" as defined in the WCA).

Dismissal Governed by Employment Law

The Supreme Court of the Netherlands has (most recently in April 2005) ruled that termination of the corporate position of a managing director automatically results in the simultaneous termination of the contractual employment relationship between the business and the managing director, unless the managing director/employee is ill at the time of receiving the invitation of the shareholders meeting (or unless parties explicitly agree differently). In such case the employment contract exists also after his or her dismissal by the shareholders until the employer has validly terminated the employment contract in line with the rules of Dutch employment law.

The employment contract of a managing director can be terminated without the prior approval of the CWI.

The Cantonal Judges Formula is often used to establish the amount of compensation a managing director should receive upon termination of the contract. Some employment contracts include a provision with respect to the financial compensation to be paid to a managing director upon termination (golden parachute arrangements). Such a clause is valid but does not exclude the possibility for the managing director to demand a higher compensation in court. It is not possible for a managing director to claim reinstatement on the grounds of the manner of dismissal being apparently unreasonable. If the director feels that he or she was wrongfully dismissed by the shareholders, he or she can initiate proceedings, demanding compensation claiming unreasonable dismissal.

SECTION V

What prohibitions exist against discrimination on a basis of age, race, gender, disability, pregnancy, and other factors? What are the rights of employees, applicants, or former employees who believe that they have been discriminated against?

Equal Treatment Regulations

Act on Equal Treatment and Other Regulations

The Netherlands has extensive legislation regarding equal treatment. Articles 7:646 and 7:648 DCC contain provisions regarding equal rights for men and women and part-time and full-time employees. Article 7:649 DCC prohibits the unequal treatment of workers on fixed-term contracts.

In addition to this section in the DCC, the Act on Equal Treatment (*Algemene Wet Gelijke Behandeling*) is also applicable. This act prohibits unequal treatment with respect to religion, belief, political opinion, race, sex, nationality, sexual orientation, or marital status. This prohibition applies to discrimination at work in the exercise of a liberal profession, in offering goods and services, and in providing educational or career guidance. Recently two new acts have become effective: the Act on Equal Treatment of Disabled or Chronically Ill People and the Act on Equal Treatment in Employment (Age Discrimination).

Equal Treatment on the Grounds of Handicap or Chronic Illness

The Act on Equal Treatment of Disabled or Chronically Ill People entitles people who have a disability or suffer from a chronic illness to effective alterations to enable them to play a full role in society, and prohibits discrimination against them in the terms and conditions of their employment and training.

Discrimination is also prohibited with regard to the conditions for and access to the professions and for the performance of and development within the professions.

The prohibition on discrimination does not apply if the discrimination:

- Is necessary to protect health and safety;
- Relates to a regulation, standard, or practice that is aimed at creating or maintaining specific provisions and facilities for the benefit of persons with a disability or chronic illness;
- Concerns a specific measure that has the aim of granting persons with a disability or chronic illness a privileged position in order to neutralize or ameliorate existing disadvantages and the discrimination is proportionate to the objective;
- Is indirect and is objectively justified by a legitimate aim, and the means used to achieve that aim are appropriate and necessary.

Equal Treatment Irrespective of Age in Employment, Occupation, and Vocational Training

On May 1, 2004, the Equal Treatment in Employment (Age Discrimination) Act came into force. This act is an implementation of an EU directive and provides for equal treatment irrespective of age in employment, occupation, and vocational training. Under this act it is prohibited to discriminate on the basis of a person's age with regard to the terms and conditions of employment and training.

Age distinction will be permitted only if the distinction is objectively justifiable. For this, the applied criteria must be appropriate and necessary and serve a legitimate cause. The prohibition on discrimination furthermore does not apply if the discrimination:

- Is based on employment or labor-market policies to promote employment in certain age categories, provided such policies are laid down by or are introduced pursuant to an Act of Parliament;
- Relates to the termination of an employment relationship because the person concerned has reached the pensionable age under the General Old Age Pensions Act (age of 65) or a more advanced age laid down by or pursuant to an Act of Parliament or agreed between the parties;
- Relates to the age of admission or to the pensionable age laid down in the pension plan, or to the establishment of different ages for admission or entitlement for employees or for groups or categories of employees;
- Is based on actuarial calculations in the context of pension plans that make use of age criteria.

Compliance with the Law

The Equal Treatment Commission decides on complaints of unequal treatment. Individual employees and employers, trade unions, and works councils may file a complaint with the Equal Treatment Commission, which will then be investigated by this Commission. Filing of a complaint is free of charge and a lawyer is not required. The Equal Treatment Commission may also conduct an investigation on its own initiative. It should be noted that courts are not bound by the decisions of the Commission (and frequently rule otherwise). It is not necessary to first file a complaint with the Commission; it is also possible to take the matter straight to court.

Equal Treatment with Respect to Employment

Equal Treatment in Recruitment and Selection

In the Netherlands an employer is not allowed to discriminate between job applicants on the basis of religion, race, conviction, sexual orientation, civil status, working hours or temporary or permanent contract, age, or handicap.

Equal Pay and Equal Conditions of Employment

In the Netherlands employees who perform work of equal value are entitled to equal pay. The employer has to make sure that equal pay is given for work of equal value. Pay has to be calculated on the basis of equal criteria. The calculation of pay must be made in a transparent manner. When an employer uses criteria that lead to differences in pay for specific employees, the employer must have a justification. However, it is possible that an employee doing work of equal value does not earn exactly the same as a colleague. The employer has to justify this difference in pay.

SECTION VI

On the Horizon: What key labor and employment law developments should an employer doing business in the Netherlands anticipate occurring in the coming years?

Recent Amendments

As of March 1, 2006, the rules that apply in case of a dismissal for economic reasons are as follows: the CWI will grant permission only if the so-called age-reflecting principle (*afspiegelingsbeginsel*) is applied (unless all of the employees are dismissed). For a further explanation, see page 163.

As of June 1, 2005, the possibility for an employee to take a long term (unpaid) care leave for the care of a partner, child, or parent with a life threatening disease was added to the Work and Care Act (*Wet Arbeid en Zorg*). The duration of this leave can be six times the working time of the employee per week calculated over a total period of twelve months. The employer can only refuse the request of an employee for a long term care leave for reasons of important business interest.

Pending Legislative Proposals

Legislative Proposal with Regard to the Noncompetition Clause

A legislative proposal to amend the legislation on noncompetition clauses is being considered. In this legislative proposal the rules regarding noncompetition clauses will be tightened.

Important elements of this legislative proposal are

- The term of the noncompetition clause will be limited to a maximum of one year;
- The employer will have to pay a reasonable compensation if, after the termination of the employment contract, the employer wants the employee to be bound by the clause;
- The compensation is not payable in the event:
    - The employee is liable for damages in respect to the termination of the contract;
    - The employer notifies the employee prior to the termination of the contract that the employer will not invoke the noncompetition clause;
    - The employer notifies the employee after the employee has terminated the contract that the employer will not invoke the noncompetition

clause, and the employee agrees to the expiration of the obligation to pay compensation. The court can nullify a noncompetition clause in the event the employee refuses to agree to the expiration of the obligation to pay compensation on unreasonable grounds;
  - The employer, in case of an employment contract for a definite period of time, notifies the employee a month before the termination of the contract that the employer will not invoke the noncompetition clause;
- The noncompetition clause must contain the term, the activities to which it applies, the geographical scope, and the amount of compensation.

Amendment to the Works Councils Act

The Dutch government has proposed to amend the Working Hours Decree (*Arbeidstijdenbesluit*) following the ruling of the European Supreme Court on September 9, 2003, in the so-called Jaeger-case.[8] In the Jaeger-case the European Court ruled that "sleep-over shifts" should be accounted for when calculating the maximum working time of an employee per week. Among other things, the amendment provides for a longer maximum working time.

NOTES

1. The conditions that have to be provided are specified in Article 7:655 Dutch Civil Code (hereinafter DCC).
2. Articles 7:634 up until 7:642 DCC contain detailed provisions relating to the employee's holiday entitlement and his or her rights to exercise it.
3. In this chapter, purchase, transfer, or sale of a business includes part of a business, unless clearly indicated otherwise.
4. This European Directive has been renewed in 1998 (European Directive No. 98/50) and 2001 (European Directive No. 2001/23).
5. Pursuant to Article 2 of the Act on the Declaration of General Applicability or Nonapplicability of Provisions in Collective Bargaining Agreements (*Wet op het algemeen verbindend en onverbindend verklaren van collectieve arbeidsovereenkomsten*).
6. Supreme Court 26 June 1998, JAR 1998/199 (Taxi Hofman-case).
7. The Cantonal Judges Formula does not have statutory effect.
8. HvJ EG 9 September 2003, nr. C 151/02, JAR 2003/226 (Jaeger-case).

CHAPTER 11

Labor and Employment Law in Spain

Vicente Calle
Alfredo Aspra Rodríguez

In Spain, the rights and obligations pertaining to employment relations are governed by

- The legal provisions and regulations of the State;
- Collective bargaining agreements, which may be specific for a certain industrial or professional sector or apply to a certain company, and which rank after the legal provisions and regulations of the State;
- The will of the parties expressed in the employment contract, provided that its purpose is lawful and that no conditions are stipulated that are less favorable or contravene the aforementioned legal provisions and collective bargaining agreements; and
- Local and professional custom and usage.

SECTION I

My client wishes to establish a manufacturing facility in Spain and will need to hire a workforce. What are the key legal issues involved?

Collective Agreement to Be Applied

Collective bargaining agreements have the binding force of Law and establish a minimum, which the employee may not waive.

Under interprofessional agreements or collective bargaining agreements, the most representative trade unions and employer associations at the national or autonomous community levels may establish the structure for collective negotiation, as well as the procedure for the settlement of dispute in events of conflict between collective agreements of different scopes of application.

In this respect, collective bargaining agreements are binding on all employers and workers included within their scope of application, for their entire term of effectiveness, in important aspects such as timetable and working time, shift work, remuneration system, working system and yield, paid and unpaid leaves of absence, vacations, etc. Thus, they may be changed only by reaching agreement with the workers' legal representative, or failing this, with the workers affected—but the conditions established by a bargaining agreement may never be worsened.

In practical effect, collective agreements are actually "laws" that govern the day-to-day contractual affairs in the provision of professional services between workers and employers.

In general terms, there is always an applicable collective agreement. It is the company's decision to determine which one it will apply, based on the activity it performs and its territorial scope (e.g., a metal industry in Madrid will have to apply precisely the existing collective agreement for the metal industry in Madrid, unless a company decides to negotiate a collective agreement at company level).

Labor Contracts

A labor contract is an agreement between the employer and the worker whereby the latter undertakes to render certain services for the employer and under the employer's direction in return for remuneration.

Formalization and Characteristics of the Labor Contract

Capacity to Contract

- Persons of legal age (18 years).
- Persons under 18 years who are legally emancipated.
- Persons over 16 years and under 18 years:
  - If they live independently with the express or implied consent of their parents or guardians.
  - If they have the authorization of the parents or of those who have them in their charge.
- Foreigners, in accordance with the legislation applicable to them.

Form of the Contract

Labor contracts are valid whether oral or in writing. They must be recorded in writing when so required by statute or specific regulation. This applies in particular to work experience and trainee contracts, part-time, indefinite-term contracts for seasonal work, contracts for partial replacement of semiretired workers with registered unemployed workers, domestic labor contracts, contracts for a specific project or service, and insertion contracts, as well as those of workers hired in Spain to serve Spanish companies abroad.

Contracts for a fixed period of time that exceeds four weeks must also be in writing. If this requirement is not observed, the contract will be presumed to be entered into for an indefinite period and on a full-time basis, in the absence of proof to the contrary.

Either of the parties may demand that the contract be entered into in writing, even throughout the course of employment.

Term of the Contract

The labor contract may be for an indefinite period or for a fixed term, where legally possible.

Trial Period

The establishment of such a period is optional. If agreed, it must be in writing in the contract. The length varies depending on the category of employees, but in any case the maximum is six months.

Workers' Information

When the labor relation with the worker exceeds four weeks, the employer must provide the latter, in writing, with the essential elements of the labor contract and the principal conditions of performance of the labor obligation, within two months from the date of commencement of employment.

The following aspects must be included:

- The identity of the parties to the labor contract.
- The date of commencement of the labor relation and, in the case of a temporary labor relation, the foreseeable term.
- The company's registered office or, where relevant, the address of the employer and the workplace where the worker habitually renders services. If the worker habitually renders services at different workplaces or in mobile or itinerant workplaces, these circumstances must be stated.
- The category or the occupational group of the job held by the worker or the characterization or brief description of such job, in terms that allow the specific content of the work to be ascertained with sufficient accuracy.
- The initial basic salary and additional salary payments, as well as the intervals at which they are to be paid.
- The duration and distribution of the ordinary working day.
- The duration of the vacation and, where relevant, how vacation is determined.
- The prior notice periods that, where relevant, must be observed by the employer and the worker in the event of termination of the contract. If it is not possible to provide this information at the time of supplying the information, the means by which such prior notice periods are to be determined.
- The collective labor agreement applicable to the labor relation.

Right of the Workers' Legal Representatives to Information regarding Contracts

A basic copy of the contracts, which must be executed in writing (except for contracts governing senior management special relations, of which notification is sufficient), must be supplied within ten days to the workers' legal representatives, who will sign it for the purpose of proof that it has been supplied. They must also be notified within the same period of extensions of such contracts, as well as notices of termination.

A basic copy of the contract is one that excludes personal data of the employee (e.g., domicile, ID number).

Part-Time Contracts

The labor contract will be deemed to be entered into on a part-time basis where the provision of services is agreed for a number of hours per day, per week, per month, or per year less than the working hours of a comparable full-time worker. "Comparable full-time worker" means a full-time worker of the same company and workplace, with the same type of labor contract, who performs the same or a similar job. If there is no comparable full-time worker in the company, the full-time working hours provided in the collective labor agreement applicable, or in the absence thereof, the statutory maximum working hours, shall be deemed to be the full-time working hours.

Hiring of Executives

Definition

Executives are defined as personnel who exercise powers belonging to the legal ownership of the company, relating to its general objectives, independently and with full responsibility.

They are considered to be employees but of a special kind, as their position is between the board of directors and the rest of the company.

Persons who purely and simply hold the post of member of the board are not considered senior executives.

Basic Characteristics

- This labor relationship is based on the mutual trust of the parties, who adapt the exercise of their rights and obligations to the requirement of good faith.
- It is governed by what is agreed by the parties and the legislation in this respect.
- Any matters not governed by the legislation applicable to it or by an agreement between the parties shall be governed by the provisions of civil or mercantile legislation and its general principles.
- The contract is executed in writing, in duplicate. A trial period may be agreed that may not in any event exceed nine months, if its term is indefinite.
- In the absence of a written agreement, the labor relation will be deemed to be of this nature where the worker hired carries out these duties.
- Where the senior executive has received specialized professional training at the company's expense for a certain period of time, it may be agreed that the employer is entitled to damages if the former leaves the job before the term established.

- The senior executive may not enter into other contracts with other companies, in the absence of the employer's authorization or a written agreement to the contrary.
- The term of the noncompetition agreement after the termination of the contract may not exceed two years, and is valid only if the following requirements are met:
  - The employer has an effective industrial or commercial interest in it.
  - Adequate compensation is paid to the senior executive.
- Notification of these contracts must be made to the workers' legal representatives.
- The contract may be terminated at the request of either of the parties, in which case three months' advance notice must be given. If the termination occurs due to the employer's withdrawal from the contract, the worker will be entitled to the indemnity agreed in the contract. In the absence of an agreement, the indemnity will be equal to seven days' pay per year of service, up to a limit of six months' pay.
- If the dismissal is declared unjustified, the amounts agreed in the contract will be observed. In the absence of such agreement the indemnity will be 20 days' pay per year of service up to a maximum of 12 months' pay.
- The remuneration of these personnel enjoys the salary guarantees established by the Wage Guarantee Fund and the rules on the settlement and payment of salaries established apply to it. The amount equivalent to the national minimum wage may not be attached.

Salaries and Benefits

The salary is the total compensation received by workers, in cash or in kind, for the professional provision of their labor services, whether reflecting actual work, irrespective of the form of remuneration, in cash or in kind, or the rest periods that may be taken into account as work.

The structure of the salary is established by collective bargaining or by the individual contract and must include the basic salary and additional salary payments.

The salary taken altogether and calculated overall, i.e., with all its complements, may in no case be lower than that provided in the reference collective bargaining agreements applicable to the company (for example, the metal agreement for the Madrid Community) though it can be improved by the employer by means of different mechanisms: higher fixed salary, variable salary depending on targets, salary in kind (company car, restaurant vouchers), improved benefits (private health insurance), etc.

Trade Unions

Trade unions have constitutional recognition under the Spanish Constitution (Article 28.1). They are essential to the functioning and understanding of Spanish labor law.

Trade unions seek to defend and improve the working conditions of their protégées or, using a more actual expression, the collective promotion of workers.

Their basic and most important function may be defined as compensating for the power of the employer by producing, in agreement with it, a set of legal-labor provisions, i.e., collective bargaining agreements, which is therefore a legislative power.

Union presence in companies is twofold: on one hand, through the Workers' Committees, which is a body elected by and from company's employees, and on the other hand through what are called Union sections, which are officers designated by the union from the company's employees.

The capacities of these union bodies in the company could be classified as (1) negotiating authorities, (2) information and/or consultation authorities, (3) surveillance and control authorities, and (4) other authorities and powers.

The great importance of the trade unions in Spanish labor law should be stressed as they act as valid and legitimate counterpart to the employer in the adoption by the employers of all manner of measures of employment or affecting the contractual relation that always exists between the employer and the worker, such as

- Massive layoffs (redundancy procedures);
- Negotiation of collective bargaining agreements, both those applicable at the company level and those of a business or professional sector scope;
- Temporary and/or final postings of workforces;
- Strikes and temporary suspensions of employment contracts (lockouts); and
- Any other measure that may materially affect the contractual relations existing within the performance or provision of professional services by the employer.

SECTION II

My client is acquiring an existing business in Spain. How do I assess the existing workforce and consider changes?

Initial Assessments

It will first of all be necessary to assess the situation of the managers of the company, specifically the special contractual conditions tying them to the company, for the purpose of being able to assess their change of conditions or even termination of their contracts with the company (these aspects will be dealt with in further detail below).

Second, and prior to transfer of companies, it will be necessary to analyze the type of conditions, both collective and individual, governing in the Spanish company, so as to be able to determine the impact (fixed and variable costs) that that operation implicitly entails.

In this regard, it is a good idea to analyze (1) the collective bargaining agreement that is the object of application in the Spanish company (if it is a company agreement, or a sector agreement at the state level, or even if there are various sector agreements at the provincial or autonomous community level due to the fact that the company has plants or offices in various regions); (2) the existence of collective specific agreements for certain matters that would improve the conditions of the agreement regarding topics as important as salaries, working hours, working day, vacations, and so on (both with a particular group of workers and with all the employees of the company); and (3) the existence of special contractual conditions with certain workers, agreed on an individual basis, that would affect questions as important as salary, working hours and day, and so on.

Having assessed all these questions, one may find a duplication of jobs as a result of the existence of synergies of the market/sector where the company operates (as a consequence of the transfer). Or, it may appear that the company could substantially alter the work conditions of the employees of the Spanish company, with the aim of improving its competitive situation on the Spanish market by means of a better reorganization of its resources. In that case, different procedures exist in Spanish labor legislation to carry out those changes.

Reduction of Personnel

The reduction of personnel should be arranged, legally, by means of a collective dismissal or by individual elimination of the jobs sought to be reduced—even if it were as a group, as we will see. In any event, it is not a matter of free choice, as will be explained below.

The transfer, by itself, cannot constitute the basis for the dismissal; there must be economic, technical, organizational, or production reasons that could justify the transfer.

Collective layoff means the termination of labor contracts based on economic, technical, organizational, and production-related reasons, when in a period of 90 days, the termination affects at least

- Ten workers in companies that employ less than 100 workers.
- Thirty workers in companies that employ 300 or more workers.
- Ten percent of the workers in companies that employ between 100 and 300 workers.

The above-mentioned reasons will be deemed to exist where the adoption of the proposed measures contributes, if economic reasons are considered, to overcoming the company's negative economic situation—or, if they are technical, organizational, or production-related reasons, to guaranteeing the future viability of the company and of employment in it through a more suitable organization of resources.

The procedure to be followed is the so-called "Collective Layoff Procedure." Termination of employment agreements will follow the individual procedure.

Termination by Elimination of the Job

The formal requirements that must be observed in a termination of a contract due to the elimination of the job are

- Written notification to the worker stating the reason for terminating his or her contract (economic, technical, organizational, or production-related);

- An indemnity to the worker of 20 days' salary per year of service, dividing pro rata by months the periods of time below one year, with a maximum of 12 months' salary; and
- Advance notice of 30 days, calculated from the delivery of the written notification until the actual termination of the labor contract. If this prior notice period is not observed, the employer will pay financial compensation, in full or pro rata to the period for which prior notice is not given. A copy of the prior written notice will be given to the workers' legal representatives.[1]

The Collective Layoff Procedure

From an eminently practical perspective, the essential characteristics of this procedure, provided in Article 51 of the current Workers' Statute and of Royal Decree 43/1996, of January 19, 1996, are as follows: The employer must negotiate the appropriateness of the terminations of the contracts and the terms applicable, with the workers' legal representatives (Workers' Committee, personnel delegates) or, if there are no representatives, with the workers themselves. In addition, the authorization of the competent labor authority must be obtained.

The minimum statutory indemnity is 20 days' salary per year of service, subject to a maximum of 12 months' salary. There is no maximum statutory indemnity, but rather the final amount will be the subject of negotiation between the employer and the workers' representatives.

Change in Salary and Benefits Structure

Throughout the duration of the labor relation, circumstances may give rise to modifications in the terms of the contract relating to functional mobility, geographical mobility, or substantial modifications of the terms of employment.

Functional Mobility

Functional mobility refers to a job change within the same professional group, between different professional groups or professional categories, or a change of duties not agreed or included in the previous points.

Geographical Mobility

Geographical mobility is the transfer or posting of the worker to another workplace, in a different city, which involves a change of residence by the worker. A transfer occurs where the worker (who has not been specifically hired to render services in companies with mobile or itinerant workplaces) is allocated to a different workplace of the same company that requires changes of residence on a definitive basis, or when a posting exceeds 12 months in a period of three years.

Transfers must be for economic, technical, organizational, or production-related reasons. Companies may temporarily post their workers for these reasons, or due to hiring relating to the business activity, to other workplaces that require residence in a town other than that of their habitual residence, provided that this period is less than 12 months in the course of three years.

Substantial Modifications of the Terms of Employment

The management of the company, when there are proven economic, technical, organizational, or production-related reasons, may initiate a procedure to approve substantial modifications of the terms of employment. The measure must follow a collective or an individual procedure similar to that for the collective dismissal.

Modifications affecting the following subjects, inter alia, will be considered substantial modifications of the terms of employment:

- Working hours
- Timetable
- Shift-work system
- Remuneration systems
- System of work and output
- Duties, where they go beyond the limits of functional mobility

The reasons referred to in this chapter will be deemed to exist where the adoption of the proposed measures contributes to improving the company's situation through a better organization of its resources, to favoring its competitive position in the market, or to improving its response to demand.

Individual termination decisions are fundamentally tied to the terminations of job contracts, given that there exist many situations in which, both for reasons of confidence and due to the requirements of the absorbing company, the latter places its own people in certain jobs, with changes being carried out at all levels of the company.

SECTION III

My client wishes to sell its existing facility. What restrictions do we need to consider?

Legal Regime of the Succession of Employer

In the light of labor law, any legal transaction that implies the transfer of business, tangible and intangible assets, and personnel of a company or part of it to another that will continue the transferred business is apt to be considered an event of "succession of employer" under Article 44 of the Workers' Statute.

If the transfer may be statutorily classified as an event falling within the scope of Article 44 of the Workers' Statute, a series of major legal labor consequences would arise, among which are

- Enforceability of the transfer;
- Legal subrogation of the new employer to the rights and obligations of the transferred workers in effect at the date of transfer; and
- Joint and several liabilities for labor obligations.

Requirements to Apply the Subrogation Contemplated in Article 44 of the Workers' Statute

The statutory event requires two essential requirements to be met:

Subjective: Change of owner of the company, workplace, or independent production unit, from the former employer (assignor) to the new employer (assignee). The type of transaction used for the transfer is irrelevant (assignment, contribution of business or business unit, purchase and sale, etc.).

Objective: Actual delivery of the set of essential operating factors of the employer, permitting the continuation of the business activity. These factors should conform to the company as a whole, or to its workplace, or to an independent production unit of the company.

In addition to these two requirements, it will be necessary for the transaction not to be performed for fraudulent purposes to the detriment of the rights of the workers.

Article 44 authorizes three types of succession of employer:

1. Of the company as a whole.
2. Of a workplace.
3. Of an independent production unit (IPU).

The company and the workplace, as units to be transferred, in general give rise to no problems of interpretation to establish whether or not a succession of employer has occurred.

Nevertheless, the definition of the term "Independent Production Unit" has given rise to major difficulties in those cases where the production unit in question is not clear, and to a certain extent is mingled with the business as a whole and the means and organization of the company are globally considered.

In principle, the IPU should comply with the definition given in Article 44 of the Workers' Statute of the term "employer" for the purposes of succession: "an economic entity that should maintain its identity, understood as a set of organized means to perform an essential or ancillary economic business."

Labor Effects and Consequences of the Succession of Employer

- **Enforceability of the transfer:** The effects of succession are imposed on all the parties in the transaction (assignor, assignee, and workers) by legal imperative. Consent from the worker is not required for the transfer.
- **Legal subrogation of the new employer to the rights and obligations in effect for the transferred workers at the date of the transfer:** The assignee is under the legal obligation to observe both the individual and the collective working conditions in effect in the assignor company for the transferred workers (length of service, professional category, salary, working hours, nonsalary accruals, working system, etc.).
- **Applicable collective bargaining agreement:** The collective agreement that applied in the company, workplace, or independent production unit transferred will continue to apply until it expires or a new one comes into force.

- **Situation of the workers' representatives after the succession:** The mandate of the legal representatives elected in the transferring company will be maintained only when the scope of their representation (the workers that elected them) is fully maintained. For example: transfer of the entire workplace or company. If only some of the workers are transferred and these are included in the workplace of an assignee that has its own representatives, the representatives transferred forfeit their status as such. If, as a result of the succession, the assignee increases the number of workers but the assignee does not have the number of representatives as required by Article 66 of the Workers' Statute (which sets forth minimum numbers of representatives based on the number of workers), then the employees may propose that an election of representatives be held.

Formal Obligations of the Succession of Employer

Notification and Information to the Workers' Representatives

The assignor and the assignee should inform the legal representatives of their respective workers subject to the change of owner of the following circumstances:

- Intended date of transfer;
- Reasons for the transfer;
- Legal, economic, and social consequences of the transfer for the workers; and
- Forecast measures in respect to the workers.

Harmonizing Management Measures

The company (assignee and assignor) should decide whether or not to adopt management measures affecting the manner in which the workers were providing their work.

These measures may be of many different kinds (material changes, collective dismissals, etc.) and it must be established whether any changes are due to the transfer or otherwise, since Article 44.9 contemplates a specific consultations procedure for measures adopted due to the succession.

These criteria should be interpreted prudently and in accordance with the principle of good faith, taking into consideration in each event the protection sought by the provision and the reasonable connection with or independence from the change of employer.

Possible measures to be adopted due to the transfer:

- **Material changes of the working conditions:** Transfers, working hours, timetable, shift system, remuneration system, work system, yield, and duties, among others. The procedure information and consultation to implement these measures should comply with the specific formalities contemplated in Articles 40.2 and 41.4 of the Workers' Statute.
- **Other statutorily classified measures:** When provisions exist that are applicable to other measures (such as collective dismissals or suspensions of

contract for economic causes) and these expressly contemplate an information and consultation procedure, this procedure should be adopted, despite the fact that Article 44.9 of the Workers' Statute has not provided this expressly.

- **Nonspecific measures:** Doubts may arise when employer decisions may affect the manner in which the work is provided and do not fall within the two above categories, such as adaptations of professional profiles, new engagements, application of guidelines to be followed with the clientele, uniformity, ethical codes, use of computer means, and nonmaterial amendments.

These decisions in ordinary circumstances could be made (1) by the employer alone (because of its management authority) on occasions without need for any formality, (2) by the employer with notification to the workers' representatives (for example, for plans to make new contracts; Article 64.1.1 of the Workers' Statute), and (3) by the employer after requesting a report from the workers' committee (for example, to establish professional training plans or to implement a work control system; Article 64.1.4 of the Workers' Statute).

Article 44 of the Workers' Statute, seeking to increase the ordinary guarantees, attempts to reinforce the protection afforded to the workers affected by the subjective novation of employer. The executive powers of the employer are restricted or conditioned in this case, so that decisions that may be adopted at the employer's discretion in ordinary circumstances are subject to the participating procedure described above.

SECTION IV

My client wishes to replace its senior manager(s). What restrictions do we need to consider?

One of the most particular features of the legislation governing senior management personnel is the wide margin of freedom allowed to the parties. Rights and obligations pertaining to the employment relation will be governed by the will of the parties, subject to the provisions of the Royal Decree.

The termination process demonstrates clearly these freedoms to self regulate. The Royal Decree for senior management personnel, unless agreed otherwise in the contract, places senior management in an inferior position as compared with ordinary workers. Unilateral termination of senior management without cause gives rise to an economic cost of seven days of salary per year worked, up to the maximum limit of six months of salary. In contrast, ordinary employees may receive 45 days per year worked, up to a maximum of 42 months of salary in the event of dismissal declared to be unfair, for objective or disciplinary causes.

As a result, when the legislation governing senior management personnel came into force, the majority trend was to include in employment contracts clauses stipulating a higher indemnification than that established by law. The term *blindado* ("golden parachute") applied to the commitment to pay a higher economic compensation in any event of unilateral termination by the employer (except for fair dismissal) or resignation by the executive for cause.

However, agreements containing golden parachute clauses, in Spanish business practice, establish indemnification not only higher than that of the Royal Decree but also higher than that established by the Workers Statute for unfair dismissal.

One of the main issues that is discussed during negotiations to engage senior management personnel is regarding these clauses, not only in the event of unfair dismissal (exceeding 20 days of salary in cash per year of work) but also for unilateral termination by the employer, and resignation by the top executive for cause.

Legal Requirements regarding Indemnity for Dismissal

In this section we analyze the formal dismissal procedure that must be adopted by the employer when dismissal is unjustified, i.e., in which there is an obligation to pay indemnity to the worker as a result of the employer's unilateral termination.

When the dismissal is declared unjustified, the employer, within five days from the notification of the judgment declaring such lack of justification, may opt either to reinstate the worker, paying the salaries for the duration of the proceedings (the worker's salary for the days between the date of dismissal and the date of notification of the judgment), or to pay the following sums (which must be established in the judgment):

1. Indemnity of 45 days' salary per year of service, periods of less than one year being divided proportionally according to months, up to a maximum of 42 months' salary.
2. An amount equal to the sum of the salaries not received from the date of dismissal until notification of the judgment declaring it unjustified, or until the employee finds other employment, if such placement was prior to such judgment and the employer proves what was received, in order for it to be deducted from the salaries for the duration of the proceedings.

Legal Restrictions regarding Dismissal without Justified Reason

In Spain, there is no employment at will. Hence, dismissals must be based on cause.

The absence or insufficiency of cause is considered as an unfair dismissal, with few exceptions related mainly to discrimination or pregnancy. In general, the effect of a dismissal without reason in Spain is that the employer must pay to the worker indemnity of 45 days' salary per year of service, subject to the limit of 42 months' salary.

Other formalities are necessary, since otherwise a dismissal could be classified as void, the reinstatement of the worker at the company being mandatory.

Thus, the dismissal must be put in writing to the worker, stating the facts justifying the dismissal and the date on which it will take effect.

Other formal requirements for the dismissal may be established by collective labor agreement.

A dismissal that is motivated by any of the causes of discrimination forbidden by the Constitution or by law, or that violates the fundamental rights and public liberties of the worker, will be void.

A dismissal will also be void in the following cases:

- That of workers during the period of suspension of the contract due to maternity, risk during pregnancy, adoption or fostering, or that were notified on such a date that the prior notice period ends within such period.
- That of pregnant workers, from commencement of the pregnancy until commencement of the period of suspension referred to above, and that of workers who have requested reduction of the working day for nursing infants or have requested leave of absence to care for children.

The terms of the previous paragraphs will apply unless, in both cases, the dismissal is declared to be justified by reasons not related to the pregnancy or to the exercise of the right to the above-mentioned leave.

If the dismissal is declared void, the worker will be immediately reinstated.

Following the provisions of the Workers' Statute, the labor contract may be terminated by decision of the employer, through a dismissal based on a serious and culpable breach of the worker. The following are considered breaches of contract:

- Repeated unjustified absenteeism or lack of punctuality;
- Insubordination or disobedience at work;
- Physical or verbal abuse of the employer, fellow employees, or family members who live with them;
- Breach of contractual good faith or abuse of trust in the performance of the work;
- Willful and continuous diminution in normal or agreed job productivity;
- Habitual drug or alcohol abuse that adversely affects job performance; and
- Harassment due to racial or ethnic origin, religion or convictions, disability, age, or sexual orientation of the employer or of persons who work in the company.

SECTION V

What prohibitions exist against discrimination on a basis of age, race, gender, disability, pregnancy, and other factors? What are the rights of employees, applicants, or former employees who believe that they have been discriminated against?

Prohibited discrimination is defined as follows:

- Any distinction, exclusion, or preference based on race, color, gender, religion, political opinion, or national or social origin that has the effect of annulling or altering the equality of opportunities or of work, employment, and occupation;
- Any other distinction, exclusion, or preference having the effect of annulling or altering equality of opportunities or treatment in access to employment or occupation, along with any distinction that is not objectively justified by the employer, among groups or employees who perform the same professional duties within a company (for example, giving more

vacations to one worker than to another who performs the same job with the same length of service and salary and contractual conditions).

Likewise, Article 17 of the Workers' Statute provides that "provisions or regulations, clauses of collective labor agreements, individual agreements, and unilateral decisions of the employer that contain unfavorable discrimination due to age or when they contain favorable or adverse discrimination in employment, as well as in remuneration, working hours, and all other terms of employment based on gender, origin, marital status, race, social status, religious or political ideas, membership or nonmembership of trade unions and adhesion to their agreements, kinship to other workers of the company, and language within the Spanish State shall be deemed to be void and without effect."

The antidiscriminatory rule applies both at the precontractual or employment stage and during the performance of the contract by the worker already employed. Thus, discrimination is unlawful

- Before the labor contract comes into existence; and
- During the course of the labor relation once employed, using the terminology of Article 42(c) of the Workers' Statute.

Both times are clearly defined in Article 3 of European Directive No. 2000/78, referring on the one hand to "conditions for access to employment, including selection criteria and recruitment conditions," and on the other hand to "employment and working conditions, including dismissals and pay." The discrimination may have its source in provisions of regulations, clauses of collective labor agreements, individual agreements, and employers' decisions.

If the worker provides evidence to the competent "labor" court of the existence of discriminatory conduct by the employer, the remedies against such discriminatory act would consist of

- The declaration of nullity of the discriminatory decision and the discontinuance of any practice of this kind;
- Indemnity for the damage caused, in accordance essentially with the rules of precontractual liability; and
- The restoration of the situation at the time prior to the occurrence of such discrimination.

SECTION VI

On the Horizon: What key labor and employment law developments should an employer doing business in Spain anticipate occurring in the coming years?

In general the following could be mentioned:

- Greater flexibility in the Spanish system of collective bargaining, which provides greater discretion for the parties when negotiating the rules under which the obligations and rights both of the worker and of the employer, will be developed.

- The establishment in labor law of full specific legislation regarding cases of mobbing or psychological harassment, in order to avoid the deprival of both workers and employers of the right to defend themselves.

Finally, we provide the address of various Web pages that deal with the regulation of labor law in Spain and that may be of great assistance to any lawyer specializing in labor matters in any other country:

- http://www.westlaw.es
- http://www.aranzadi.es

We also draw attention to the following handbooks:

- Alfredo Montoya Melgar, *Manual del Derecho del Trabajo* (2004).
- Manuel Alonso Olea and María Emilia Casas Baamonde, *Manual del Derecho del Trabajo* (2004).
- *Guía Laboral y de Asuntos Sociales,* published annually by the Ministry for Labor and Social Affairs.

NOTES

1. The majority of case law considers that when the Workers' Statute refers to the prior written notice, in reality it is referring to the written notice of termination itself, since the prior notice is a period that may or may not exist as it may be replaced by payment of the relevant salaries. In the end, the purpose of the rule is simply to allow control by the workers' representatives of the number and reasons for terminations performed for those reasons, which is possible only by being aware of the content of the written notice of termination itself.

An employer's breach of this requirement would involve the declaration of the termination as unjustified, and not as void.

CHAPTER 12

LABOR AND EMPLOYMENT LAW IN THE UNITED KINGDOM

NICHOLAS DENT

SECTION I

My client wishes to establish a manufacturing facility in the United Kingdom and will need to hire a workforce. What are the key legal issues involved?

Employment Contracts

There is no requirement to provide employees with a written contract of employment. However all UK employees are entitled to a written statement of the main terms and conditions of their employment within two months of commencing the employment (this is not a contract of employment but it does provide evidence of the terms of the contract). There is no financial penalty for failing to do so, but it is good practice to do so and is the best evidence of the terms agreed to with the employee. Otherwise the terms of the employee's contract of employment will have to be deduced from oral evidence.

The statement should cover the following issues:

- Names of employer and employee;
- Start date, period of employment, and place of work;
- Rate and dates of remuneration;
- Length of notice required;
- Hours of work;
- Holidays and maternity pay;
- Title of the job and brief description;
- Sick pay;
- Grievance, disciplinary, and dismissal procedures.

In addition, the company will need a standard offer letter and, as it grows larger, an employee handbook containing its employment policies. The offer letter will be a simple document attaching a statement of terms but also setting out:

- The date by which the offer must be accepted;
- The obligation on all employees to provide appropriate identification, in order to comply with the requirements of UK immigration law;[1]

- If applicable, any contractual arrangements specific to signing, e.g., a guaranteed bonus.

Employee handbooks are commonly divided into a contractual section, setting out matters that are to be binding on employees, such as confidentiality provisions, restrictive covenants, and pension arrangements, and a noncontractual section that includes employment policies, such as an equal opportunities policy, disciplinary and grievance policies, and Internet and IT policies. On account of the significant work involved in drawing up an employee handbook, employers tend not to introduce handbooks until they have about 50 employees or more.

Hiring Managerial Employees

All of the same basic employment issues apply when hiring managerial employees as when hiring nonmanagerial employees. In addition, significant issues are likely to include restrictive covenants, the amount of severance payment due on termination of employment, and bonus arrangements.

Severance Payments

It is not usual in the UK for there to be a fixed severance clause in the contracts of managerial employees. Instead, the employee will have a notice period (i.e., a period of advance warning of termination of employment that the employer is required to give the employee). For managerial employees it will rarely be less than three months, but may for senior management be up to one year.

In practice managerial employees often do not work out their notice, but are paid a termination payment in lieu of notice. Unless the contract has a "payment in lieu of notice clause" (see below), the payment will amount to damages for breach of contract and the employer may be able to reduce the payment due by arguing that the employee should have mitigated his loss by finding alternative employment during the notice period.

The main reason for including a payment in lieu of notice clause (giving the employer the discretion to terminate employment with immediate effect and make a payment equivalent to salary for the notice period) is to ensure that the restrictive covenants that apply on or after the termination of employment (see below) are enforceable. If the covenants are to be enforceable, the employer must have terminated employment in accordance with the terms of the contract. What this means is that if the employer is unlikely to wish the employee to serve out his or her notice, then it should include a payment in lieu of notice clause in the contract. However, this will effectively turn the notice period into a fixed severance payment, as the company will no longer be able to apply mitigation.

Bonuses

Most bonus arrangements will be discretionary. The contract should state in the clearest possible terms that the employee has no contractual right to a bonus, and is not even eligible for consideration for the bonus unless the employee is still in employment and not under notice on the bonus payment date after the end of the bonus year.

Even if the bonus plan is said to be discretionary, the English courts will require any discretion to be exercised in a manner that is not arbitrary or capricious. For this reason employers should preferably document the basis on which they have determined bonuses in each year, in case this is subsequently challenged, even if the rationale for bonus decisions is not shared with the employees at the time.

Garden Leave

If the employer wishes to be able to send the employee home and require him or her not to do any work during the notice period, then it will usually need to include a "garden leave" clause in the employment contract. The longest period of garden leave that an employer is likely to be able to enforce through the courts is six months, even where the notice period is longer than six months. The employer will need to continue paying the employee salary and benefits in the normal way during a period of garden leave. The employer will also be able to enforce restrictive covenants in addition to enforcing garden leave (see below).

Restrictive Covenants

Covenants restricting the activities of employees after the end of their employment generally need to be considerably more limited than the standard in the United States if they are to be enforceable in the UK courts. Restrictive covenants are in restraint of trade and therefore the courts will enforce them only if they are reasonably necessary for the protection of a legitimate business interest of the employer. Accordingly the enforceability of the covenants will depend on the specific circumstances of employer and employee. However, as a rule of thumb:

- Noncompetition covenants, which seek to prevent employees from working for a competitor within a certain period, are difficult to enforce and will be enforceable only if the employee has knowledge of confidential information that he or she will inevitably use when working for a competitor. In many circumstances, the courts will regard nonsolicitation, nonpoaching, and nondealing covenants as sufficient protection for the employer and refuse to enforce a blanket noncompetition covenant. If the employee gives the covenant in the context of selling a business to the new employer, or if the covenants are linked into the acquisition of stock rights, then there is likely to be a degree more flexibility.
- Nonsolicitation and nondealing covenants, which prevent the employee from soliciting business from clients and doing business with them, will generally be enforceable if they are stated to apply for a year after termination. They will need to be limited to soliciting business of the same kind as the employee was involved in, and to clients with whom the employee had dealings in the 12 months prior to termination.

- Nonpoaching covenants, preventing the employee from seeking to hire other employees, need to be limited to specific categories of senior employees whose departure would damage the business and should also be limited to those employees with whom the employee has had business dealings in the 12 months before termination.

Wages and Benefits

There is a national minimum wage for all employees in the United Kingdom. This is currently set at £4.85 for employees over 21 years old, £4.10 for employees 18 to 21 years old, and £3.00 for employees 16 and 17 years old, and is reviewed by the government annually.

Employers with five or more employees must give employees access to a stakeholder pension if there is no company pension plan that all employees can join within one year of starting their employment with the business. Stakeholder pension plans are generally provided by insurance companies and pension fund managers.

All employees have a statutory entitlement to 20 days' paid vacation a year: at present this includes the eight UK public holidays, but the law is shortly to be changed to make the 20 days in addition to public holidays. It is common to find 25 days' vacation entitlement in many British contracts. Additional fringe benefits found in a contract are normally individually negotiated. An employer must generally pay statutory sick pay of £66.15 a week when an employee is absent for four or more calendar days in a row on grounds of illness.

Labor Unions

These are called trade unions in the United Kingdom. All employees are free to join a trade union if they choose.

There are two ways in which trade unions can gain recognition:[2]

1. **Voluntary recognition:** An employer may voluntarily agree to recognize trade unions. In this case collective bargaining often extends to matters such as terms and conditions of employment, physical conditions of work, equipment, dismissal, suspension, allocation of work, matters of discipline, union membership, facilities for officials of trade unions, and bargaining machinery and other procedures.
2. **Statutory recognition:** There is a statutory procedure for trade unions to gain recognition in organizations with 21 or more employees for the purposes of collective bargaining. If the employer does not voluntarily recognize the trade union, under the statutory procedure it may ultimately be forced to do so if the unions can satisfy certain conditions. Statutory recognition provides for consultation with regard to pay, hours, and vacation (other matters may also be included by agreement).

A recognized trade union has a number of rights, including the disclosure of information for the purposes of collective bargaining and occupational pension plans and rights to information and consultation on layoffs and TUPE transfers (see below).

Employees who are members of a trade union have certain rights, e.g., to take time off work for union activities and training without unfair dismissal or unlawful detriment.

Various forms of industrial action (e.g., a meeting to consider proposals for strike action) may also be lawful in prescribed circumstances.

Collective Agreements

A collective agreement is any arrangement or agreement made by or on behalf of one or more trade unions and one or more employers or employers' associations that relates to one or more of the following: conditions of employment, physical conditions of work, equipment, dismissal, suspension, allocation of work, matters of discipline, union membership, facilities for officials of trade unions, and bargaining machinery and other procedures.

If a collective agreement is reached voluntarily between the parties the presumption (rebuttable) will be that there was no intention to create legal relations, unless the agreement is in writing and there is a clear intention that it should be treated as legally binding. Where an employer recognizes a trade union under the statutory plan, and is forced to comply with the statutory model for collective bargaining, this *will* have effect as a legally enforceable contract made between the parties, unless the parties agree otherwise. The only remedy for breach will be an order for performance of the obligation under the agreement.

Collective agreements may form the basis for the individual worker's contract of employment if it is agreed between the parties that they should do so.

Works Councils

Under the European Works Council Directive (implemented into UK law in 1999), groups employing at least 1,000 workers in the European Union with at least 150 in each of two Member States are required to establish a European-level information and consultation procedure, or European Works Council (EWC).

Once the thresholds have been reached, the regulations will apply only if central management is situated in the United Kingdom. If European central management is not based in the United Kingdom, the law of another EU country may apply to the establishment of the EWC. Under UK regulations the obligation to initiate negotiations to establish an EWC or alternative information and consultation procedure is triggered when a request is received from employees or employees' representatives. The function of an EWC is to facilitate the information and consultation of employees in Community-scale undertakings on a wide range of issues, e.g., the economic and financial structure, the situation, and the probable trend of employment within the undertaking.

New National Works Councils are also being introduced in the UK (see National Works Councils (NWC) under Section VI below). As of April 2005, UK employees have a new right to minimum standards of information and consultation in the workplace, e.g., on the employment situation and prospects and on any decisions likely to lead to substantial changes in work organization or contractual relations.

SECTION II

My client is acquiring an existing business in the United Kingdom. How do I assess the existing workforce and consider changes?

In order to assess the workforce the acquirer will need to carry out due diligence. Due to issues of confidentiality and data protection, information about employees will often initially be anonymous.

There are a couple of key concepts of UK employment law that will be central to any assessment of the existing workforce:

- **TUPE:** A key issue when considering making changes to the workforce upon acquiring an existing business is whether the acquisition was the purchase of a business to which the Transfer of Undertakings (Protection of Employment) Regulations 1981 (TUPE) applied. TUPE applies when a business or undertaking, or part of one, is transferred and retains its identity after the transfer. The effect of TUPE is to transfer contracts of employment automatically to the purchaser, so that the contracts continue as if originally made between the employees and the purchaser. TUPE also gives employees a number of other rights, as outlined below. It is important to note that TUPE does not apply to a share acquisition.
- **Unfair dismissal:** Over and above the right to receive the period of notice of termination of their employment set out in their contracts, all employees with one year's service have the statutory right not to be unfairly dismissed. A dismissal will be fair if it is for a fair reason and a fair procedure is adopted in effecting the dismissal. The five fair reasons are conduct, capability, illegality, redundancy, and "some other substantial reason." The last two are relevant in this context.

Compensation for unfair dismissal has two elements (1) a statutory basic award (maximum £8,100), based on the employee's age, week's pay (maximum £270), and length of service (maximum 20 years) and (2) a compensatory award (maximum £55,000). The compensatory award is calculated principally on the basis of the financial loss suffered by the employee as a result of the termination of employment.

Making Changes to Key Managerial Positions

Share Sale

There is often discussion with senior management about their future roles as part of the negotiations on the acquisition. If not, then this discussion will be one of the first tasks to be undertaken postacquisition. These discussions should be stated to be on a "without prejudice" basis (i.e., off the court record) if they are likely to lead to termination of employment. If the only role for an existing senior executive will be at a reduced level, there may be some flexibility in the contract to change the executive's role, but many changes will give executives the right to claim constructive dismissal. If, following a share sale, an executive agrees to a change in role and/or employment terms, this should be documented in a revised form of service agreement. As TUPE does not apply to share sales, no special procedures need to be followed.

If any executives are to be terminated, their severance packages will principally be determined by their contractual notice period (see Section I above). Due diligence should have identified whether the executives have a change of control clause in their contract giving them the right to enhanced severance payments on termination (or a change of role) in the aftermath of a change of control, and perhaps even the right to resign with a severance payment whether or not their roles are affected.

It is advisable to document the agreement on severance in a "compromise agreement"—a form of agreement under which the employee takes legal advice and then gives a valid release of all contractual and statutory claims arising on termination of employment. The compromise agreement will often also address restrictive covenants, bonus arrangements, and any period of garden leave that the purchaser requires.

Asset Sale

The considerations above apply. In addition, TUPE applies to senior management employees as much as to other employees. Accordingly, if an executive agrees to a change to the employment contract, this change will as a matter of law be ineffective. Executives who have agreed to sign new service agreements will often therefore enter into compromise agreements (with both seller and purchaser as parties) under which their old employment is terminated with effect from completion, and then sign the new service agreements with the purchaser, which come into effect at completion.

This procedure could theoretically be adopted to effect valid changes to the terms of all employees in the context of an asset sale, but it is rarely either logistically practical or, from an employee-relations perspective, the best way for a purchaser to introduce itself to its new workforce.

Carrying Out a Workforce Reduction

Share Sale

Employees who have been employed for two years or more are entitled to statutory redundancy pay (SRP). This is calculated in the same way as a basic award for unfair dismissal (see above), subject to the same cap of £8,100; employees are not entitled to both payments. Employers often enhance SRP on a discretionary or contractual basis. Due diligence should have determined whether a purportedly discretionary redundancy arrangement has become contractual by virtue of consistent custom and practice.

To avoid unfair dismissal liability, there needs to be a genuine redundancy situation and the purchaser needs to adopt a fair redundancy process. There is a redundancy situation where (1) the business ceases; (2) the employer ceases to carry on the business at the place where the employee is employed; or (3) the employer's requirements for employees carrying on the type of work the employee does at the place where the employee is employed are to cease or diminish. A fair procedure will involve the employer:

- Using fair selection procedures when selecting employees for redundancy (where the purchaser has a preexisting business into which the new business is being integrated, the purchaser will need to consider equitably both the newly acquired employees and the purchaser's existing employees);
- Giving the employees advance warning that their employment is likely to terminate by reason of redundancy; and
- Consulting with them on this and the possibility for alternative employment.

Where an employer is proposing a collective redundancy—to lay off 20 or more employees in the same location within a period of 90 days or less—it is obliged to provide specified information and then consult with the trade unions or, where there is no recognized union, with employee representatives elected for this purpose. Consultation should cover ways of avoiding the redundancies, the process and timing proposed (including the method of selecting the employees to be laid off), and ways of mitigating the effect (for instance, by locating alternative employment or making enhanced redundancy payments.)

Failure to consult can lead to a tribunal awarding a protective award of up to 90 days' pay (uncapped) to each employee affected. However, the penalty is solely financial and there is no mechanism for requiring the employer to reverse the process and carry out consultation.

Asset Sale

All the factors outlined above are relevant. In addition, under TUPE, any dismissals that take place in connection with the transfer are automatically unfair, unless the employer can show that the dismissal was for an economic, technical, or organizational (ETO) reason entailing a change in the workforce. In fact, a genuine redundancy situation will usually amount to an ETO reason, so the difference in practice is not often substantial.

TUPE also imposes an obligation on the parties to an asset sale to cooperate in consulting with employee representatives on the transaction and its implications. See Consulting with Labor Unions or Works Councils under Section II below.

Reorganizing the Workforce

Share Sale

If the purchaser wishes to change employees' job location or job responsibilities, many of the same considerations relevant to workforce reductions will apply.

If the location where the job is to be carried out will be changing only marginally (for instance, a different location in the same town), the employment contracts are likely to be flexible enough, either expressly or impliedly, to allow the employer to change this after discussion and consultation with the employees in question. Where the change is more radical, the employees' current roles will be redundant, and whether it will be fair to require them to relocate will depend on all the facts of the case (transport links, the type of role, etc.).

How much flexibility there is to change an employee's functions depends on the terms of the contract, but generally the employer will not have the contractual right to force an employee to take on a role that amounts to a demotion. If there are genuine business reasons for the reorganization, and a fair procedure is adopted in introducing the changes, then it should be possible to avoid liability for unfair dismissal.

Asset Sale

Under TUPE, a reorganization for genuine business reasons may constitute an ETO reason, and thus not be unfair, again so long as fair procedures for carrying out any dismissals are followed.

Changing the Wage and Benefits Structure

Share Sale

As a matter of contract law, employees must agree to a change in the terms of their contract, preferably in writing. Some benefits may be provided on a discretionary basis or with some discretion reserved about changing the terms of the plan. Even where this is the case, the purchaser will need to give advance warning and generally act reasonably, or else run the risk of constructive dismissal claims for breach of the term of "mutual trust and confidence," which is implied in all employment contracts.

Where changes are minor and employees are unlikely to object, many purchasers tend simply to notify employees of the changes, without requesting consent.

The last resort for employers who have not been able to persuade employees to agree to a change in their contracts is to serve notice to terminate employment and simultaneously make a formal offer of employment on the new terms. This will be effective to change the contractual terms but a claim for unfair dismissal is always a potential issue.

Asset Sale

Under TUPE, posttransfer variations to terms and conditions of employment are ineffective as a matter of law if the variations are by reason of the transfer, even if the employees voluntarily consent to the changes. If the purchaser wishes to harmonize employee contracts with those of its preexisting workforce, it should wait for a certain period after the acquisition before doing so. To be legally secure, the purchaser should change the employment terms only for a reason not connected to the transfer—for instance, as part of a general review of the employee handbook to update for developments in the law and market practice, applicable to all employees.

Company pensions plans are an exception to this rule. There is no obligation at present under TUPE on a purchaser to replicate pension arrangements. For good employee relations, purchasers will often want to set up a plan that provides substantially comparable benefits to employees. Whatever the purchaser decides to do, this will be a key issue on which it will need to pass details to the seller for the collective consultation exercise. TUPE is due to be revised over the next year to require the employer to set up a plan that provides substantially comparable benefits to employees.

If any changes are intended to noncontractual benefits or working practices, details of the purchaser's plans should be passed to the seller for the collective consultation exercise.

Consulting with Labor Unions or Works Councils

Share Sale

Other than TUPE consultation, the same considerations apply. At present there are no obligations to consult on a share sale, but after 2005 there is likely to be an obligation to consult with the works council where one exists (see Section VI below).

Asset Sale

As described above, the parties to an asset sale have an obligation to inform and consult collectively on the transaction and its legal, social, and economic implications for employees, either with the union or, if there is no recognized union, with elected representatives. The primary obligation to inform and consult on the transfer is the seller's, but the purchaser has an obligation to inform the seller about any measures it is envisaging taking in relation to the employees after completion. A key measure will be whether the purchaser is planning to make any job cuts; another is proposed changes in pension provision. There need be no agreement with the representatives, just consultation in good faith with a view to reaching agreement.

Liability for breach is solely financial, up to 13 weeks' pay per affected employee. Unless an indemnity is included in the sale agreement, liability for a failure to consult by the seller will transfer to the purchaser under TUPE. There may also be an obligation to consult with the European Works Council if one exists.

If collective redundancies are proposed, there is a separate consultation obligation as outlined in Carrying Out a Workforce Reduction above. This can be satisfied as part of one combined consultation exercise, but in the event of breach there is the potential for two separate legal liabilities.

As of April 2005 employers also have to consult with the works council (where one exists) on probable developments within the undertaking (see Section

VI). The manner and content of consultation will depend on the terms of reference agreed when the works council was set up.

Any collective agreement made between a seller and a recognized union is automatically transferred to the purchaser.

SECTION III

My client wishes to sell its existing facility. What restrictions do we need to consider?

Assessing Employment Contracts

Whether the sale is a share sale or an asset sale, all rights and liabilities in connection with employment contracts are assumed by the purchaser (in an asset sale, by the operation of TUPE). However, in an asset sale, criminal liabilities and most liabilities relating to company pension plans are not transferred.

The purchaser will seek warranties about the seller's employment history and may seek an indemnity to cover the risk of employment claims as a result of acts or omissions of the seller before the sale completes. Where the overall commercial deal is that the purchaser is assuming all historic liabilities (as is usual in a share sale) then the seller will normally resist giving an employment indemnity. In an asset sale, where historic liabilities more commonly remain with the seller, it has become conventional for the seller to give an indemnity for all precompletion employment liabilities in return for a similar postcompletion indemnity from the purchaser.

Consulting with Government

There is an obligation to notify the Department of Trade and Industry in writing whenever 20 or more redundancies are proposed at one location within a period of 90 days or less. Otherwise there are no general requirements to consult with the government on employment issues.

Consulting with Trade Unions or Works Councils

The consultation obligations mirror those applicable on the purchase of a company or business under Section II above.

Negotiating with a Purchaser: Special Labor Issues

The seller will be asked to provide warranties regarding employment issues. In many circumstances, the seller may be able to argue that individual employment issues are immaterial in the context of the sale price and that very few warranties are genuinely necessary. The seller may have to provide indemnities to cover all claims arising in relation to employment claims relating to periods before the business was sold.

The seller may also wish to offer retention bonuses to retain key managers for the period leading up to the sale in order to ensure that the transaction proceeds smoothly to completion. If these are the same managers whom the purchaser wishes to retain after the facility is sold, and the purchaser is consulted on the structure of the retention arrangements, it may be possible to negotiate that some or all of the cost of the retention payments be paid by the purchaser.

SECTION IV

My client wishes to replace its senior manager(s). What restrictions do we need to consider?

Employment Contracts

The cost to the company of dismissing senior managers will depend on the interaction of the contractual notice period and any relevant statutory rights. Senior managers are likely to have longer notice periods in their contracts than ordinary employees, they may have options, and they may have a payment in lieu of notice clause. If the contract is silent as to notice or there is no written contract, then the applicable notice period will be what is "reasonable" subject to the statutory notice provisions.[3] Although the notice period is the single most important factor in determining the severance offer, other contractual issues are also relevant, as outlined below.

Discrimination Issues

The same discrimination issues apply to senior managers as apply to all other employees. See Section V below.

Statutory Severance Pay Requirements

There are none except for statutory redundancy payments (see Section II). However, there are a bundle of contractual and statutory rights attaching to senior management positions that dictate the level at which the severance offer should be pitched: the contractual notice period and whether there is a payment in lieu of notice clause (see Section I); whether there are restrictive covenants in the contract that the company wishes to enforce; how long it is likely to take the executive to find another similar job; whether the company wishes to put the executive on garden leave for part of the notice period; what bonus or share rights the executive has; whether there are any discrimination issues or other potentially sensitive issues; and whether the company is looking for a quick and amicable deal or is prepared to engage in some robust negotiation with the risk of some publicity.

When a deal is reached, a compromise agreement should be signed including a full release of contractual and statutory claims, together with other provisions such as confidentiality undertakings, a nondisparagement clause, and perhaps an agreed form of press release.

Statutory Restrictions on Dismissal without Cause

Employers are unlikely to avoid unfair dismissal liability if they dismiss an employee without cause (see Section II). Employees can claim reinstatement as part of an unfair dismissal claim, but the Employment Tribunal is extremely unlikely to order reinstatement of an executive.

As explained in Section II, the compensatory award for unfair dismissal is subject to a cap of £55,000 and is calculated by reference to financial loss: Any contractual payments offered will be taken into account and the employee is not entitled to double recovery.

SECTION V

What prohibitions exist against discrimination on a basis of age, race, gender, disability, pregnancy, and other factors? What are the rights of employees, applicants, or former employees who believe that they have been discriminated against?

There are a number of statutes that set out an employer's responsibilities in the area of discrimination. Unlawful discrimination is generally prohibited at every stage of employment: advertising vacancies, engagement of employees, promotion and other opportunities, and in making a decision to dismiss. Some discrimination laws also cover postemployment discrimination.

The following areas of discrimination are currently prohibited under UK law:

Age

See Section VI below, which deals with pending legislation on age discrimination. At present there is a voluntary Code of Practice on Age Diversity but this does not have legal force. New laws will be introduced in 2006.

Race

The Race Relations Act of 1976 makes discrimination on racial grounds unlawful. Racial grounds are defined in the Act as any of the following: color, race, nationality, or ethnic or national origins.

Gender

The Sex Discrimination Act of 1975 makes discrimination on grounds of sex or marital status unlawful. The Act is worded in terms of discrimination against women, though it is intended that the Act should be read as applying equally to the treatment of men. The Act also covers discrimination against transsexuals[4] and people who intend to undergo or are undergoing gender reassignment.[5]

The Equal Pay Act of 1970 enables men and women to claim equal pay as against a comparator of the opposite sex in like work and also eliminates sex discrimination in the terms of their contracts of employment.

Sex discrimination can also cover maternity and pregnancy discrimination on the basis that it is unique to women.

Disability

The Disability Discrimination Act of 1995 provides that discrimination on the basis of disability is unlawful. Under the Act a person has a disability if he or she has a physical or mental impairment that has a substantial and long-term adverse effect on his or her ability to carry out normal day-to-day activities.

Sexual Orientation

The Employment Equality (Sexual Orientation) Regulations of 2003 provide that discrimination occurs on grounds of perceived as well as actual sexual orientation. The Regulations cover discrimination on grounds of orientation towards persons of the same sex (lesbians and gays), the opposite sex (heterosexuals), and the same and opposite sex (bisexuals). The Regulations also cover discrimination by association, i.e., discrimination on grounds of the sexual orientation of those with whom a person associates (for example, friends and family).

Religion or Belief

The Employment Equality (Religion or Belief) Regulations of 2003 prohibit discrimination on grounds of religion, religious belief, or similar philosophical belief. It is thought that the broad definition is deliberate and is unlikely to prove controversial. The Regulations cover discrimination on grounds of perceived as well as actual religion or belief and discrimination by association.

Other Areas of Discrimination

Less favorable treatment or discrimination is also prohibited on various other grounds under UK law, including the following:

- Trade Union membership and activities;
- Part-time workers or fixed-term employment; and
- Various rights to family or dependant leave, for example:
  - Maternity leave;
  - Paternity leave;
  - Adoption leave;
  - Parental leave;
  - Dependant care leave; and
  - Flexible working arrangements for parents of children under six years old.

Types of Discrimination

There are basically four types of discrimination that apply in most cases:

1. **Direct discrimination** occurs if a person is treated less favorably than other persons on the basis of the discriminatory feature, e.g., race or gender.
2. **Indirect discrimination** occurs where a provision, criterion, or practice disadvantages people of a particular group (e.g., on grounds of their sexual orientation or religion) and is not justified as a proportionate means of achieving a legitimate aim.
3. **Victimization** is less favorable treatment because of something an individual has done under or in connection with the protected legislation (e.g., giving evidence in a tribunal case).
4. **Harassment** is unwanted conduct that violates an individual's dignity or creates an intimidating, hostile, degrading, humiliating, or offensive environment.

Disability discrimination is slightly different in that there is no definition of indirect discrimination as shown above. Instead, there is a duty under the Disability Discrimination Act of 1995 to make reasonable adjustments where any arrangements made by or on behalf of the employer or physical features of premises occupied by the employer place a disabled person at a disadvantage in comparison with a nondisabled person. A failure to comply with this duty is an additional form of discrimination.

The Disability Discrimination Act of 1995 also defines as disability-related discrimination a situation where an employer treats a disabled person less favorably, for a reason relating to the disabled person's disability, than he or she treats (or would treat) others to whom that reason does not (or would not) apply, and cannot show that the treatment was justified.

Disability-related discrimination is not the same as direct discrimination that occurs when the reason for the less favorable treatment is the disabled person's disability (rather than a reason that relates to the disability). Disability-related discrimination, unlike direct discrimination, may be justified in some circumstances.

Positive discrimination is not permitted under any of the discrimination laws detailed above (except to the extent that there is a duty to make reasonable adjustments under the Disability Discrimination Act of 1995).

Grievance and Claim Procedures

Employees who feel that they have been discriminated against may be required to initiate a statutory grievance procedure before bringing a claim in the employment tribunal.

Employees can issue a questionnaire before they bring a claim in order to gather more information to determine whether they believe it is worth bringing a claim in the employment tribunal. They can also issue the questionnaire after commencing litigation in order to gather more evidence.

There is, generally, no minimum service requirement for bringing a discrimination claim in the employment tribunal. The normal remedies for discrimination claims include an order declaring the rights of the complainant, a recommendation for the respondent to take action to remove or reduce the adverse effect upon the complainant, and/or an order for compensation. In most cases the level of compensation is not subject to an upper limit.

There is generally a three-month time limit for bringing a discrimination claim in the employment tribunal.

SECTION VI

On the Horizon: What key labor and employment law developments should an employer doing business in the United Kingdom anticipate occurring in the coming years?

There are three main issues on the horizon: implementation of National Works Councils, age discrimination, and amendments to the Working Time Directive.

National Works Councils (NWC)

Regulations under the EU Information and Consultation Directive will from April 2005 give UK employees a new right to minimum standards of information and consultation in the workplace.

The Regulations apply only to companies with 50 or more employees and are being introduced on a phased basis.

Number of Employees	*Date That Regulations Come into Effect*
At least 150	6 April 2005
At least 100	6 April 2007
At least 50	6 April 2008
Less than 50	Regulations will NOT apply

However, employers will be under an obligation to establish an NWC only when a valid request is received from a minimum of 10 percent of the workforce (subject to a minimum of 15 employees and a maximum of 2,500 employees). Employers can take the initiative and create an information and consultation forum to improve employee relations or to take a larger role in determining the shape a future NWC will take. There may be advantages for employers in seeking an NWC agreement before they receive a request: for instance, the only penalties for breach will be those set out in the agreement, rather than compensation of £75,000 and the risk of an order requiring compliance as would otherwise apply.

The emphasis of the regulations is on implementing voluntary agreements: if an employer receives a valid request from employees, it has to enter negotiations for an NWC agreement, but there are no stipulated contents to such an agreement and the parties can agree on whatever they choose. If the employer and the negotiating team appointed by the workforce are unable to reach a negotiated agreement, there are standard fallback provisions, which provide for:

- An employee committee to be set up comprising between two and 25 representatives (one per 50 employees);
- Information on the recent and probable development of the undertaking's activities and economic situation;
- Information and consultation on the situation, structure, and probable development of employment within the undertaking and on any anticipatory measures envisaged, in particular where there is a threat to employment (such as redundancies);
- Information and consultation on decisions likely to lead to substantial changes in work organizations or in contractual relations;
- Information to be given to employees "at such time, in such fashion and with such content" as is appropriate to enable them to conduct an adequate study and, where necessary, prepare for consultation.

Age Discrimination

A voluntary Code of Practice on Age Diversity in employment already exists. However, from 1 October 2006 new legislation will be brought in to outlaw discrimination on the basis of age in employment and vocational training (see http://www.agepositive.gov.uk). The new rules are still the subject of government consultation so exact details are not known. Particularly controversial is the question of whether employers should be able to set a compulsory retirement age.

Age discrimination applies to all parts of the spectrum—young people, older people, and everyone in between.

In its consultation document, the government has stated that it does not want to outlaw initiatives that improve opportunities for people to enter or return to work or training. Nor does it want to ban employment practices that can be reasonably and objectively justified (for example, for health and safety reasons or where a business has a number of persons approaching retirement age at the same time).

Working Time Directive

The European Commission is proposing to revise the EU Working Time Directive. A key area of speculation has been the future of the so-called "opt-out" that has enabled the UK to disapply the weekly working time limit (48 hours on average over a 17-week reference period) with prior worker consent. The current proposals envisage retaining the opt-out but curtailing its use considerably.

NOTES

1. This include passports, national identity cards, and residence permits. For the exact requirements see Schedules 1–3 of the Immigration (Restrictions on Employment) Order of 2004, S.I. 2004/755.

2. "Recognition" means the process by which an employer accepts a trade union as entitled to act on behalf of a particular group (or groups) of workers for a particular purpose, most commonly an agreement by the employer to undertake collective bargaining.

3. Employed for one month or more but less than two years: a minimum of one week's notice. Employed more than two years: one week's notice for each year of continuous employment up to a maximum of 12 weeks.

4. Following the case of P v. S and Cornwall County Council, [1996] IRLR 347.

5. Sex Discrimination (Gender Reassignment) Regulations, 1999, S.I. 1999/1102.

CHAPTER 13

Labor and Employment Law in the United States

Philip M. Berkowitz
Anders Etgen Reitz

SECTION I

My client wishes to establish a manufacturing facility in the United States and will need to hire a workforce. What are the key legal issues involved?

The labor and employment laws of the United States are regulated both on a federal and state level. Thus, in many cases, relevant labor and employment issues differ from state to state.

Unlike most other countries, there is a general presumption of "at will" employment in all states with the exception of Montana. At-will employment means that either the employer or the employee may terminate the employment relationship without notice or cause (see Statutory Restrictions on Dismissal without Cause under Section IV).

Employment Contracts

There is no general obligation in the United States for the employer to issue employment contracts. As the at-will employment is only a presumption that may be rebutted by other circumstances, it is generally recommended that the employer use caution when drafting an employment contract, as this may imply more protection than available under the at-will doctrine.

Employment contracts should therefore only be issued in situations where special terms and conditions not covered by the company's general employment policies apply. This could be the case if the employer wishes to impose a non-competition clause or a fixed-term employment, or if the employee is awarded more favorable terms, such as severance pay, and change-of-control clauses.

It is, however, generally recommended that the employer issue general employment policies stating the terms and conditions of the employment relationship. Such policies may include rules of conduct, disciplinary actions, safety rules, harassment policies, substance abuse policies, discharge or grievances procedures, holiday regulation, and sickness procedures. When drafting such employment policies, it is important to consider the language carefully because it may provide a basis for unintended implied rights such as termination-for-cause requirements, special grievances procedures, and probation periods. It is for this reason that the policies generally state that they do not constitute a contract and that the employer reserves the right to modify or even deviate from them.

Changes in employment contracts generally require acceptance from the employee unless the changes can be reasonably justified or the employer previously has reserved the right to change the contract. The same may be the case with employment policies. However, here the courts are more willing to accept unilateral changes as the terms often also have been introduced unilaterally. In both cases it is recommended that the employer reserves its right to make future changes. If the employer contemplates changes it is advised that reasonable notice be given as this will allow unsatisfied employees to voice their concerns and may influence the courts' view on the enforceability of the changes.

Fixed-term contracts are generally considered to be terminable only for cause. It is therefore advised that such agreements be phrased carefully to avoid unintended employee protection. Alternatively, they may provide for termination at will, and set forth the employee's specific rights in those circumstances—which may include payment of less severance than would otherwise be implied by the term of the contract.

Arbitration agreements are most common when hiring managerial employees. In some companies, they are also part of the general standard employment contracts. The advantage of arbitration, beside costs, confidentiality, and duration, is that it may lessen the likelihood of an award of punitive damages claims. The courts generally accept such clauses if they are procedurally fair and not in violation of public policy.

The issue of whether to require arbitration of disputes is a complex one that goes beyond the scope of this article. Many employers disfavor arbitration, despite its varied advantages, because the employer may not have access to the same level of discovery and because of the limited ability to have the arbitrators decide dispositive motions, among other reasons.

Hiring Managerial Employees

Managerial and supervisory personnel are excluded from the protection of the National Labor Relations Act (NLRA) (see Labor Unions later in Section I) and most often also from federal statutes such as the Fair Labor Standards Act (FLSA). This gives the parties more freedom to determine the terms and conditions of the employment. However, such employees will most likely not be considered independent contractors and will still be protected by the antidiscrimination statutes (see Section V). It is important to remember that even though managers may not be protected by some of these statutes, lower-level employees applying for a managerial position may still be covered. In addition, it is somewhat disputed whether some groups such as partners in accounting and law firms are independent contractors or employees.

When hiring managerial employees, it is more common to draft employment contracts, as the need for special provisions is likely to be higher. Examples of such provisions could be restrictive covenants, conflict-of-interest clauses, arbitration agreements, and confidentiality provisions.

Restrictive covenants, such as noncompetition clauses, are generally enforceable in most states. However, overbroad clauses may be denied enforcement by the courts. Therefore, it is important when drafting such provisions to consider the reasonable necessity of the imposed restrictions in regard to the duration and the geographic scope.

When hiring managerial employees, it is often common to grant some form of financial participation scheme, such as bonus plans, stock option plans, or other kind of financial instrument. There is generally freedom of contract when drafting such schemes. However, as the plans may fall under the complicated requirements of the Employee Retirement Income Security Act (ERISA), the language of such plans should be carefully considered.

Wages and Benefits

Minimum Wages

Under the FLSA, most companies are required to pay a minimum wage to the employees, and the salary must be paid on time. There are a number of exceptions or exemptions to the Act, one of the most important of which is employees paid more than a certain salary. In addition to minimum wage requirements, the employees covered under the Act must be paid at time and a half for each hour worked over 40 hours a week irrespective of whether the overtime was requested by the employer. Finally, the FLSA sets standards for working time and time off, which should be followed carefully.

Holidays and Vacation

Private companies are not required to grant paid vacation or holidays. In many cases, employees are not granted paid vacation the first year. Thereafter, the amount of paid vacation may vary from two to four weeks per year. If the employee is granted vacation or holiday with salary, specific rules may apply. In some states, holiday entitlement becomes vested as it accrues and will be payable upon termination. Other states may accept forfeiture provisions in the employment policies.

Leave

Under the Family and Medical Leave Act (FMLA), employees with more than 12 months' seniority may be entitled to 12 weeks of unpaid leave per 12-month period for a number of family and medical-related matters, including the birth or adoption of a child or a serious "medical condition" of the employee or someone with whom the employee is "associated" such as a family member. The employer is required to hold the job or a similar position during FMLA leave.

Under the Uniformed Services Employment and Reemployment Rights Act (USERRA), employees may be entitled to up to five years' unpaid leave to serve in the military. The Jury System Improvements Act (JSIA) also requires employers to provide leave for employees who are called to serve on a jury, in some states with paid leave.

Illness

Employers are not legally required to pay salary during illness. Most employers do offer paid leave for a limited period of time, ranging from less than full salary to full salary, and others allow a certain amount of paid sick days per year. Under certain state laws, the employer may be required to insure the employee against short-term illness.

Pension and Insurances

The employer is not required to offer pension or other retirement benefits to the employees. However, if the employer does provide a pension plan it may fall under the complicated provisions of ERISA, which requires that the pension plan be in writing. Some pension plans are subject to favorable tax treatment, such as the so-called 401(k) plans. For that reason, ERISA plans are most often drafted by tax and ERISA attorneys.

Employers are not legally obligated to offer health insurance. However, as health insurance is costly and the employer may get better rates by grouping the employees, these kinds of insurance plans are often offered as a valuable employment benefit. Employers that do provide health insurance may be required to continue the benefits under the federal Consolidated Omnibus Budget Reconciliation Act (COBRA) for a certain period after termination of the employment relationship. Special discrimination issues should also be considered (see Section V), as the pension or insurance plan may indirectly disfavor a protected group of employees.

Labor Unions

Under the NLRA, which covers most companies of a certain size, a labor union may seek to establish support by the majority of workers in an appropriate unit. This is usually done through elections amongst the employees or by the employers' voluntary recognition. The cases regarding establishing and recognizing unions mostly concern the issue of what constitutes an "appropriate" unit. In cases where more than one union seeks to represent the employees, the employer should be careful not to recognize one of the unions, as this may violate the rights of the employees to choose their own representative.

If a union is successful in obtaining certification as the majority representative, the employer is obliged to recognize its authority as the exclusive bargaining agent of so-called mandatory subjects of bargaining, i.e. wages, hours, and terms and conditions related to wages.

Regardless of the presence of a union, employees are generally protected when engaging in concerted activities with the purpose of establishing better terms and conditions of employment. The employer is prevented from interfering with this right and any defensive actions should be considered carefully.

Collective Agreements

As the exclusive bargaining agent, the employer must bargain in good faith with the certified union on matters related to wages, hours, and terms and conditions of employment. The employer is not required to enter into a collective bargaining agreement, but the employer must have a good faith intention to reach an agreement. This may require the employer to participate in a minimal number of meetings with the union, to provide sufficient information, to consider proposals, and not to take unreasonable positions solely to avoid an agreement.

When the parties have exhausted their abilities to reach an agreement, the parties are at "impasse" and unilateral terms and conditions may be implemented by the employer, with the risk of strikes, lockouts, etc. During a strike, the employer is permitted to hire permanent replacements unless the strike is the result of an employer's unfair labor practice, in which case it can only hire temporary replacements during the length of the strike.

If a collective bargaining agreement is signed, the employer is generally prevented from unilaterally changing the terms and conditions for the duration of the agreement. Should the parties wish to change the agreement, specific procedures apply, which, among others, require the party requesting renegotiations to issue a written notice 60 days prior to the expiration. The prohibition against amendments in general concerns only the subjects covered by the agreement of "fully discussed" during the negotiations. No-strike clauses are enforceable if they are made explicit in the collective bargaining agreement.

There are no statutory requirements of what must be in a collective bargaining agreement. However, besides mandatory and permissive subjects of bargaining, the parties may wish to include terms and conditions that are deemed "unlawful" subjects. The nature of the contemplated terms should therefore be examined carefully before signing.

There is no permanent arbitration institution for labor disputes in the United States. However, arbitration clauses are common in collective bargaining agreements. The courts generally accept such clauses if they are procedurally fair and not in violation of public policy.

Works Councils

Works councils generally do not exist in the United States in the known form introduced by the European Union (EU), where employees and management are required to meet and consult about day-to-day issues arising in the organization. Such consultation bodies are generally not allowed under the NLRA to the extent that the purpose of the meetings is to "deal" with working conditions. As such activities may be viewed as unlawful interference by the employer, it is recommended that the purpose and content of any such meetings between management and the employees be carefully monitored so as to contain only exchange of information, brainstorming, suggestions, and other unilateral mechanisms.

SECTION II

My client is acquiring an existing business in the United States. How do I assess the existing workforce and consider changes?

As in most other countries, it is common to carry out a due diligence procedure to assess the existing workforce in a target company. This is especially the case in a stock deal where the buyer generally assumes all employer liabilities, but also in an asset deal where the buyer may assume liability for the seller's conduct prior to the closing. The personal data protection in due diligence procedures is generally not nearly as strong as in the EU, for example, and therefore the buyer may request detailed information about employees.

Generally, there are no federal statutes regulating transfer of business as known in other countries; however, some states have enacted regulations in this regard for specific industries, such as New York for building service workers. In most other situations, the courts have developed certain protections of employees in target companies, but the general rule is still at-will employment, which entitles both seller and buyer to terminate employees without notice or cause.

Making Changes to Key Managerial Positions

As a result of the at-will employment doctrine, the buyer is generally not required to hire the employees in the target company if the sale is carried out as an asset deal. In a stock deal, the buyer generally assumes all liabilities as a successor employer and any change in management must be done through terminations. The NLRA does not protect managers and supervisors (see Hiring Managerial Employees under Section I). However, the application of these exclusions should be considered carefully on a case-by-case basis. In addition, individual contracts and employment policies may also protect the managerial employees from termination due to change of ownership, which makes the due diligence process crucial to the success of the takeover.

Any discussions with senior management regarding their role in the company going forward should be carried out with care so as to avoid an implied protection against termination. When contemplating termination of senior management it is important to avoid conflicts with the Age Discrimination in Employment Act (ADEA), which protects employees over 40 years old (see Section V); ERISA, which protects employees from termination close to vesting of employment benefits; and the Older Workers Benefit Protection Act (OWBPA), which protects older workers from losing their retirement benefits.

Carrying Out a Workforce Reduction

As most employees are subject to at-will employment (see Statutory Restrictions on Dismissal without Cause under Section IV), the buyer is generally free to carry out a work reduction in the acquired company regardless of whether it's an asset or a stock deal, provided that the buyer is not acting in bad faith or violating antidiscrimination statutes (see Section V). Unless otherwise agreed, the employees are generally not entitled to special notice or severance, with the exception of particular federal or state notice statues as discussed below.

The federal Workers Adjustment and Retraining Notification Act (WARN) applies to reductions that result in plant closings or that exceed 50 employees within a 90-day period in companies with (1) 100 or more full-time employees or (2) 100 or more full- or part-time employees who aggregate work at least 4,000 hours per week exclusive of overtime.

Under WARN, the employer is required to give a minimum of 60 days' notice before terminating the employment relationship, unless the layoffs were caused by unforeseeable events, a natural disaster, or similar exception in the Act. Unlike the NLRA (see Hiring Managerial Employees under Section I and Making Changes to Key Managerial Positions under Section II), WARN also covers management and supervisors.

The employer is required to give notice to (1) the affected nonunion employees, (2) representatives of affected unionized employees, (3) the state's dislocated worker unit, and (4) the local government where the layoffs are executed. Each of the notices is subject to specific requirements.

According to WARN, the employer's obligation to provide 60 days' notice is transferred to the buyer at the date of sale. Any employees who are still employed with the seller at the effective date of the sale shall be considered an employee of the buyer. This means that if the buyer does not wish to hire all the seller's employees and is not able to have the seller perform the terminations prior to the sale, the buyer will be required to follow the WARN procedure.

Violation of the employer's duties under WARN may result in civil penalties for each day of violation. In addition, the employer may be forced to give back pay and benefits to the affected employees for the 60-day period. It is therefore recommended that the duties and liabilities under the Act be considered in the transfer agreement. The employees may waive their rights under WARN in exchange for adequate consideration. Some states have enacted their own WARN statutes, which may provide for better protection of the employees.

In a stock deal where the employees are represented by a certified union, the buyer may be forced to recognize the union and bargain over the effects of the contemplated reduction in workforce. This may also be the case in an asset deal if the majority of employees in the target company are transferred to the buyer. If the target company has entered into a collective agreement, this may prevent a reduction in workforce.

Aside from the general concerns regarding termination of employees in protected groups (see Section I), no employees enjoy special protection against workforce reductions. Union-represented employees are not immune from termination, but the collective agreement may require the employer to show legitimate business reasons for the terminations and some collective agreement may expressly prevent reductions in workforce.

Reorganizing the Workforce

The buyer's contemplation to reorganize the workforce gives rise to many of the same considerations as changing employment contracts and employment policies (see Employment Contracts under Section I) and as reductions in workforce (see Carrying Out a Workforce Reduction under Section II). There is generally no statutory protection against the buyer's unilateral changes in employment terms and conditions.

In a stock deal, the buyer should carefully consider the existing employment contracts and employment policies to determine whether unilateral changes are permitted (see Employment Contracts under Section I). If the employees are covered by a collective agreement, the employer will be required to follow the special procedure for renegotiating the terms with the union (see Collective Agreements under Section I). If no collective agreement has been reached but a certified union exists, the employer may be required to recognize the union as the exclusive bargaining agent and may have a duty to bargain in good faith about the proposed changes.

In an asset deal, the employer is generally not required to offer the same terms of conditions, but should the employees be covered by a collective agreement, the buyer may be expressly required to assume the seller's obligations under the agreement.

Relocating the workplace generally does not require acceptance from the employees. However, relocation resulting in plant closings or mass layoffs may be subject to special WARN procedures (see Carrying Out a Workforce Reduction under Section II) unless (1) the employer offers to transfer the affected employees to another location within a reasonable commuting distance with no more than a six-month break in employment or (2) the employer offers to transfer the affected employees to a more distant site within the same time and the employees accept the offer within 30 days of the offer, the closing, or the layoff, whichever occurs later. There may additional requirements under state law.

Of course there exists the risk that relocating the workplace would be challenged as an unlawful excuse to eliminate employees in a particular preferred group, e.g., age, race, or gender.

Changing the Wage and Benefits Structure

Unlike reorganizations of the workforce (see above), the wage and benefit structure may be considered contractually protected terms. The employer may be required to give proper notice in order to change the wages and employment benefits. If the employees are protected against dismissal, this may prevent unjustified changes in the employees' compensation. Employers may, however, lawfully reserve to themselves the right to make unilateral changes in compensation or benefits.

In a stock deal, this means that the buyer is recommended to seek consent from the employees before introducing wage and benefit plans to the target company's employees or otherwise ensure that proper notice is given. If the employees are covered by a collective agreement, the same issues arise as with reorganizations (see above). Consent, however, is implied by the employees' decision to remain employed after notice is given.

If the benefit plan is covered by ERISA or OWBPA, the employer may be forced to follow special procedures contained in the plan documents, which should be followed carefully.

In an asset deal, as with reorganizations in workforce, the buyer is not generally obligated to offer the same terms and conditions as the target company, unless such rights are expressly or impliedly agreed by the seller (see Reorganizing the Workforce above).

Consulting with Labor Unions or Works Councils

There is generally no special requirement that the buyer must consult with the unions or employee representatives due to the purchase of assets or stocks in a target company.

In an asset deal, collective agreements do not transfer automatically unless expressly provided in the collective agreement. The buyer may therefore generally introduce new terms and conditions to the seller's employees. However, the buyer may be required to recognize the union and bargain in good faith over the terms and conditions if a majority of the seller's employees is transferred (see Making Changes to Key Managerial Positions under Section I). If the buyer contemplates major restructurings or reductions in workforce, the buyer may be required to bargain over the effects of these changes (see Reorganizing the Workforce under Section II) and to give notice to the union representatives under WARN (see Carrying Out a Workforce Reduction under Section II).

In a stock deal, the buyer is generally obligated to assume all obligations of the target company and any change in collective terms and conditions must be bargained over with the union (see Collective Agreements under Section I).

Regarding works councils, see Works Councils under Section I.

Consulting with Government

There is generally no obligation to consult with the authorities regarding the employees in connection with the transfer of business irrespective of whether it is a stock or an asset deal.

Should the transfer of business result in reductions in workforce, the buyer may be required under WARN to give notice to the local government where the layoffs take place (see Carrying Out a Workforce Reduction under Section II).

SECTION III

My client wishes to sell its existing facility. What restrictions do we need to consider?

Assessing Employment Contracts

The most important consideration for a seller of a target company with employees is usually the ability to transfer all of its liabilities and obligations toward these employees.

In a transfer of assets, the liabilities generally transfer at the time of closing, unless otherwise agreed. The seller may in some cases also be liable for events after closing, such as the buyer's obligations under WARN to notify the employees of mass layoffs (see Carrying Out a Workforce Reduction under Section II) and under antidiscrimination statutes when hiring employees from the target company (see Section V). It is therefore recommended that the seller ensures the indemnification for such claims through the use of warranties and preclosing conditions.

Consulting with Government

See Consulting with Government under Section II.

Consulting with Trade Unions

The seller is not generally required to notify the unions of the contemplated sale of the target business regardless of whether it is carried out as a stock or an asset deal unless otherwise provided in a collective agreement.

An asset deal resulting in reduction in the seller's workforce or other material changes in working conditions may require the seller to negotiate with a certified union over the effects of these changes (see Carrying Out a Workforce Reduction under Section II).

If a collective agreement exists and is not transferred to the buyer, it may continue to run regardless of the transfer of employees. The employer is therefore recommended to contact the union to dissolve the agreement.

In a stock deal, there is principally no change in the identity of the employer and therefore no grounds for consultation unless the buyer introduces changes. If the seller assumes preclosing obligations to reduce the workforce, etc., the same rules apply as to the buyer (see Carrying Out a Workforce Reduction under Section II).

A collective agreement would, in a stock deal, transfer to the buyer, unless expressly provided otherwise in the agreement. If the seller remains obligated under the agreement then it is recommended that the transfer agreement include a provision for indemnification by the buyer.

Negotiating with a Purchaser: Special Labor Issues

In a stock sale, the buyer may want to ensure that the seller guarantees that all conduct prior to the closing has been lawful and that any claims arising from the preclosing period will be carried out by the seller, who will indemnify the buyer of any such claims. If a reduction in workforce is foreseeable, the buyer may request that this reduction be done by the seller, who then bears the risk of discrimination claims, etc. In contrast, the seller may wish to transfer all liabilities to the buyer and avoid liability for postclosing conduct.

In an asset transfer, the buyer generally would assume liabilities only toward the employees that the buyer hires, and then only for postclosing events. The seller may be interested in ensuring that it is not held liable for the buyer's hiring of employees in violation of antidiscrimination statutes (see Section V) and may even require the buyer to offer all employees a position to avoid possible exposure of liability in a termination process. The buyer may be interested in retaining maximum flexibility in determining which employees to offer a position and at the same time avoiding any liability as a result of the seller's termination of the remaining employees. The buyer may wish to have the seller carry out the necessary reduction in workforce prior to closing to avoid any exposure. Often the target company's key employees are vital for the future business and so it may be important to the buyer to require the seller to make certain efforts to ensure the retention of these employees up to closing. This is often done by having the seller introduce bonus plans, etc., subject to a successful transfer.

SECTION IV

My client wishes to replace its senior manager(s). What restrictions do we need to consider?

Employment Contracts

In general, replacing senior managers imposes the same concerns as making changes in key managerial positions (see Making Changes to Key Managerial Positions under Section II). As the managers are excluded from the NLRA (see Hiring Managerial Employees under Section I), there is no concern of union interference or protection of management (concerted) activities. Employment of managers is presumptively at will, and there is no general statutory protection against replacing managers (see Statutory Restrictions on Dismissal without Cause under Section IV).

Nevertheless, it is very common that senior managers have some protection in their individual employment contracts (see Hiring Managerial Employees under Section I). Contractual protection includes clauses like period of notice and just cause requirements, grievances procedures, exit clauses, transfer of control, severance pay, garden leave, etc.

In cases where the contract requires breach or similar justified cause to terminate the contract, it is important to note that the senior management may be protected to some extent by a business judgment rule and that poor business decisions may not necessarily entitle a replacement unless bad faith is established.

Discrimination Issues

Management is also protected under the antidiscrimination statutes (see Section V) and the employer should carefully consider the reasoning for the replacement, especially as ADEA protects managers over 40 years old, ERISA protects managers close to vesting of employment benefits, and Title VII of the Civil Rights Act protects against sex and race discrimination, among others.

Statutory Severance Pay Requirements

Generally, senior managers are also subject to at-will employment (see Statutory Restrictions on Dismissal without Cause below) and there is no statutory requirement to pay severance unless the employer is contractually obligated to do so.

Often the employer has good reason to ensure the amicable exit of senior management to avoid any external exposure. In such cases, severance pay is often combined with confidentiality agreements. The employer may want to arrange for agreed press releases, and the manager may be interested in a reference. It is generally recommended that a severance agreement be drafted reflecting the final settlement of all claims.

Statutory Restrictions on Dismissal without Cause

Under the at-will employment doctrine, there is presumptively no requirement to justify the dismissal of senior management.

This presumption is very strong and deviated from only in specific circumstances, such as situations where an explicit or implied contract or collective agreement states otherwise, in situations where the employer is preventing the employee from engaging in protected concerted activities, or to exercise rights under statutes such as

- NLRA;
- FLSA;
- ERISA;
- FMLA;
- WARN;
- Consumer Credit Protection Act (CCPA);
- Civil Service Reform Act (CSRA); and
- State and federal whistleblower statutes, etc. (see Whistleblower Law under Section VI).

In addition, under court-developed common law, the employment relationship does imply an obligation of good faith and fair dealing. If the termination is a result of bad faith motivation, the employee may claim breach of contract or tort (depending on the state in which the employee works).

Should the courts find the dismissal to be unlawful or wrongful, the manager may claim back pay, compensatory and punitive damages, or front pay depending on the basis for the claim. Reinstatement claims are rare in senior management claims, as the company may have justified business reasons to refuse reinstatement.

SECTION V

What prohibitions exist against discrimination on a basis of age, race, gender, disability, pregnancy, and other factors? What are the rights of employees, applicants, or former employees who believe that they have been discriminated against?

There are a number of federal, state, and local laws protecting minority groups against discrimination in the United States. The dual system may cause conflicts between federal and state regulation. In some cases state regulation offers less protection than the federal statutes, and in those situations federal regulation should be followed. Where state and local laws offer greater protection (e.g., prohibiting discrimination on the basis of sexual orientation), those laws should govern. The most common federal statutes protecting against discrimination are

- Americans with Disabilities Act (ADA), protecting against discrimination of employees with disabilities;
- ADEA, protecting employees age 40 and over from discrimination because of age;
- Title VII of the Civil Rights Act (Title VII), protecting employees from discrimination because of race, color, religion, national origin, sex, and pregnancy; and
- Equal Pay Act (EPA), protecting employees from wage discrimination due to sex

Classification of Discrimination Cases

Discrimination cases are generally divided into

- **Disparate treatment cases:** Intentional discrimination based on illegal/protected criteria.
- **Disparate impact cases:** Unintentional adverse effect on protected group due to a neutral employer practice.
- **Harassment cases:** Harassment based on the characteristics of a protected group.
- **Retaliation cases:** Prohibiting retaliation for asserting protection under discrimination and harassment law.

Disparate Treatment Cases

Disparate treatment generally requires that the employee initially produce sufficient evidence of the employer's unlawful intention. However, circumstantial evidence is often sufficient. In a failure-to-hire case, the applicant must further establish that he or she (1) is within the protected group, (2) applied for the job,

(3) was qualified for the job, and (4) was denied the job, and (5) the employer continued to accept applications for the job. This evidence requirement has been applied with natural modifications to other employer decisions such as discharges, denial of promotion, etc. Disparate treatment cases may also include situations where the employee has been forced to resign due to the employment practice of so-called constructive discharge, which is recognized by some states.

The employer may rebut the presumption of discrimination by showing (1) the employee was treated the same as employees outside the protected group, (2) the applicant would not have been hired due to other nondiscriminatory factors, or (3) the employer's action was justified by the so-called Bona Fide Occupational Qualification (BFOQ) defense. To establish a BFOQ defense, the employer must prove (1) a relationship between the job requirement and the job performance, (2) the necessity of the job requirement for successful job performance, and (3) that the job performance affected is the essence of the employer's business operation. The BFOQ defense is very limited and the burden of proof is on the employer.

Disparate Impact Cases

Disparate impact requires the employee to show that a neutral employment practice adversely affects members of a protected group. Cases often involve employment requirements such as height, weight, education, performance on standardized tests, or other seemingly neutral practices that presumably give a valid prediction of the necessary employee characteristics but, due to social, cultural, or historical reasons, affect one minority group significantly differently from the majority.

The employer may rebut the presumption of discrimination by showing (1) that the neutral employment practice did not adversely affect the protected group or (2) that the neutral employment practice was justified by business necessity. The first defense often involves a battle of statistics to find the relevant group of affected persons. In regard to the second defense, the courts require significant proof of the necessity once the employee has established that the employment practice adversely affects a protected group. (However, in age discrimination cases, the employer need only show that the practice was based on a "reasonable factor other than age").

Harassment Cases

The discrimination statutes also protect members of the protected groups for harassment in the workplace based on the characteristics of this group. The employee must establish that one or more supervisors engaged in harassment that resulted in demotion, termination, or denial of benefits or that the harassment created a hostile work environment. In hostile working environment cases, the employer may have an affirmative defense to liability if the employer has exercised reasonable care in attempting to prevent, and promptly correcting, workplace harassment, and the employee unreasonably failed to take advantage of such opportunities. For this reason, it is recommended that the employer put into place sufficient antiharassment policies.

Retaliation Cases

Most discrimination laws, as other employment protection statutes (see Statutory Restrictions on Dismissal without Cause under Section IV), contain provisions that protect employees in asserting their rights under the act. Retaliation cases generally fall under employee opposition or participation cases. In opposition cases, employees are generally protected when complaining or protesting against an employer practice if they had reasonable and good faith to believe that the employer's practice was unlawful under the act. In participation cases, employees are generally protected when filing charges, testifying, etc. against the employer in a discrimination case, even if the charge is later shown to be without merit.

Enforcement

Discrimination cases are enforced by the Equal Employment Opportunity Commission (EEOC) or by private actions. Before bringing a lawsuit under Title VII, the employee must exhaust his or her administrative remedies through EEOC. A charge of discrimination must be filed with the EEOC (or a local, state, or municipal agency) within 300 days of the act of discrimination. The EEOC has no authority to impose remedies. However, some state and local agencies do have the power to award relief.

Discrimination cases are often subject to so-called class actions where a few individuals bring the case on behalf of a larger group. As Title VII and ADEA allow the employee to demand a jury trial, these factors significantly increase the potential exposure of discrimination disputes. Mandatory arbitration covering discrimination cases is generally permitted. The employer may consider imposing arbitration on its employees, as it limits the risk of exposure because punitive damages claims is generally not awarded. The courts generally accept such clauses if they are procedurally fair and not in violation of public policy.

The discrimination statutes may provide for back pay, compensatory damages, punitive damages, reinstatement, or front pay. Punitive and compensatory damages are available only for disparate treatment cases under Title VII and ADA and are capped to a specific amount dependent on the size of the company. Under ADEA, the employee may instead be awarded liquidated damages up to the same amount as back pay.

SECTION VI

On the Horizon: What key labor and employment law developments should an employer doing business in the United States anticipate occurring in the coming years?

Electronic Discovery and Obligations of Counsel

The explosion in the use of e-mail has created tremendous burdens on companies and on employment counsel in particular in the conduct of labor and employment litigation.

In the United States, the courts permit broad discovery of documents, as well as taking depositions and other quite burdensome and expensive disclosures. Thus, any foreign employer should expect that its documents and databases may be subject to broad disclosure, to the extent that the employer maintains documents or other materials, electronic or otherwise, that are relevant to the matter.

With the advent of e-mail and electronic document retention devices such as hard drives, this process has become far more expensive, time consuming, and risky. One recent decision of the United States District Court of the Southern District of New York—a particularly influential trial-level court—has been watched closely by employment lawyers. In *Zubulake v. UBS Warburg LLC,* described by the court as "a relatively routine employment discrimination dispute," the court went a long way in quite literally making the rules with regard to preservation and production of electronic discovery in civil litigation.

The court ruled that once a party *reasonably anticipates litigation,* it must *suspend* its routine document retention/destruction policy and put in place a "litigation hold" to ensure the preservation of relevant data. However, that is only the beginning of counsel's obligations. Indeed, counsel must oversee compliance with the litigation hold, actively monitoring the client's efforts to retain and produce relevant documents.

The court made clear that counsel must take a hands-on approach to overseeing these obligations. This, according to the court, will invariably involve speaking with information technology personnel. It will also require that counsel interview key witnesses to determine how they stored information. For example, some employees may print out relevant e-mails and retain them as hard copies, while others may create separate computer files. As the court stated: "Unless counsel interviews each employee, it is impossible to determine whether all potential sources of information have been inspected."

While the client "must bear responsibility for a failure to preserve," nevertheless the court pronounced that counsel is more likely than the client to be "conscious of the contours of the preservation obligation." To assure the client's compliance, the court ruled, counsel must actively supervise the client's activities in this regard.

In this case, the court decided that the employer had failed to preserve e-mail records, and issued an "adverse inference" instruction: i.e., the jury was to be instructed to draw an inference adverse to the employer in determining why the e-mails were not retained. In April 2005, the jury returned a verdict in favor of the employee in the amount of $29 million.

Whistleblower Law

Sarbanes-Oxley ("SOX") is an extraordinarily extensive, comprehensive, and burdensome federal law passed in the wake of the Enron and similar scandals, designed to make companies more accountable to shareholders for their internal financial controls. In addition to imposing quite substantial internal corporate governance obligations on publicly traded companies, the law also provides a remedy for employee "whistleblowers."

Specifically, SOX provides a remedy to employees who are retaliated against for having brought to the attention of their employers or other investigators conduct that they believe violates securities laws or constitutes a fraud on shareholders (see Statutory Restrictions on Dismissal without Cause under Section IV).

In the wake of SOX's passage, employers are renewing their attention to internal corporate compliance programs that provide employees (all of whom are, after all, potential whistleblowers) an avenue for bringing alleged wrongdoing to the company's attention so that it may be investigated and remedied.

"Qui Tam" Lawsuits

Another extraordinary federal statute, the federal False Claims Act (FCA), has received renewed attention from employers. The FCA prohibits making fraudulent claims for payment or approval to the United States government or to the armed forces of the United States, and further prohibits related activities such as conspiracy to receive payment for a false or fraudulent claim and participating in such a fraud.

Lawsuits brought under the FCA, called "qui tam" cases, may have even broader significance to employers in terms of potential liability and adverse publicity. The FCA does not merely provide whistleblowers with a cause of action; it goes far beyond that, making whistleblowers potential partners with the U.S. Department of Justice, which prosecutes the action on behalf of the employee and shares in the recovery.

Under the FCA, whistleblowers may recover between 15 and 25 percent of the amount recovered against their employer, whether by settlement or otherwise, depending on the extent to which the employee "substantially contributed to the prosecution of the action."

Consequently, recoveries to individual plaintiffs in cases like these, given the extraordinary way in which they may be awarded, are often in the tens of millions of dollars.

Like SOX, the FCA prohibits retaliation against whistleblowers, and permits a civil action to recover back wages as well as "any special damages sustained as a result of the discrimination," including attorneys' fees and costs.

The potential liability presented by the FCA, as well as SOX's whistleblower provisions, are more than ever the focus of in-house counsel. Counsel are reviewing their internal practices to assure zero tolerance for fraudulent business practices. Companies are also establishing policies and procedures to encourage employees to complain about any adverse employment action based on protected conduct, to report internally any alleged violations of law, and to assist in any investigation of alleged violations.

INDEX

FROM THE ABA SECTION OF INTERNATIONAL LAW

For more information on or to order any of these books,
visit our web site at www.ababooks.org or call toll-free 1-800-285-2221